D1103153

Bob Gordon grew up in southern California and first began listening to jazz and the musicians discussed in this book while at high school in the 1950s. He served as a musician in the US Navy from 1961-6, subsequently returning to school to receive a BA in English from California State College at San Bernardino and an MA from the University of California at Riverside. He has taught jazz history courses at San Bernardino Valley College and is a member of both the National Association of Jazz Educators and the Los Angeles-based Jazz Heritage Foundation. He is currently Director of Archives for the American Jazz Symposium.

jazz
west coast
The Los Angeles Jazz Scene of the 1950s

Quartet Books

First published in Great Britain by Quartet Books Limited 1986
A member of the Namara Group
27/29 Goodge Street
London W1P 1FD

Reprinted 1990

Copyright © by Robert E. Gordon 1986
This book is sold subject to the condition that it shall not,
by way of trade or otherwise, be lent, re-sold, hired out, or
otherwise circulated without the Publisher's prior consent
in any form of binding or cover other than that in which it
is published and without a similar condition including
this condition being imposed on the subsequent
purchaser. This book is published at a net price and is
supplied subject to the Publishers Association Standard
Conditions of Sale registered under the Restrictive Trades
Practices Act, 1956

British Library Cataloguing in Publication Data
Gordon, Robert *1938–*
Jazz West Coast: the Los Angeles Jazz scene of the 1950s.
1. United States, Jazz, history
I. Title
781.650973

ISBN 0-7043-0129-6

Reproduced, printed and bound in Great Britain by
BPCC Hazell Books
Aylesbury, Bucks, England
Member of BPCC Ltd.

CONTENTS

For Lynn

Jazz West Coast

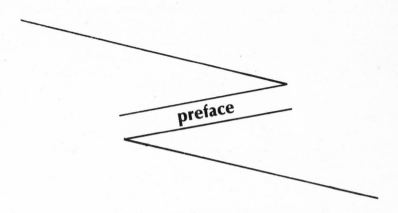

preface

In the early 1950s the attention of the jazz world was focused on Los Angeles. Baritone saxophonist Gerry Mulligan had gained fame (and a spread in *Time* magazine) by forming a pianoless quartet; his new group was drawing standing-room-only crowds nightly to an intimate club called The Haig. Several miles away in the town of Hermosa Beach, bassist Howard Rumsey and a crew of ex-Kentonites drew equally enthusiastic crowds to an old waterfront bar, the Lighthouse Cafe. Independent record companies – Pacific Jazz and Contemporary in the vanguard – sprang up like fast-food franchises and issued a seemingly endless torrent of albums by these and other Los Angeles-based musicians. In this hothouse atmosphere experimentation was rife, and attempts to adapt the instruments and techniques of the concert hall to jazz were tried, sometimes with a fair amount of success. The jazz press was – at first – also highly enthusiastic about the new sounds from the Coast. Somebody coined the term 'West Coast jazz' to describe the music being produced in California, and the tag stuck.

Naturally enough, the surfeit of attention and critical praise lavished on this music drew an eventual reaction. Jazz writers began to point out (quite correctly) that many of the experiments had little to do with jazz, and that much of the music from the Coast lacked the fire and intensity associated with the best jazz performances. As the decade wore on, the term West Coast jazz came increasingly to be used as a pejorative, and musicians and record companies alike hastened to disassociate themselves from the label. By the early sixties, the general consensus seemed to hold that any jazz recorded in Los Angeles in the fifties was suspect. Unfortunately, this latter attitude has prevailed for so long it has somehow taken on the weight of dogma. Grover Sales, in a concise (and admirable) introduction to jazz published in 1984, is merely repeating the popular wisdom when he writes: 'For all their technical expertise, most of the West Coast group recordings for Contemporary and Pacific Jazz today strike us as bloodless museum pieces, a neatly packaged soundtrack for the cold war.'[1]

It is just here that I disagree with the accepted critical stance, and this book is an attempt to restore some balance to the commonly-held picture of the Los Angeles jazz scene. My disagreement, by the way, is not total. If I could change the word 'most' to 'many', I would gladly concur with Mr Sales. There were indeed many failures among the recordings of the West Coast school, many pretentious attempts at grafting the techniques of nineteenth- and twentieth-century concert music to jazz scores. There were also many bland and innocuous recordings that lack even a hint of the fire that constitutes the lifeblood of jazz. But there were also successes, and a great many recordings of the period deserve better than to be vilified or forgotten simply because they were once branded with the label West Coast jazz.

Moreover, the Los Angeles jazz scene of the fifties was by no means monolithic. Leonard Feather has quite correctly spoken of a jazz underground of musicians whose aims were at odds with those of their more popular contemporaries. Bands such as the Curtis Counce Group and musicians like Sonny Criss, Harold Land, Teddy Edwards, Carl Perkins and Hampton Hawes kept the flame lit throughout those years, playing a brand of jazz as fiery as any on the East Coast. It is true that these musicians were seldom grouped with the West Coast school, but they were often tarred with the same brush and were overlooked or undervalued simply because they chose to remain in LA. At the same time an even more exclusive group, centred on Ornette Coleman, managed to record a few albums that pointed out new directions for jazz. It seems obvious that the LA jazz scene of the fifties was more variegated than current jazz criticism would lead one to believe.

In fact the 1950s, contrary to the popular stereotype, were exciting years for jazz in Los Angeles. I have tried to give the reader some sense of that excitement. More importantly, I have tried to give readers whose only knowledge of 'West Coast jazz' comes from curt dismissals in the jazz histories some idea of the multi-faceted and deep nature of the Los Angeles jazz scene in those years. There is evidence of reawakening interest in jazz of the period, and many albums recorded in LA during the fifties are being reissued today. This seems a good time to look at such recordings with an unjaundiced eye.

A word here on dope. Musicians have long been annoyed by writers who dwell on the use of narcotics among jazz musicians, pointing out – quite correctly – that several occupational groups (the medical profession included) have a higher incidence of users. This was true even in the 1950s, when the use of narcotics was considered a scandalous aberration by the public at large; it is undoubtedly true today, when the use of controlled substances is epidemic among a wide spectrum of the population. Nevertheless, the number of jazz musicians using heroin or other hard drugs during the forties and fifties was quite large (it has since declined dramatically), and it is impossible to discuss the chequered careers of musicians like Charlie Parker and Art Pepper without acknowledging their addiction. In these cases, and in the few others I mention in passing, the facts are well known and have already been published elsewhere. Some of the other musicians discussed in this book were also ensnared by narcotics in earlier years but have since managed to break free. If it was not germane to the music they produced, I have not discussed their personal problems.

I'd like to take this opportunity to acknowledge some of the debts I've incurred while researching and writing this book. Red Callender, Buddy Collette, Bob Cooper, Harold Land, Shorty Rogers and the late Shelly Manne all found time in busy schedules to talk with me. Their interviews allowed me to give the reader a glimpse of the LA jazz scene from a musician's point of view. Woody Woodward, Richard Bock's right-hand man at Pacific Jazz during the fifties, shed valuable light on that label's recording sessions. I'm especially indebted to Herbie Harper and to Larue Watson, Clifford Brown's gracious widow, both of whom opened doors that might otherwise have remained closed to me.

1·

diz and bird in lotus land

Modern jazz burst upon the Los Angeles scene in the December of 1945, when trumpeter Dizzy Gillespie brought his all-star sextet west from New York for an eight-week engagement at Billy Berg's Hollywood nightclub. For once, the term all-star was not a publicist's exaggeration: the group featured some of the outstanding talent available in the burgeoning movement known as bebop. Sharing the front line with Gillespie was Charlie Parker, the fiery young genius of the alto sax. These two founding fathers of modern jazz (ages twenty-eight and twenty-five) were in turn backed by the powerful rhythm section of pianist Al Haig, bassist Ray Brown and drummer Stan Levey, augmented by vibraphonist Milt Jackson. Despite this powerful line-up, however, the Hollywood audiences proved to be apathetic; their response was not commensurate with the musicians' talents.

Opening night at Berg's was the exception; the house was packed and the crowd wildly enthusiastic. The fans and younger musicians who had been introduced to Parker and Gillespie through phonograph records were impatient for a 'live' performance, and they were amply rewarded for their wait. Charlie Parker, who had missed the first couple of sets, made a belated but dramatic entrance, wending his way through the crowd while improvising furiously on the intricate chord progressions of 'Cherokee'. Memories of that evening still bring smiles to those fortunate enough to have been there. The remainder of the engagement, however, was all downhill. The musicians and hard-core cognoscenti who had formed the bulk of the opening-night crowd returned as and when they could, but there weren't enough of either successfully to support the band or the club. The mood of Billy Berg's regular patrons ranged from indifference to outright hostility. Most of them obviously preferred the nightclub's other act, Slim Gaillard, who was alternating sets with the Gillespie band. 'What they were used to in California was Slim and Slam, Eddie Heywood entertainment as opposed to pure music,' Stan Levey recalls. 'Everybody was asking, "Well, where is the vocalist?" That was the thing. "Who's going to do the singing here? Who's gonna tell the jokes?" ... The pure jazz enthusiasts were all there, but the numbers were small.'[1] Overwhelmed by the complexities of the new music being played by Gillespie and company, the club's regulars stayed away in ever-increasing numbers.

In addition, the musicians had brought some problems with them from New York. Charlie Parker, the man known to musicians and fans alike as 'Yardbird' or simply 'Bird', was undeniably a genius, but he was an erratic and sometimes irresponsible genius. Dizzy had foreseen some difficulties in this area and in fact had added Milt Jackson to the band for just that reason. 'I actually took six guys to California instead of the five I had contracted for,' Gillespie remembers, 'because I knew – them matinees, sometimes [Parker] wouldn't be there and I didn't want management on my back ... I'd say, "Look, you don't have Charlie Parker's name on the contract, and you want five guys. You've got five guys on the stage."'[2] As an added hedge, Gillespie also hired tenor saxophonist Lucky Thompson, who was working in Los Angeles at the time. All of these precautions proved well taken. Parker was often late and sometimes missed entire evenings.

Most of the altoist's erratic behaviour could be traced to his heavy drug dependency. It was no secret to the musicians or to the inner circle of jazz fans that Charlie Parker used heroin. This had not been a major problem in New York, since heroin was – at that time – both plentiful and relatively inexpensive. In Los Angeles it was neither. Much of Charlie's time and energy was spent in searching for his daily supply. When he finally found a dependable source, the pressure was relieved somewhat. None of this helped the band's already strained relations with the nightclub, however. When the engagement finally limped to a close in February, it was a toss-up as to who felt more relieved: the musicians, the patrons or Billy Berg himself.

Measured solely by the response at Berg's, the trip would have to be judged a failure, and indeed the New York musicians were (deservedly) soured on Los Angeles for some time thereafter. Fortunately, however, the matter didn't end there. If the bulk of the audiences were unreceptive, there were always a few listeners who grasped the message, and those few were the ones who counted. Pianist Hampton Hawes was only one of many Los Angeles musicians who dated his vocation as a jazz musician from the time he first saw the Gillespie band at Billy Berg's. Hawes, a teenager at the time, was particularly struck by the playing of Charlie Parker. 'When I first heard him in Billy Berg's in 1945 I couldn't believe what he was doing,' Hawes would later recall, 'how anyone could so totally block out everything extraneous, light a fire that hot inside him and constantly feed on that fire.'[3] In fact, Hawes could remember the specific moment during that opening night when he was hooked. 'Bird played an eight-bar channel on "Salt Peanuts" that was so strong, so revealing that I was moulded on the spot, like a piece of clay, stamped out.'[4] Nor were such experiences limited to those physically present at the club. Another aspiring pianist, John Lewis, remembers listening intently to radio broadcasts from Berg's that reached his home in Albuquerque, New Mexico. Shortly afterwards, Lewis moved to New York, where he eventually landed a job playing with Gillespie.

The influence of both Gillespie and Parker was spread even further by records of the two cut while in California. This was no small accomplishment, for the discography of modern jazz was alarmingly scanty at the time. Although both Gillespie and Parker had played and recorded with big bands at the tail end of the swing era – Dizzy with Teddy Hill, Cab Calloway and Lucky Millinder from 1937 on, and Bird with Jay McShann in 1941 and 1942 – there were few truly representative small-group recordings featuring either of the two extant at the close of 1945. Most of the recordings that were available involved musical compromises of one sort or another. Usually these took the form of mixing established swing-era musicians with the young lions on a recording date. The results were interesting but often unsatisfying to fans of either persuasion. Only a handful of sides cut for the Guild and Savoy labels offered full-scale evidence of what the youthful revolutionaries were capable of. The Guilds (reissued later on the Musicraft label), which included such classics as 'Groovin' High', 'Salt Peanuts', and 'Hot House', had been cut

7

early in 1945. A Savoy recording session in December – just previous to Gillespie's and Parker's departure for California – had produced two classic blues performances, 'Now's the Time' and 'Billie's Bounce', as well as Parker's incredible work-out on the familiar 'Cherokee' chord progressions, 'Koko'. The time seemed ripe for further recording.

Unfortunately, the first California recordings featuring Gillespie and Parker did little to further the cause. As 1945 drew to a close, the two were invited to record with Slim Gaillard, their co-headliner at Billy Berg's. Gaillard played guitar and other assorted instruments, but his speciality was humorous vocals – he was best known for his hit 'Cement Mixer'. One of his typical numbers, 'Flat Foot Floogie', had been a best-seller for Decca before the war. At that time he had been teamed with bassist Slam Stewart (Slim and Slam); now Gaillard proposed to record the piece on his own for an obscure Los Angeles label called Bel Tone. The other musicians brought in for the date were Jack McVea on tenor sax, pianist Dodo Marmarosa, bassist Tiny Brown and drummer Zutty Singleton. In addition to the remake of 'Flat Foot Floogie', the group recorded a similar novelty entitled 'Popity Pop (Goes the Motor-Sickle)', and two relaxed instrumentals, 'Dizzy Boogie' and 'Slim's Jam'. Although none of the tunes could be considered a masterpiece, each contains short solos by both Parker and Gillespie and so is of some historical interest. 'Slim's Jam', the best performance of the four, is indeed a miniature jam session which features droll spoken introductions for each soloist by Gaillard.

Gillespie and Parker were also recorded in concert with a Jazz at the Philharmonic troupe while in California. The promoter of these events, Norman Granz, had been a film editor for MGM in 1944 when he first got the idea of transferring the excitement of a jam session from the confines of a nightclub to the concert stage. These concerts were originally held in the Los Angeles Philharmonic Auditorium, a staid hall that usually offered the more sedate strains of symphonic music. Later the concerts were held at various locations, but the original name stuck – usually shortened to JATP in print. A typical line-up at a Jazz at the Philharmonic concert would consist of eight or nine musicians jamming spontaneously on warhorses of the jazz repertoire. The fans got to see and hear many 'names' for their money, since Granz hired (for the most part) only well established swing and modern jazz musicians. The three JATP concerts presented in the winter and spring of 1946 were truly all-star affairs, featuring variously such players as tenor saxophonists Lester Young, Coleman Hawkins and Charlie Ventura, altoist Willie Smith, and trumpeters Buck Clayton, Howard McGhee and Al Killian. Both Parker and Gillespie appeared at the first of these concerts, held in January, and Charlie was aboard for two in March and April as well.

Again, the records made at these concerts are more of historical than musical interest. It's certainly fascinating to hear Bird and Diz trading solos with the giants of the previous generation, and Charlie must have been especially thrilled at sharing the stage with his boyhood idol from Kansas City, Lester Young. Still, the JATP format tended to work against the modernists. The drummer at the first two concerts was Lee Young (Lester's brother), whose rhythmic concept was somewhat out of date. Certainly Lee's plodding swing-era style, with its four-to-the-bar thumping on the bass drum, must have been an extreme annoyance to both Gillespie and Parker, particularly on the up-tempo numbers. Gillespie comes off the better of the two, since the extrovert JATP atmosphere favours his bravura trumpet style, but Parker did not fare at all well in this milieu. The subtle complexities of his style were often overshadowed by the raucous honking and squealing of the other hornmen, and of the two styles, the audience obviously preferred the latter. Charlie would never be the crowd pleaser that, say, Illinois Jacquet would later become. Bird's one great solo from these JATP bashes – a blues-tinged romp on 'Lady be Good' – rates only polite applause from the restive audience.

If the Slim Gaillard and Jazz at the Philharmonic sides had been the only records cut by Gillespie and Parker during their stay in California, and if they had both returned to New York immediately following their gig at Billy Berg's as planned, the trip would rate only a footnote in the history of modern jazz. The events of the frenetic week in February, however, conspired to change all that. These events were sparked by an unexpected source: an enthusiastic jazz fan who proposed to start a record company specifically to record the giants of modern jazz.

Ross Russell was the owner of a small record store in Hollywood, Tempo Music Shop, which catered solely to jazz collectors. Tempo had been patterned after New York's famed Commodore Music Shop, the world's first jazz record store. Russell had started the shop with a small sum saved during his tour with the Merchant Marine during the war, using his own record collection as the nucleus of the store's inventory. He was somewhat nonplussed to find his store a battleground in the wars then raging between the followers of classic jazz and the younger crowd that favoured bebop. Russell admits that he was originally in the Moldy Figs' camp, but he was gradually weaned over to the modernists' side. Several nights at Billy Berg's, listening to Bird and Diz in person, completed his conversion. The thought now occurred to him to record the new music. Again, he had in mind the Commodore Music Shop, which recorded traditional and swing-era musicians on its own label.

Russell found a partner (Marvin Freeman, a Los Angeles attorney) who was willing to help raise the necessary money, and Dial records was born. Russell wanted to record Dizzy's band before it left California, so a recording session was hurriedly arranged. George Handy, pianist and arranger for the Boyd Raeburn orchestra, was contracted to supervise the session and gather the musicians. Handy even suggested adding Lester Young to the line-up, which would have produced a spectacular all-star date. The Gillespie band closed at Berg's on Monday 4 February, and a rehearsal was called for the next evening. Unfortunately, Lester Young was not to be found. The rehearsal itself was something of a madhouse; word of the session had leaked out and scores of assorted hipsters, fans and hangers-on milled about the studio in a chaotic herd. Empty bottles clanked to the floor and the pungent smell of cannabis wafted through the air. Somehow, amid all the confusion, a test-pressing of 'Diggin' for Diz' – a Handy original based on the familiar 'Lover' changes – was recorded by a septet consisting of Gillespie, Parker, Lucky Thompson, Handy himself on piano, guitarist Arvin Garrison, Ray Brown and Stan Levey. Unfortunately, this was the only time that Gillespie and Parker were to appear together on Dial records.

The actual recording session was set for Thursday. A few hours before recording was scheduled to begin, however, George Handy phoned Russ Russell to admit that he could find neither Lester Young nor Charlie Parker and asked that the session be scrubbed. Russell relates what happened next:

> Luckily I reached Dizzy Gillespie at his hotel, which was in another part of Los Angeles altogether, and Dizzy said, 'Well, man, why didn't we do business between ourselves all along?'

He asked if I still wanted to make the date, and I said, 'If we can.' He said all right, he'd have everybody out there. And less than an hour later they were out there, in Glendale, over fifteen miles, and this included Ray Brown's bass, Stan Levey's drums – and I guess the biggest hassle of all was Milt Jackson's vibes, which was roped on the top of somebody's automobile. Bird wasn't on this date at all.[5]

The band recorded five numbers, using material they had been playing nightly on the Billy Berg's gig.

'Confirmation', the first tune recorded, is a Charlie Parker original, one of the few thirty-two measure tunes of his *not* to have been based on the chord changes of a standard show tune.

The introduction Diz uses was soon to be recorded in his own right as 'Oop-Bop-Sh-Bam'. After a remake of 'Diggin' for Diz', which features a marvellously relaxed solo by Gillespie, the group cut two equally impressive takes of the trumpeter's 'Dizzy Atmosphere', taken at a typically break-neck tempo. These alternate takes were issued on two sides of a Dial 78, retitled 'Dynamo A' and 'Dynamo B'. Perhaps to relax, the group next recorded a humorous bop-flavoured version of 'When I Grow

Too Old to Dream', complete with tongue-in-cheek vocal chorus. (When the side was released, the last word of the title was intentionally omitted on the record label.) Finally, the sextet cut a languid version of Thelonious Monk's haunting 'Round about Midnight'. Because Gillespie was already under contract to another company, these sides were attributed to the Tempo Jazzmen, and the trumpet player was listed as one 'Gabriel'.

The very next day, Dizzy and the rest of the band returned to New York, but once again without Bird. Charlie had been missing for several days and couldn't be located even through the musicians' extensive grapevine. Seats had been booked on an airliner for Friday, but Bird failed to show. Gillespie made one last-ditch effort to find the altoist, sending Stan Levey out in a cab. Levey remembers running up a hefty fare during the fruitless search. When it became evident that Parker wasn't going to make it, Gillespie left Charlie's ticket and some money at the hotel desk, and the rest of the musicians left for the Apple.

Charlie Parker remained out of sight for several more days. Some time during that period he cashed in his airline ticket and committed himself to an extended California residency. The usual explanation is that he needed the money for drugs. It may, however, have been nothing more than another manifestation of his live-for-the-moment philosophy. Whatever the reason, it was a mistake, for Charlie was temperamentally unsuited to the small-townish, often racist ambience of post-war Los Angeles. None the less, he was now stuck and had to make the best of it. Charlie landed a job at the Club Finale, an after-hours, bring-your-own-bottle club located in the Little Tokyo section of Los Angeles. The section had become something of an annexe of the black community during the war, when several black businesses had moved into stores vacated by Japanese-Americans (who had been interned for the duration). Charlie was joined at the Finale by the young Miles Davis, something of a protégé of the altoist back in New York. Miles had come west with the Benny Carter orchestra specifically to be with Bird. The pair were backed by a tight rhythm section of locals: pianist Joe Albany, bassist Addison Farmer and drummer Chuck Thompson. As word of the gig spread, the Finale became a frequent stop for visiting jazzmen who dropped by to listen and to sit in with the band. Stan Getz, Zoot Sims, Gerry Mulligan, Serge Chaloff, Sonny Berman, Shorty Rogers or Charlie Ventura were likely to stop in on any given night, as the Woody Herman or Gene Krupa or Boyd Raeburn orchestras would swing through town. LA's own Sonny Criss, Gerald Wilson, Dexter Gordon, Teddy Edwards, Red Callender or Roy Porter were always ready to jam if the occasion arose.

Ross Russell was a frequent patron of the Finale. He had missed the chance to record the Gillespie–Parker group, but he saw his opportunity to make up for that. Russell talked with Parker, and the altoist was signed to a contract with Dial. Arrangements were then made for a recording session to take place late in March. Charlie picked his sidemen from the pool of musicians who were frequent visitors to the Finale club. Besides Miles Davis, he called Lucky Thompson, guitarist Arvin Garrison, bassist Victor McMillan and drummer Roy Porter. Pianist Dodo Marmarosa was a last-minute sub for Joe Albany, who had walked out in the middle of a set the night before following a heated argument with Bird.

The first tune recorded was an original of Charlie's, 'Moose the Mooche'. A typical bebop tune with sinuous melody and jagged rhythms, 'Mooche' was named after a local character, one Emery Byrd. A victim of polio in his youth, Byrd ran a combination shoeshine stand and record shop on Central Avenue, the mainstem of LA's black community. He could often been seen wheeling himself in and out of the nightclubs along the Avenue in a wheelchair. The shoeshine stand and wheelchair were also ideal covers for Byrd's real vocation: dealing drugs. He was in fact Parker's LA connection. The next tune to be recorded was a relaxed performance of one of Charlie's more lyrical compositions, 'Yardbird Suite'. Then came Little Benny Harris's tune 'Ornithology', a number based on the chord changes of the bebopper's national anthem, 'How High the Moon'. Harris was a trumpet player from Detroit who had toured with Diz and Bird in the Earl Hines orchestra, and the title is an obvious tribute to Parker. The germ of 'Ornithology' is a phrase lifted from a solo of Parker's on Jay McShann's 'Jumpin' Blues'. One of the alternate takes of 'Ornithology' was issued by Dial under the title 'Bird Lore'.

There had been three different takes of 'Moose the Mooche' and four takes each of 'Yardbird Suite' and 'Ornithology'. The large number of repeats was due to Parker's insistence on perfection in the ensemble portions of the performance. Bird's solos were apt to be as brilliant on his first attempt as on his

fourth or fifth try, but the same couldn't always be said of his sidemen. The final tune to be recorded that evening was Dizzy Gillespie's 'Night in Tunisia'. Like many of Dizzy's compositions, 'Night' features a complex pattern of rhythms and counter-rhythms. Ross Russell later described the difficulties that ensued during its recording:

'Night in Tunisia' took two, possibly three, hours to get pulled together and to record. It proved to be very difficult for everyone in the studio except Bird. We made five takes and a number of false starts. After we made the first take and Bird took that wonderful alto break, we listened to the playback, and we knew that the rest of it was so ragged we couldn't possibly release it. Bird said, 'I'll never make *that* break again.' Actually, he didn't make it quite as well, or at least not with the blinding brilliance and wonderful sense of suspense and climax he had in the first take. Later on, we released that fragment, that first break, on an LP intended only for collectors.[6]

It might be added that Bird's alto break on the version that was ultimately released was only a little less impressive than that first take.

The session had been a great success, and a second recording date was tentatively agreed on. Unfortunately, extra-musical complications were to turn that second date into a disaster. Shortly after the first session the LA Police Department vice squad launched a crack-down on drugs. Heroin, always hard to obtain and expensive in Los Angeles, became prohibitively so. One of the casualties of the crack-down was Emery Byrd. With his connection gone, Charlie tried to kick his habit cold turkey. He switched to a cheap California port wine to help ease the transition. It was not an improvement. In truth, Charlie had adapted to his addiction; he was able to function normally when a steady supply was assured, and was in trouble only when that supply was endangered.

Then, as if these difficulties weren't enough, the engagement at the Finale club came to an abrupt halt. Owner Foster Johnson, a dancer and ex-vaudevillian, ran the club as a sideline. He enjoyed listening to the music and occasionally dancing to the musicians' improvisations. When the vice squad started dropping by to check out his clientele, Johnson decided he didn't need the extra hassle and pulled out. The musicians showed up for their job one night and found the place locked and shuttered. Once again, Charlie dropped out of sight. He was found a few days later rooming in a converted garage in one of the shabbier neighbourhoods of the city's ghetto. His furnishings consisted of a decrepit spring bed, a small throw rug and a battered dresser, all set in the middle of a concrete floor.

That Charlie made it through the next few months at all can be attributed almost entirely to Howard McGhee. Howard, one of the pioneer trumpet players of modern jazz and at this time second in popularity only to Dizzy Gillespie among the modernists, took Charlie under his wing. It was not a responsibility to be taken lightly. Like any other black musician, Howard had difficulties of his own. He and his wife Dorothy, a blonde ex-model, were constantly hassled by the Los Angeles police. A mixed couple was quite enough to bring most officers of the time to an apoplectic rage. The McGhees were once arrested for sitting together at a James Cagney movie in the 'white' section of downtown LA.

Howard and Dorothy brought Charlie into their modest bungalow, then made arrangements to reopen the Finále club. This time there would be no bottles; it would be strictly a paid-admission jazz club. The band consisted of Howard, Charlie, Dodo Marmarosa, Red Callender and Roy Porter. Dorothy McGhee collected the one-dollar fee at the door, and the night's take was divided among the musicians. Through the early summer months of 1946 the job provided sustenance for Charlie, yet it was a far cry from the standards a man of his artistic stature deserved. In the meantime, although he shied clear of heroin, whisky had replaced port wine as a self-prescribed medicine and was wreaking havoc on his body. Physically and emotionally, Parker was a very sick man. He had developed nervous tics and muscular spasms; while playing a solo his horn was apt to jerk into the air, or he might suddenly spin off to one side.

All of Charlie's problems came to a head the night of 29 July, at the infamous 'Lover Man' session. He had been badgering Ross Russell for another recording date for some time but Russell, knowing Charlie's physical condition, had been putting him off. Howard McGhee finally told Russell that Charlie was going downhill fast, and that if there were to be any recording done it would have to be soon. Arrangements were hastily made, and on the appointed night the musicians and a few interested onlookers gathered at the studio. Pianist Jimmy Bunn and bassist Bob Kesterton replaced Finale regulars Dodo Marmarosa and Red Callender for the recording. Howard, Charlie and Roy Porter completed the quintet. Bird was obviously in bad shape. He sat slumped in a chair to one side, seemingly oblivious of the proceedings. Finally Howard took charge and suggested a tune called 'Max Making Wax'. The tempo was set at a blistering pace. Normally, extremely rapid tempi were Charlie's forte, and the only problem he had was finding musicians who could keep up with him. But on this night his deteriorating body betrayed him. Moreover, the rest of the musicians were distressed and unnerved by Charlie's obvious difficulties. The supposedly unison statement of the theme on 'Max' is terribly ragged, and the volume drops sharply as Bird's alto jerks off-mike from time to time. The take was obviously not worth issuing, but there seemed little chance of an improved performance on a second try. Ross Russell instructed the engineer simply to record every bit of music played and to adjust his levels as best he could.

After a short break the musicians decided to try the ballad 'Lover Man'. Charlie, in the meantime, had taken some barbiturates in an attempt to settle his protesting muscles. Pianist Jimmy Bunn began a quiet introduction, but Bird missed his cue and came in a few bars late. Charlie's tone on the performance is haunting, the equivalent of a vocalist about to burst into tears. He stays close to the melody at first, then gains a measure of confidence and launches into flight. The notes come in flurries, in seemingly random phrases that manage somehow to fit into a satisfying whole. It's a technique that Charlie often used on ballads, but here he seems dangerously close to losing control altogether. He's the high-wire artist, working without a net, who slips and stumbles, yet never falls. The performance, with all its obvious faults, is strangely and deeply moving.

'The Gypsy', a ballad that Charlie had been playing nightly at the Finale, came next. Here Charlie lost the control he had tenuously gained on 'Lover Man'. His performance is deliberate and plodding, a walk-through that takes no chances whatsoever, dull as Sunday-morning TV. Charlie's final tune was the minor-key 'Bebop', taken at a disastrously fast tempo. The ensemble passages are exceedingly sloppy and Charlie's solo simply peters out; even two great choruses by Howard McGhee aren't enough to save the piece. Charlie brought the tune to a close with an unnerving whimper on his alto, then collapsed in a chair – obviously finished for the night. Off in another corner, one of the few visitors sat taking notes. This was Elliott Grennard, Hollywood correspondent for *Billboard*, and he would later pen a prize-winning short story for *Harper's* entitled 'Sparrow's Last Jump', based on the evening's events.

Charlie was driven back to the hotel he was staying at by a man named Slim, the custodian and equipment man at the Finale. Slim was charged with putting Bird to bed and staying with him for the night. In the meantime, Russell and the musicians hoped to salvage the session with some quartet recordings. After a short break for sandwiches, Howard and the rhythm section quickly ran down two new tunes. The musicians, freed from the earlier tensions, were finally able to relax, and the recording went apace. The first tune, released under the title 'Trumpet at Tempo', was Howard's fiery improvisation on 'Back Home in Indiana'. The second piece, 'Thermodynamics', was a relaxed reworking of an obscure minor-key Ellington tune. Ross Russell thought these performances of little commercial value, due to their thin instrumentation, but they are minor bebop classics, and their reissue on a Spotlite LP has been enthusiastically greeted by collectors.

The session finished, Russell drove by Charlie's hotel to see how the altoist was doing, but Bird had disappeared. The story, pieced together afterwards, was this. Slim had indeed put Charlie to bed but, contrary to directions, had then left. A short time later Charlie had appeared in the hotel lobby seeking change for a pay telephone, there being no phones in the rooms. Unfortunately, he was stark-naked. Charlie seemed unaware of his state of undress and couldn't understand the commotion he was causing. The manager, after a short shouting match, persuaded Charlie to return to his room. A short time later the scene was repeated, and this time the manager led Charlie back to his room and locked him in. About half an hour later, smoke was seen billowing from beneath the door of the room. The manager called the fire department then rushed up to the room and unlocked the door. Charlie had fallen asleep while smoking and his mattress had caught fire. A fire engine soon arrived, followed closely by the police. Charlie, roused from a drugged sleep and still naked, wandered about shouting at the people who were invading his privacy. He was promptly sapped by the police for his trouble and driven off to be booked. Russell tried desperately to find Charlie to bail him out, but the police weren't co-operating.

Charlie was finally located, ten days later, in the Psychopathic Ward of the Los Angeles county jail. He was charged with committing arson.

The upshot of the affair was that Charlie was ordered to be confined for six months at Camarillo State Hospital. As traumatic as the experience must have been, it probably was a fortunate thing to have happened to Charlie at the time. He had been going downhill fast, and it's conceivable that the stay at Camarillo may have saved his life. Camarillo is a small town halfway up the coast between Los Angeles and Santa Barbara. It boasts the sort of weather that city fathers and Chambers of Commerce dream about. The state hospital lies several miles out of town, nestled between the foothills and truck farms. At the time, it was considered the country club of the state hospital system, housing neither dangerous psychotics nor the criminally insane. Physically, Charlie prospered during his stay. The regular hours, balanced diet, healthful climate and above all the absence of drugs and alcohol all helped to restore his wellbeing. As his health improved, however, Charlie was increasingly agitated by the confinement. Hospital officials dragged their feet over Bird's release, unconvinced that he could face the rigours of the outside world. Finally, Ross Russell, by agreeing to have Charlie released into his custody, managed to get Charlie sprung. He was released towards the end of January 1947.

Once again, Howard McGhee came through. Howard had just contracted to bring a band into the Hi-De-Ho club on Western Avenue. He promptly offered Charlie a spot in the group as co-leader, at a salary of two hundred dollars a week. Charlie was never more ready, and soon proved that he hadn't lost his touch while at Camarillo. Despite the importuning of the pushers and local hipsters, he stayed clear of drugs, although he did continue to drink heavily. He just wanted to make the gig and save a little money so he could make it back to New York. He was physically fit and blowing better than ever. It seemed like an auspicious time to record.

Ross Russell and Charlie discussed a 'farewell' recording session. They planned on using the cream of the musicians then available on the Coast. Howard would be on trumpet, of course, and as a third horn they planned to use the rising young tenor saxophonist Wardell Gray. The rhythm section would consist of Dodo Marmarosa, guitarist Barney Kessel, bassist Red Callender and Don Lamond, Woody Herman's fine drummer.

Arrangements for this session had just about been set when Charlie suggested adding a vocalist, a young baritone he had heard in a Central Avenue club named Earl Coleman. This panicked Ross Russell. He didn't want or need a vocalist, and felt sure one would wreck the session. Thinking quickly, he came up with a counter-offer. Why not record Earl Coleman at a separate session devoted strictly to his vocals? To Russell's relief, Charlie agreed.

Russell phoned around and soon came up with a rhythm section for the vocal date. The Erroll Garner trio, with Erroll on piano, Red Callender on bass and Harold 'Doc' West on drums, was available. Russell talked with Garner, who agreed to play the session if he could cut a couple of additional trio sides. Everything was set. The musicians met at the C.P. MacGregor studios in Hollywood on 17 February. Three hours of studio time had been reserved, and it took two hours to record acceptable takes of the two Earl Coleman vocals, 'This is Always' and 'Dark Shadows'. The first is a ballad in the Billy Eckstine mode and the second a blues. Despite Russell's misgivings, the two sides have held up well over the years – especially 'Dark Shadows', which features a moving chorus by Bird. However, by the time the two tunes were completed, Earl Coleman's voice was failing. Russell recalls what happened next:

> At that point, Earl had had about enough; his pipes were beginning to give out on him. So Charlie Parker kinda cranked up, and they tossed off a blues. They did three takes – bang, bang, bang. The first two were too fast. Garner didn't like the tempo, and we slowed the takes down a little. One of the fast takes was released as 'Hot Blues', and the slow, 'Cool Blues'. As soon as that was finished, they made an ad lib improvisation on 'I Got Rhythm'. Three takes on this – bang, bang, bang. The interesting thing is that Bird played a little differently with Erroll Garner. Some of the very hip people didn't like what happened; but I think a very interesting performance resulted on this date.[7]

Russell's memory is a bit hazy here; the 'I Got Rhythm' number was in fact taken first. Back in top form, Charlie reeled off superior solos on each take, and all three versions eventually found their way on to 78s under the title 'Bird's Nest'. There were actually four takes of the blues. As Russell mentions,

Garner felt uncomfortable with the tempo on the first two. (These were later released as 'Hot Blues' and 'Blowtop Blues'.) On the slower third and fourth takes, however, the band cooks as if the musicians had been working together for years. The third take, chosen for release, is one of Parker's great recorded performances. Bird's solo on 'Cool Blues' swings hard yet is utterly relaxed, while Erroll forgets his usual mannerisms and really digs into the guts of the blues.

In fact, despite Russell's initial misgivings, the entire date turned out to be an unqualified success. The two impromptu performances by the quartet were critical as well as popular successes; 'Cool Blues' won the *Grand Prix du Disque* when it was released in France the following year. The two Erroll Garner Trio selections, 'Pastel' and 'Trio', were equally well received. And to top everything off, Earl Coleman's version of 'This is Always' became a surprise hit, outselling everything in the Dial catalogue.

Charlie's farewell session took place a week later, on 26 February. The day before there had been a short rehearsal at the studio. Charlie had brought in a new tune which he had scribbled down while riding over in the cab. Most of the session was spent in running down the new tune, a blues with a complex, sinuous melody line. The rehearsal ended with the musicians mumbling over the difficulty of the new piece. Next day, Charlie was late for the actual recording session. Howard McGhee found him a couple of hours later asleep in his bathtub, fully clothed, where he had crashed the night before. Back at the studio, Charlie revived himself with black coffee while Howard rehearsed the rest of the band on three originals he had brought in for the date. Finally Charlie was ready and they started working on his new tune. It took five attempts to get an acceptable take. Charlie's solos on all five were top-notch, but the ensembles were ragged on the first four, as the other musicians struggled with the complex rhythms of the melody line. All of the solos on the final take are extremely relaxed, as if the musicians could breathe easier once the tortuous head had been negotiated. The tune was released under the title 'Relaxin' at Camarillo', and it is a classic statement of the blues in the modern jazz idiom.

The other three tunes recorded during the session are all fine, workmanlike performances, but they suffer in comparison with 'Relaxin''. The next tune, 'Cheers', is a slightly-above-medium piece with an undistinguished, boppish melody. 'Carvin' the

Bird' is another blues, slightly faster but less intense than 'Relaxin' at Camarillo'. As jazz writer Ira Gitler has noted elsewhere, it's Bird who does the carving. Wardell Gray, whose tenor sax exhibits a Lester Youngish tinge throughout the date, comes on very much like Prez in his solo on 'Carvin''. The final tune, 'Stupendous', is based on the old standby ''S Wonderful'. All in all it was a very successful date and a fitting farewell to the Coast for Parker.

A few days later Charlie finally caught a plane back to New York. His stay in California hadn't been a happy one, and he was more than eager to return to a milieu where his talents were more appreciated. Physically, he was in much better shape when he left than when he had arrived, but that would prove to be a short-lived respite; he later returned to drugs. Musically, he was at the top of his form, and it is generally agreed that the years 1947 and 1948 saw the peak of Bird's creativity. The records he cut in New York in those years for Dial and Savoy are considered among his greatest legacies. The Dials that Charlie cut in California are worthy additions to his canon, and the best of them ('Ornithology', 'Night in Tunisia', 'Cool Blues' and 'Relaxin' at Camarillo') rank with any records he ever made.

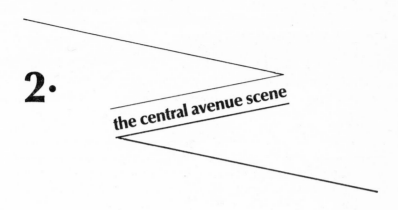

2.
the central avenue scene

As word of the ill-fated gig at Billy Berg's and of Charlie Parker's subsequent troubles in California spread, Los Angeles came to be saddled with a square reputation it didn't entirely deserve. One statement of Charlie's came to be widely quoted at the time. Shortly after he had returned to New York, Charlie told Leonard Feather, 'Finally on the Coast I didn't have any place to stay, until somebody put me up in a converted garage. The mental strain was getting worse all the time. What made it worst of all was that nobody understood our kind of music out on the Coast. I can't begin to tell you how I yearned for New York.'[1] But while it seems obvious that Bird's talents weren't appreciated by the audience at Billy Berg's, it simply is not true that nobody understood modern jazz on the Coast – as Parker himself knew well enough. Unfortunately, this kind of blanket condemnation was all too often taken at face value.

One of the problems was that the response of the Hollywood audience was accepted as typical by the true believers back east. In truth it was typical of only one portion of the LA audience. There *were* enthusiastic supporters of jazz in Los Angeles in those post-war years; they just weren't to be found among the regulars in the Hollywood nightclubs. Several miles to the south of the Hollywood hills – and all but unknown to the mass of white Angelenos – a wealth of nightclubs, restaurants and after-hours spots served up a steaming potpourri of jazz nightly. These clubs were clustered along or near the mainstem of LA's black community, Central Avenue, in a setting that rivalled New York's famed 52nd St.

The focal point of the Avenue was the Club Alabam, a favourite of the crowds for several decades. The Alabam had been founded (as the Apex Club) in the twenties by drummer-bandleader Curtis Mosby, and featured dancing and entertainment nightly. During the boom years of World War Two Lee Young led the house band; his lead altoist for a time was a white teenager just beginning to make a name for himself in jazz circles, Art Pepper. Art described the Alabam as:

> one of the old-time show-time places, a huge room with beautiful drapes and silks and sparklers and coloured lights turning and flashing. The bandstand was plush and gorgeous with curtains that glistened. The waitresses were dressed in scanty costumes, and they were all smiling and wiggling and walking around, and everywhere you looked you saw teeth, people laughing, and everybody was decked out. It was a sea of opulence, big hats and white fluffy fur.[2]

There was a balcony and a spacious dancefloor and, along one wall, an eighty-foot bar.

Clustered nearby were such clubs as Lovejoy's, the Downbeat, Memo, Bird in the Basket, Last Word and Turban Lounge. Lee Young remembers:

> They had so many little clubs. Next door to the Alabam was a Mexican restaurant, and it had a piano in the back, and piano players used to go in there, and I'm speaking about *Art Tatum*. Adjacent to that was the Downbeat. Within two blocks they had about six clubs where musicians were working, and so, like, we used to take long intermissions and go across the street and listen. We'd go next door and they'd come over to hear us play. It was a West Coast 52nd St, but you never really heard of Los Angeles that much, then, where music was concerned.[3]

There were, in addition to the regular nightclubs, numerous after-hours rooms, bottle clubs (bring your own bottle; they'd supply the set-ups) and restaurants that featured jazz of one style or another.

Dizzy Gillespie and Charlie Parker both knew of the Central Avenue scene, of course, because they'd go down after their job at Berg's and jam with the locals. They had no difficulty finding musicians ready and eager to play. Dexter Gordon – LA's most famous native son – was out of town when the Dizzy Gillespie Sextet dropped by, but musicians like Sonny Criss, Teddy Edwards, Wardell Gray, Bobby and Jay McNeely, Art and Addison Farmer, Howard McGhee, Al Killian, Dodo Marmarosa, Hampton Hawes, Charles Mingus, Chuck Thompson and Roy Porter were available at a moment's notice.

There was at least one first-rate bebop combo playing in the Los Angeles area even before Diz and Bird arrived. This was the Howard McGhee Sextet with tenor saxophonist Teddy Edwards. McGhee and Edwards were recent settlers on the Coast who shared similar backgrounds. Howard was born in Tulsa in 1918, but grew up in Detroit. There he attended Cass Technical School, which also numbered jazzmen Wardell Gray and Milt Jackson among its alumni. Maggie served the usual apprenticeship in the big bands of the period, starting with road trips and one-nighters in territorial bands in the late thirties. In 1941 he joined Lionel Hampton and subsequently spent time in such name bands as Andy Kirk's Clouds of Joy, Charlie Barnet, Georgie Auld and Count Basie. He settled in New York in 1944, just in time to join the brewing bebop revolution. Originally heavily influenced by Roy Eldridge, Maggie forged an original style for himself that combined the bravura flash, broad tone and vibrato of the trumpet masters of the thirties with the fluid agility and advanced harmonic ideas of Dizzy Gillespie. Howard quickly made a name for himself on the 52nd St scene, and when Coleman Hawkins formed a combo for a West Coast tour Maggie was picked for the trumpet slot.

The Coleman Hawkins Quintet (McGhee, Hawkins, Sir Charles Thompson, Oscar Pettiford and Denzil Best) played an extended engagement at Billy Berg's in early 1945. The band featured a fascinating synthesis of swing and bop, and apparently was conservative enough to find favour even with the crowds at Berg's. More importantly, the group recorded while in California, and the sessions – one for Asch and three for Capitol – produced some outstanding examples of jazz in transition from the swing to modern idioms. On ballads like 'Stardust' and 'Talk of the Town' the group is cast in a traditional mould, yet the up-tempo numbers – such as 'Bean Stalkin' ' from the Asch session and 'Rifftide', 'Hollywood Stampede' and 'Bean Soup' from the Capitol dates – find the band in a boppish mode.

When Coleman Hawkins returned to New York in March,

McGhee decided to stay on in Los Angeles. He wanted to form a band along the lines of the Hawkins group, using many of the same arrangements, and it was here that Teddy Edwards entered the picture. Teddy was born in Jackson, Mississippi in 1924. He took up alto sax at the age of eleven, and was soon playing professionally with local bands. In 1940 he moved to Detroit, where one of his jobs was with the Stack Walton band. Howard McGhee was also in the Walton band, as were Wardell Gray, Matthew Gee and Al McKibbon. Teddy moved to California in 1944 and settled in Los Angeles, where he soon renewed his acquaintance with McGhee. Maggie called on Edwards when it came time to form his band. 'They had a library,' Teddy remembers, 'and Howard wanted to use most of that. He couldn't find anybody he liked, so he persuaded me to give the tenor a try.'⁴ Teddy took up the larger horn and found it a challenge because, 'while changing horns I also had to learn the band's book at the same time. This was kinda tough, but it taught me a lot.'⁵

The group played jobs around Los Angeles throughout 1945 and 1946. Work wasn't always steady, but McGhee had a way of finding gigs if any were available. The personnel varied but usually included McGhee, Edwards, Dodo Marmarosa or Vernon Biddle on piano, Stanley Morgan, guitar, Bob Kesterson, bass, and Roy Porter on drums. During the spring and summer of 1946 Howard spent some time playing with Charlie Parker (as we have seen) in an attempt to keep Bird's head above water. Following Charlie's breakdown and departure to Camarillo, however, Howard was once again free to work with his own group. By October of 1946 he and Ross Russell agreed that the band was ready to record.

The musicians gathered at the C.P. MacGregor studio in Hollywood on 18 October. Dodo Marmarosa was the pianist and studio veteran Arvin Garrison sat in on guitar; McGhee, Edwards, Bob Kesterson and Roy Porter completed the band. Dodo Marmarosa – the nickname is a diminutive of 'Dodobird', which referred to the pianist's rather large head and slight frame – was one of the brilliant group of white pianists (Al Haig, George Wallington and Joe Albany were the others) who helped spearhead the bop revolution. His given name was Michael. Bob 'Dingbod' Kesterson was a free spirit who commuted to gigs, bass and all, on an Italian motor scooter. With the exception of Garrison, the musicians had been playing together on and off for well over a year, and in the autumn of 1946 the band was the equal of any bebop unit on either coast.

The band cut four sides for Dial that night. The first tune was released under the title 'Dilated Pupils' and attributed to McGhee, but it is simply a remake of the 52nd St favourite 'Max Makin' Wax'. Teddy Edwards, in his recording debut, is remarkably at ease at the rapid tempo, and Maggie caps the performance with a well-balanced solo in cup mute. In fact, Howard stays in cup through all four tunes. 'Midnight at Minton's', an original of Maggie's, is a medium-tempo ballad. The highlight of the session is a blues with altered changes in the first four bars, 'Up in Dodo's Room'. Once again the tune is attributed to McGhee, but Teddy remembers that the tune was written by Hal Vernon, a Los Angeles pianist. The performance remains a favourite of Teddy's, who calls it 'one of my best solos'. The final tune is a smoking version of the bop standard '52nd Street Theme' – retitled 'High Wind in Hollywood' – in which the soloists tame the rapid chord progressions with ease. The four sides caused an immediate stir among the jazz public. Speaking specifically about 'Up in Dodo's Room', Teddy Edwards says: 'This was the first record to come out with a sound different from what groups led by Hawkins and Lester Young had been getting up till then. By this time I'd been very much influenced by Charlie Parker, and this accounted for the different sound. It surprised a lot of people at the time.'[6]

Unfortunately, the group did not record again. When Charlie Parker returned from Camarillo, McGhee once again hired the altoist to share the front line of the quintet he was leading at the Hi-De-Ho club. The pianist for that gig, incidentally, was a teenager just out of high school named Hampton Hawes. For a time – before Bird left for New York – McGhee organized an eight-piece band that included Charlie Parker and Sonny Criss on altos, Teddy Edwards and Gene Montgomery on tenors, Earl Ecklin, piano, and Bob Kesterson and Roy Porter on bass and drums. The combination sounds intriguing, but no recordings of the group seem to have been made. Shortly afterwards Bird returned to the Apple and Howard himself soon left town with a Jazz at the Philharmonic troupe. Teddy Edwards stayed on in LA. Maggie's departure left a serious void in the Los Angeles jazz scene, but it was soon filled by another young giant when LA's own Dexter Gordon returned to the fold.

Dexter had already achieved national fame as one of the

pioneers of the modern-jazz movement. He had played with Dizzy Gillespie in Billy Eckstine's roaring big band and Charlie Parker's combo on 52nd St. He had recorded with both Gillespie and Parker in a number of contexts – the best-known being his collaboration with Diz on 'Blue 'n' Boogie' for the Guild label – and had cut many sides for Savoy under his own name. He was, quite simply, the leading tenor saxophonist of the modern school.

Dexter Gordon had been fortunate from the beginning in growing up in a sympathetic musical environment. He was born in Los Angeles on 27 February 1923. His father was a well-known doctor who counted Duke Ellington and Lionel Hampton among his patients; he was also an avid jazz fan, and introduced Dexter to the music at an early age. Dr Gordon started his son off on clarinet lessons and saw to it that he studied harmony as well. At the time (that is, throughout the 1930s) the Los Angeles black community offered an exciting milieu for young musicians. Dexter would remember later:

There was a very strong musical thing in my neighbourhood and we had some very good teachers. I went to Jefferson High School with people like Chico Hamilton, Melba Liston, Ernie Royal, Vi Redd. In another neighbourhood there was a school with Charles Mingus, the Woodmans, Buddy Collette and others. In high school we had a very good teacher named Sam Brown – very dedicated. He had all these wild young dudes. We used to call him Count Brown. We had a school marching band, an orchestra that used to play light classics, plus a swing band that played stock arrangements of Benny Goodman and Basie hits.

I studied with Lloyd Reese. At that time he was playing lead trumpet with Les Hite's band. He taught Mingus too. Reese formed a rehearsal band. Every Sunday morning we used to go down to the union building and rehearse. And different people – professionals – would write charts for us to practise. Nat Cole wrote a couple for us. He was one of the local piano players at the time. So I got a foundation in music in Los Angeles. I studied harmony and theory for two or three years. Studying with Lloyd Reese was important. He taught more than exercises in the books. He gave us a broader picture and an appreciation of music. He made us more aware. He was teaching us musical philosophy.[7]

28

Lloyd Reese is remembered with affection and respect by all the musicians who studied with him. Buddy Collette, a fine reedman and one of the first black musicians to break into the lucrative confines of the Hollywood studio orchestras, credits much of his success to a thorough grounding in basics drilled into him by Reese. 'He wanted all his students to play the piano, to learn the keyboard,' Buddy says. 'He wanted you to learn all the chords to different songs in different keys, and he used the Roman numeral system so you could transpose easily. He liked you to be very versatile in reading and playing tunes, because he knew what was going to be demanded of us.'[8] Collette introduced several budding musicians to Reese, including Charles Mingus, Bobby and Jay McNeely, Bill Douglass and the young Eric Dolphy.

Dexter Gordon decided early on a musical career, dropping out of high school at seventeen to play tenor with a local group known as the Harlem Collegians. He soon got a call to join the Lionel Hampton band. One of the tenor saxophonists had suddenly given notice, and Hampton desperately needed a player. 'So Marshall Royal, who was playing lead alto in the band, called me. He and his brother Ernie were both in the band, and Ernie and I had been in the school orchestra together. I only had three days to get ready, which I'm sure is one of the reasons I got the call. There wasn't time to get someone of professional quality.' Dexter found himself in a sink-or-swim situation. 'We played the first night without rehearsal. I didn't play a right note all night. Nobody said anything. The next couple of days we rehearsed, so I got a chance to become acquainted...That was like going to college for me.'[9]

Dexter credits Marshall Royal especially as being a mentor while in the Hampton band. Marshall was ten years older than Dexter and had a wealth of experience in big bands.

There's a cat who showed me a lot – Marshall. I didn't really come to appreciate it until recently – a few years ago. He used to stay on my ass all the time in that section. I'd say, 'Oh, man, won't this guy ever get off my back?' But everything he told me was right – breathing, phrasing. 'Man, tune up, tune up, man.'[10]

Dexter stayed with Hampton for three years, then moved back to

LA and worked for Lee Young and Jesse Price, before joining Louis Armstrong's big band. While he remembers Armstrong with affection, the same couldn't be said of the band itself. 'I had more to play than with Hamp, but the band wasn't saying too much. Pops was using all those old, thirtyish arrangements... "Sleepy Time", all those funny things.' Dexter stayed with Armstrong for six months, then joined the brash new band that Billy Eckstine had formed.

> I remember coming out of Louis Armstrong's band into Eckstine's band, which was like night and day – because there was nothing but happenings, excitement and enthusiasm in Eckstine's band; whereas in Pops' band, everything was just blah. You played a job, and that was the whole thing. Of course, Pops sounded very beautiful at that time – I loved the way he sounded.[11]

The Billy Eckstine band of 1944–46 has long since taken on near-mythical overtones. Nearly every major figure of the bebop revolution put some time in with the band, including – at one time or another: Dizzy Gillespie, Fats Navarro, Miles Davis, Charlie Parker, Sonny Stitt, Gene Ammons, Wardell Gray, Leo Parker, Oscar Pettiford, Shadow Wilson and Art Blakey. The band was a showcase for Eckstine's vocals, of course, but Billy respected his musicians (he played trumpet and valve trombone himself) and gave free rein to his arrangers. Dexter joined the band on the road. They were playing the Howard Theater in Washington, DC and once again Dexter had to go in cold, without a rehearsal.

> I just went onstage and made it with them. I didn't know what was going on. And they had an opener they used to use called 'Blitz' – it was a Jerry Valentine thing, up-tempo – short for 'Blitzkrieg'. I don't think I made a right note in the whole thing, 'cause it was *flying*! Buhaina [Art Blakey] was dropping all those bombs back there. I just kept comin' out of the seat.[12]

Dexter quickly had the book down and soon became a major voice in the band. At a recording session for Deluxe in December of 1944, Dexter and Gene Ammons engage in a tenor-sax duel on a tune called 'Blowing the Blues Away'. The format of a tenor-sax chase was to become an important one in Dexter's subsequent career. Soon after the Deluxe date, Dexter left Eckstine to freelance in New York. He played with Charlie Parker's combo at the Spotlite club and on 9 February 1945, he recorded 'Blue 'n' Boogie' with Dizzy Gillespie for Guild. In the latter part of 1945 Dexter recorded extensively for Savoy under his own name. By the end of the year he was recognized by most fans as the premier tenor saxophonist in modern jazz.

Gordon returned to the West Coast in the summer of 1946, moved briefly to Hawaii for a two-month stay with the Cee Pee Johnson band, then returned to LA. He soon became a fixture on the Central Avenue scene, bringing his own brand of fiery playing to the casual jobs and numerous jam sessions that ran night and day at various clubs. These jam sessions often turned into old-fashioned cutting contests as the younger musicians tried to make a name for themselves by outplaying the established stars. Dexter was the master gunfighter who had to face a new challenge each time he took the stand. The audience and fellow musicians kept score.

One of the few musicians who could consistently keep up with Dexter was the tenor saxophonist Wardell Gray. Gray had been born in Oklahoma City in 1921, but moved at a young age to Detroit, where he attended Cass Tech and played alongside Howard McGhee in the student band. He gained further experience in territorial bands and in 1943 joined the Earl Hines big band that featured Dizzy Gillespie and Charlie Parker. Gray stayed with Hines for two years, then moved to the Coast, where he made a name for himself in a series of 'Just Jazz' concerts for promoter Gene Norman. He was a significant contributor to Charlie Parker's 'Relaxin' at Camarillo' session, as we have seen. And he was a frequent and welcome voice in the Central Avenue clubs and jam sessions.

Dexter Gordon and Wardell Gray complemented each other both musically and in their physical appearance. Both were tall, handsome men with commanding stage presence. Dexter stood six foot five and had an athlete's matching build, while Wardell – almost as tall – had a slight, willowy frame. Their musical styles seemed to match their physiques. Both had originally based their tenor styles on Lester Young's pioneering work of the thirties, although each subsequently modified his style under the influence of Charlie Parker. Dexter's tone had a harder edge to it, and his brusque solos incorporated more of Charlie Parker's fire. Wardell, especially during this period, remained more under Lester's spell; his solos were lyrical, his tone light. Both were relaxed swingers who could cope with any conceivable tempo, and each dug the other's work. In the latter part of 1946 and early 1947 they met often onstage in the Central Avenue clubs and increasingly came to be recognized as a duo simply because they would outlast and outplay the other musicians. 'There'd be a lot of cats on the stand, but by the end of the session, it would wind up with Wardell and myself,' Dexter remembers.[13]

One of the regular listeners at these events was Ross Russell, who naturally thought of the opportunity this pairing presented for Dial records. 'Dexter and Wardell were playing around Los Angeles, conducting this musical chase almost every evening,' he recalls, 'and it was creating a great deal of comment. It seemed like a good idea to get them into the studio and record it.'[14] There remained some problems, though. At the time, recording techniques and equipment were not equal to the task of recording on location, so a 'live' date was out of the question. The problem (and it remains one for jazz recordings to this day) was how to retain the spontaneity and excitement of a nightclub atmosphere in the formal and even sterile confines of a recording studio. The musicians gathered at the C.P. MacGregor studios on 12 June 1947 to see if they could overcome the difficulties. The rhythm section consisted of several regulars from the Central Avenue circuit: Jimmy Bunn, Red Callender and Chuck Thompson. As it turned out, the results of the session exceeded everyone's fondest expectations.

The tune decided upon for the tenor-sax chase was an original of Dexter's, entitled simply 'The Chase'. It was a thirty-two-bar AABA tune based – at least in the A sections – on the old Basie speciality 'Doggin' Around' (a tune that featured contrasting solos by Basie's great tenor men, Herschel Evans and Lester Young). An eight-bar introduction – Charlie Parker would use it later on his recording of 'Klactoveesedstene' – is followed by a statement of the theme in unison. The theme itself is based on a motif almost as old as jazz, the Alphonse Picou clarinet obbligato for 'High Society'. (Both Louis Armstrong and Charlie Parker had incorporated the lick in earlier recorded solos.) Dexter takes the first solo, stretching out for a complete chorus, then Wardell answers in his contrasting style. They each take one more chorus, then relinquish the mike to Jimmy Bunn. After the piano chorus, the real chase begins. Wardell leads off this time for sixteen bars and Dexter becomes the counter-puncher; this order remains as the length of the exchanges shortens to eight and then to four bars each while the excitement mounts apace. Finally there is a restatement of the theme, with the intro tagged on as a coda.

'The Chase' was released on two sides of a single 78 disc and soon became the number-one record in the Dial catalogue, outselling even Charlie Parker's sides. It also gathered a great deal of critical acclaim. Martin Williams, for instance, has written, 'It was one of those rare records that not only went beyond the studio but had an excitement that's rare even in a club.'[15] However, it did little to further the commercial careers of its principals. Dexter later attempted to analyse the situation.

> Somehow my thing with Wardell was never exploited – at least in a positive way. There was nobody to promote it. We did things together, but it would just be a different club every night. We talked about travelling together, but in those days there were few managers or promoters around who might be interested. Most of the people in the business were gangsters. And also our personal lives were pretty chaotic – we weren't the most stable people in the world.[16]

Nor was Gordon's statement about the gangland influence in jazz mere hyperbole; many nightclubs and small record companies of the time were indeed run by gangsters. In view of the success of tenor duos in later years (Sonny Stitt and Gene Ammons, Zoot Sims and Al Cohn, Johnny Griffin and Eddie 'Lockjaw' Davis) it does seem a shame that the pairing of Wardell Gray and Dexter Gordon wasn't capitalized on further.

Dexter cut three more tunes the same day, all with Wardell laying out. These quartet performances are only a little less interesting than 'The Chase'. The first, 'Chromatic Aberration', was an up-tempo original of Dexter's with (as the name suggests) a great deal of stepwise chord movement. Next came a ballad long associated with Coleman Hawkins, 'It's the Talk of the Town', showcasing Gordon's romantic approach. Finally there was another Gordon original, 'Blues Bikini'. The form is one long favoured by jazz musicians, a blues with a channel: that is, an AABA tune in which the A sections are twelve-bar blues. (In this case, a minor blues.) Dexter's solo is well constructed, with no superfluous notes. There seems to have been doubt among some jazz writers as to whether the title refers to the bathing-suit or to the island; both were in the headlines in 1947. Gordon's sardonic subtitle – 'All Men are Cremated Equal' – leaves no doubt as to which he was thinking of.

Dexter recorded two other times for Dial in 1947. The first session, which actually took place a week before the pairing with Wardell Gray, featured trombonist Melba Liston. Melba, originally from Kansas City, Missouri, had moved to Los Angeles in 1937. Only twenty-two at the time of the session, she had been playing professionally from the age of sixteen. She had started out with a community youth band organized by Alma Hightower, a great-aunt of alto saxophonist Vi Redd. Melba credits Mrs Hightower with recognizing and developing a great many talented youngsters. 'After school we would go to the playground and she would work us in theory and harmony, scales and stuff like that, and we would play stock arrangements, and she put this little big band together. We played at the YMCA, dances, churches; we'd play on street corners and pass the hat and all that kind of thing.'[17] Melba's first professional job was with the pit band of the Lincoln Theater; later she moved over to Gerald Wilson's big band; she also studied arranging with Wilson. Although she thinks of herself primarily as an arranger, her skills as a trombonist were always recognized by other musicians. Obviously Dexter thought highly enough of her to call her for the recording date. Melba herself thinks the opportunity might have been a bit premature:

> When [Dexter] got his record date, he said, 'Come on, Mama' – I think they were callin' me Mama already back then, 'cause I used to fuss with them about smokin' their cigarettes or drinkin' their wine – and they'd come and get me when something was goin' on, and I would play little gigs with them. I was scared to go in the studio, though, because I didn't really hang out with them when they were jamming and stuff. I was home trying to write, so I didn't have that spirit on my instrument as [an] improvisational person. I was really very shy. I really didn't wanna make that record session. I don't know which was worse – makin' it or trying to persuade them to leave me *out* of it. I'm happy for it now. I'd rather not *hear* it, however.[18]

With a rhythm section of pianist Charles Fox, Red Callender

and Chuck Thompson, Dexter and Melba cut two tunes on the date: 'Mischievous Lady', an original of Dexter's, and 'Lullaby in Rhythm'. Melba takes a sixteen-bar solo on 'Mischievous Lady'. She doesn't take many chances, but it's a competent performance, certainly nothing to be ashamed of. On 'Lullaby' – taken at a much faster tempo – Melba is heard only in the ensembles. In later years, as she gained experience and confidence, Melba Liston became a much sought-after performer; she was a member of the Quincy Jones all-star orchestra that toured Europe in 1959 and 1960, playing alongside such musicians as Jimmy Cleveland, Quentin Jackson, Phil Woods and Clark Terry.

Dexter Gordon's final session for Dial was held in December of 1947. This was on the eve of an American Federation of Musicians recording ban, and the record companies were scrambling to get a backlog of masters in their vaults to issue later during the ban. Once again Ross Russell (obviously thinking of the sales of 'The Chase') proposed a tenor-sax battle – this time pitting Gordon against Teddy Edwards. The rhythm section for this meeting would be pianist Jimmy Rowles, Red Callender and Roy Porter. Dexter opened the proceedings with two ballad performances, 'Ghost of a Chance' and 'Sweet and Lovely'. 'Ghost' features Dexter at his romantic best, sparked by the lush block-chording of Jimmy Rowles. 'Sweet and Lovely', taken at a faster than expected clip, features Gordon all the way.

Teddy Edwards then joined Dexter for the tenor-sax chase. Once again Gordon supplied an original line, 'The Duel', based this time on the standard 'I Got Rhythm' changes. In this case there is an alternative strain in the second eight, so the tune's format is ABCA. The order of solos is much the same as for 'The Chase': two full choruses each by Gordon and Edwards, a chorus by Jimmy Rowles, then the chase sequence – a series of increasingly shorter exchanges culminating in a chorus of simultaneous improvisation. There is less of a contrast between Dexter and Teddy Edwards than had been the case between Dexter and Wardell Gray. Both Gordon and Edwards are straight ahead, damn-the-torpedoes swingers. If there is more excitement at times on 'The Duel', there is withal a loss of warmth and relaxation compared with 'The Chase'. Still, the performance sold well and boosted the reputations of both saxophonists.

Shortly after Dexter's final Dial session, an AFM recording

ban went into effect. As had been the case with an earlier ban during the war years, the issue was the lack of royalties accruing to musicians for records played on the radio and on jukeboxes, and as also had been the case with the earlier ban, this one was only partially successful. The second ban began on 30 December 1947, and lasted until the following December. There was some clandestine recording, especially by the smaller independent labels, but for the most part the ban held. Unfortunately, it hurt the young modern-jazz movement almost as much as it did the major record companies who were its prime target. Ross Russell has argued that the ban marked the end of the bebop era. Although that's an exaggeration – many sides cut by Parker, Gillespie, Bud Powell and others in the years 1949–53 are considered classics of the genre – it does seem as if the style traced a declining trajectory from that time on.

Certainly the Los Angeles jazz scene was hurt by the ban. Ross Russell had already moved the headquarters of Dial records to New York to be closer to his major artist, Charlie Parker; the Dexter Gordon–Teddy Edwards session was in fact the last Dial date to be held on the coast. Faced with the impending curtailment of all recording, the musicians scrambled to place themselves in favourable situations. Dexter left for New York (a more promising ground for freelance jazzmen) shortly after the Teddy Edwards session, and sat out the ban in the Apple. Wardell Gray also left town the following spring to work with the Benny Goodman Sextet. Once again Los Angeles seemed destined to slip out of the ken of the jazz audience.

By 1948 Dexter Gordon, Howard McGhee, Wardell Gray and Teddy Edwards were, thanks in large part to their California recordings, well known in jazz circles. One other musician who would eventually make an even larger impact on the jazz scene was in the meantime practising his craft in relative obscurity. Charles Mingus is now recognized as a major composer and one of the finest bassists in jazz history, but much of that recognition came belatedly. In fact, many of the compositions that critics and fellow musicians lauded in the late fifties and early sixties had actually been composed – and some even recorded – a decade or more earlier in California.

Charles Mingus was born in Nogales, Arizona on 22 April 1922, but grew up in LA's southside community of Watts. His mother died when he was less than six months old, and Charles was raised by his father, a quick-tempered retired army sergeant, and a loving but religiously strict stepmother. The elder Mingus bequeathed his son not only his temper but his light skin, and so placed Charles in an ambiguous position which would cause problems throughout his life. Watts, in the 1920s, was a mixed blue-collar neighbourhood which was only beginning to receive the influx of black families that would transform it in later decades to an overcrowded black ghetto. As a child, Mingus was not fully accepted by either his black or white schoolmates, and so came to feel that he was, as both the title and contents of his autobiography make clear, *Beneath the Underdog*.

The Mingus household was self-consciously middle-class and jazz music was definitely not allowed, but Charles did get an introduction to black music by attending the neighbourhood Holiness Church with his stepmother. One of the instruments used to provide accompaniment to the gospel-style singing in the church was a trombone, and this was Charles's first choice as an instrument. Unfortunately, his initial instruction by the church's choirmaster was lackadaisical at best, and Charles had to pick his way mainly by ear. He was able to gain a shaky proficiency on the horn and brashly tried to challenge another of the neighbour-hood's trombonists, Britt Woodman, to a cutting contest. Woodman, two years Mingus's senior, came from a musical family – his father, William Woodman Sr, also played trombone, William Jr played trumpet and saxes, and brother Coney played piano – and Britt had received a thorough training on the horn. Nevertheless, he was more amused than annoyed by the youngster's chutzpah and took Charles under his wing. Britt suggested that Charles take up the cello, since one was needed in the school orchestra. This Mingus did, but again his training was haphazard and largely by ear. He did get some help from his sisters Grace, a violinist, and Vivian, a pianist, and the three formed a trio which played concerts at the Methodist church his father attended. None the less, he was later denied a spot in the Jordon School orchestra. Finally one of his classmates at Jordon, Buddy Collette, suggested that Charles take up the double bass, and thus won Mingus's lifelong gratitude and friendship. Buddy also introduced Mingus to bassist Red Callender, and for the first time (at the age of sixteen) Charles received adequate instruction on his chosen instrument.

Buddy Collette, born William Marcell Collette 6 August 1921 in Los Angeles, served as Charles's lifelong friend and mentor. He was the one person who could calm Mingus down when the bassist's explosive temperament was set off. 'We never got into a fight, we had a special relationship...' Buddy would later remember. 'In fact, sometimes when Mingus was getting into trouble and just about to go off on someone, they might say, "We're going to call Buddy," and he would say, "No, no, don't do that." '[19]

Buddy also introduced Charles to Lloyd Reese, and Mingus began studying piano and music theory with Reese. He was soon playing in Reese's Sunday-morning rehearsal band that met in the union hall of the segregated Local 767. Dexter Gordon was also in the band at the time. Buddy Collette and Mingus also played with the Al Adams band, which featured such future stars from nearby Jefferson High as Gordon, Chico Hamilton, clarinettist Jackie Kelso and trumpeter Ernie Royal. (Marshall Royal, Ernie's older brother, was playing lead alto for Les Hite at the time.) Buddy remembers Charles's intense enthusiasm throughout this period:

> He was at my house every day for two years – bringing his bass from 108th St to 96th St, carrying it on his back – to practise and jam with me. And also when we started rehearsing in Los Angeles, which was a long trip from Watts, we'd get the Red Car [Pacific Electric interurban] at 103rd St, and Mingus was so excited about playing, he'd get on the car and zip the cover off the bass, and we'd start jamming on the streetcar... He was always a very open guy with all his thoughts: 'Let's play! Are we gonna play today?' And I'd say, 'Well, OK,' and get the alto out, and the conductor and the motorman would wave – they didn't mind...

It was also during this period that Charles began to concentrate on writing, and two of his compositions that would not be recorded until decades later were written in these pre-war years: 'The Chill of Death' and 'Half-mast Inhibition'.

Following high school Charles seriously considered working for the post office (mainly due to his father's insistence) but finally opted for music – which meant several years of scuffling. When World War Two broke out many of his friends, including the Woodman brothers and Buddy Collette, joined the service. Charles failed his medical and continued to gig around Los Angeles. In 1943 he toured briefly with the Louis Armstrong orchestra, but quit when he found out the band was going on an

38

extended road trip through the South. He then worked intermittently with Lee Young's band at the Club Alabam. (Dexter Gordon and Art Pepper were in the band at the time.) He also kept up his studies on the bass, first with Red Callender, then for several years with Herman Rheinshagen, formerly with the New York Philharmonic. By 1945 Mingus was well on his way to becoming one of the finest bassists in jazz.

Charles also began to record in 1945, mostly as a sideman on pick-up sessions for obscure labels. There were dates with both Russell Jacquet and Illinois Jacquet that were as much rhythm and blues as jazz, and others that found Mingus backing vocalists Ernie Andrews and Dinah Washington. There were also dates under Mingus's own name in the summer of 1945 and January 1946 for the Excelsior label. Both were largely vocal affairs, and titles such as 'The Texas Hop', 'Lonesome Woman Blues' and 'Ain't Jivin' Blues' give the flavour of the recordings. Nevertheless, the second session produced the first recording of 'Weird Nightmare', a ballad which would become a staple in the Mingus book.

In the spring of 1946 Mingus and Buddy Collette (home from a stint as a navy bandleader) helped form a co-operative group known as the Stars of Swing, which should have – but didn't – advanced the careers of all its participants. The band did, however, have a memorable run at the Down Beat club on Central Avenue. The members of the septet were John Anderson, trumpet; Britt Woodman, trombone; Collette, alto sax; Lucky Thompson, tenor; Spaulding Givens, piano; Mingus, bass; and Oscar Bradley, drums. Buddy still looks back on the band with fondness and the sense of a missed opportunity:

It was an exceptional band because of the guys and because about five of us wrote: Mingus, Lucky, John Anderson, Spaulding Givens and myself. Lucky also had some arrangements by Jimmy Mundy for seven pieces. We rehearsed for about a month – none of the guys were busy at that point – and we'd rehearse at Mingus's house every day, five, six, seven hours. We'd go have lunch and come back and work on dynamics; we did everything possible to have a good band...It was better than anything around, because when you've got that kind of talent and you work that hard, well...So when we went into the Down Beat, people couldn't believe it; their mouths fell open. 'Huh? What is that? How could they be *this* good?' I'm talkin' about – not solo-wise, because most groups are good that way – but we were good solo-wise *and* sectionally, which you don't hear very much, because nobody spends that much time.

Unfortunately, the band didn't last much longer than its six-week engagement at the Down Beat. Worse, it was never recorded. Britt Woodman remembers that they did audition for one company, but the label soon folded and the demos were never found.

With the break-up of the Stars of Swing, Mingus returned to freelancing once more. In May 1946 there was an octet date under his leadership for 4 Star records in which 'Weird Nightmare' was again recorded (under the title 'Pipe Dream') as well as another ballad entitled 'This Subdues My Passion'. Later in the year he played a one-nighter with an otherwise all-white bebop group led by altoist Dean Benedetti; the band also included trombonist Jimmy Knepper, who would later be a mainstay of the famous Mingus groups of the late 1950s.

The following year, 1947, proved to be pivotal in Mingus's career. Early in the year he somehow managed to talk Columbia records officials into recording his composition 'The Chill of Death' with a large studio orchestra. Although the recording was never released – it was undoubtedly far too 'advanced' for the Columbia brass – it did bring encouraging comments to Charles by none other than Charlie Parker, who was present at the recording session. ('The Chill of Death' was ultimately recorded – and released this time – by Columbia in 1971.) Then in the summer of 1947 Mingus was hired by Lionel Hampton, which finally led to national recognition for the young bassist. In November the Hampton band recorded Charles's composition 'Mingus Fingers', an up-tempo number on 'I Got Rhythm' changes that featured an extended bass solo by Mingus. The recording was for Decca, which meant national distribution for the side.

Mingus toured with the Hampton band through most of 1948 (the year of the recording ban) but returned to LA to freelance late in the year. The exposure he had got with the Hampton orchestra had undoubtedly helped his reputation, but that didn't translate immediately into superior jobs; he was once again forced into a routine consisting largely of casuals and one-nighters. It was one such gig, however, that led indirectly to a momentous shake-up of the Los Angeles music scene. Sometime in 1949 Mingus was called to play for a big band backing singer Billy Eckstine in a concert at the Million Dollar Theatre. Buddy Collette remembers what happened next:

I don't know who called the band together, but Billy was coming to town and the contractor usually does that. And it was an all-white band, except for Mingus, who is very light-complected... He didn't like that and he hassled all those guys, made them all feel uncomfortable. 'Well what the heck, why aren't there any other black guys here? What are you guys, prejudiced or something?' It was the sort of thing he did; he wasn't a guy to hold his feelings. And a lotta times that's good, too, because he was saying something that most people would just [shrugs his shoulders], but he brought it out in the open. And it got to the point where guys were trying to avoid him, but it was still the truth... I probably wouldn't have said anything, but sure would have felt it: 'Hey, it would have been nice if they would have hired a few blacks.' And especially with Billy Eckstine being a black artist, because there'd be a lot of black people in the audience, and they'd be thinking, 'Hey, where are they?'

It was this incident which eventually led to the amalgamation of the segregated Los Angeles Musicians' Union locals.

Collette and Mingus discussed the situation with a few others and came to the conclusion there would never be an influx of black musicians into well-paying jobs as long as the musicians' locals were segregated. They set about rectifying that situation and immediately found that it wouldn't be easy. 'The black union was located in a broken-down building on Central Avenue, with terrible pianos, but the officials, who were older, liked it that way and said, in effect, let's keep our own union and our own building. Don't rock the boat.'[20] The dissidents also discussed the matter with some sympathetic white musicians, including percussionist Milt Holland:

He suggested joint meetings, but I knew many of our guys wouldn't come to meetings, so I suggested starting an integrated rehearsal orchestra, in this case a symphony orchestra, because that would prepare everyone for studio work. I knew I needed it, because on flute there were still things that gave me trouble. Milt said, 'Get as many blacks or other minorities as you can, and I'll fill in the other spots.' We only had about nine, so he had a lot of filling-in to do: Bill Green, Red Callender, Jimmy McCullough, Britt Woodman, Jimmy Cheatham and Percy McDavid, an excellent conductor – one of the few black orchestra conductors.

We had our first rehearsal at Town Hall... and the place was packed with press and everyone. Nobody had heard of an inter-racial symphony orchestra before. 'What? Blacks and whites playing symphony music together?' We lucked out, as you always do when you are doing something like this. Players from the LA Symphony volunteered, wanted to be part of this.[21]

Forming the orchestra was an important first step, but progress was slow; it took three years in all – the unions did not merge until 1951 – and by that time Mingus was no longer in Los Angeles to enjoy the fruits of his labours. Through 1949 he gigged around LA, taking such jobs as were available. There were recording sessions for the Dolphins of Hollywood label (named after a hip music and record store miles from Hollywood in south LA) and another for the Rex Hollywood label. These records sunk almost immediately out of sight, following the earlier 4 Star and Excelsior sides into oblivion. Discouraged by the lack of opportunities, he dropped out of music completely by the end of the year and took a job with the post office.

He was still working as a mailman the following year when Red Norvo came to town for an extended trio gig at The Haig and found himself in need of a bassist. Pianist Jimmy Rowles recommended Mingus and Charles readily accepted the job. The Red Norvo Trio (Norvo, vibes; Tal Farlow, guitar; Mingus, bass) had a very successful run at The Haig, and also cut some records for Discovery that sold quite well. The group was another manifestation of the trend towards cool jazz during this period, but it would be hard to think of a better showcase for Charles's by now phenomenal technique on bass than the trio. The dynamics were such that the bass was on an equal footing with the other instruments, and Mingus was able to use his entire arsenal, including arco solos, double-stops and counter melodies. (It was probably no accident that Gerry Mulligan, having listened to a later edition of the trio at The Haig, applied much the same principals of group dynamics and interaction to his original quartet.)

By the close of 1950, the Norvo trio was high in the polls of the trade magazines, and Charles was beginning to get some of the attention he deserved. There had been a road trip to Chicago during the year, and in the summer of 1951 the group travelled to New York for a successful run at the Embers. At this point things began to go awry. The trio was invited to appear on a series of television broadcasts from station WCBS with vocalist Mel Torme, but the station executives, fearful of offending sponsors and Southern sensibilities, decided that a white bassist would be a better choice. Red Norvo was unhappy with the decision but felt the professional opportunity was too good to miss and reluctantly went along. He did offer to retain Mingus on the job at the Embers, but Charles felt the time was right to try his hand at freelancing on the New York scene. By the next week he was working at Birdland with Miles Davis, and from that time on Charles was a permanent resident of New York City.

In the meantime, back in Los Angeles, Buddy Collette was beginning to reap the dividends of the efforts begun several years before. The inter-racial orchestra was still meeting regularly and often drew interested musicians as spectators. One auspicious night Jerry Fielding, musical director of the Groucho Marx show, dropped by just in time to catch Buddy working out on a difficult part for solo flute. As Buddy recalls the evening:

So Jerry Fielding showed up, and this night I had a flute solo...it was Bizet, and it was all harp and flute for about sixty seconds...so we get through and the bows are tapping. And after it was over, we all go out – it was in Hollywood, at Le Conte Junior High – and I walk into Fielding, and he said, 'That was nice.' And he asked if I knew Marshall Royal, and I said 'Sure, why?' And he said, 'Because I have an opening on the Groucho show and I need a saxophone player and a flautist. Too bad you don't play saxophone.' And I said, 'Well that's my instrument.' And I didn't really try to hurt Marshall, but I said, 'Marshall is not in town, and Marshall doesn't play flute.' Which was true; Marshall hadn't played flute at all then, and he had also just joined Count Basie, so he was gone. So I said, 'I just study on flute; I also play sax and clarinet.'

A couple of days later, Fielding's contractor contacted Buddy and told him he had the job. The bandleader was dubious about Buddy's reading, and set up a meeting before the first show.

We went to a little Italian restaurant and he showed me the book so that I could see what I had to do. I was glad of that, although I was a good reader by then, with all my studies and the symphonic orchestra experience. The hard part was not so much the notes, which I would make OK, but the routine they had on Groucho's show. Remember the secret word routine, when the duck would come down when a contestant said the word? The orchestra had to go immediately into the piece of music appropriate to that, and there were other routines we had to follow dependent on things that happened during the show... We tried it a few times so that I could get used to it, then walked over to meet the other musicians. They didn't know who was coming in, just that there were two new guys. They were really surprised, but friendly, and Groucho came in and said, 'Hey, I see we have a new guy.' Actually there were two new musicians but he just said *a new guy*. We got into it, and it went well; I don't think I missed anything, but if I did, it wasn't noticeable. The guy sitting next to me, first alto, said, 'Man, nice to have you around...' That's how I was hired into the studios.[22]

Things were beginning to move: Buddy Collette's personal breakthrough took place in 1950, and the merger of the unions was finally achieved the following year. By this time the matter was becoming a *cause célèbre*. A benefit at the Club Alabam featured entertainers like Nat Cole and Josephine Baker and attracted much press attention; other public figures, including Frank Sinatra, spoke out. A slate of the musicians favouring amalgamation – including Marle Young, Benny Carter, Bill Douglass, John Anderson and Collette – finally wrested positions on the board of Local 767 and forced the old-guard leadership to negotiate. At the same time supporters in the white union – Milt Holland, Phil Sobel and George Kast among them – worked towards the same end. In large part it was simply a matter of drawing the attention of the white musicians to some of the practices that had been going on. Buddy Collette pointed out:

Another thing, was that our union was like a subsidiary – it wasn't supposed to be, but if a good job happened to come in to the black union, the president would have to call the white union to see if we could take it... Also our dues, when I did

Groucho, were about half that of the white union. And when the guys found that out they screamed. 'You're paying half the money we're paying!' and I said, 'All the more reason to get together.' I didn't want to pay more money, naturally, but at least we could watch these things [and keep us] from being played against each other.

All of the pressure finally paid off in 1951 when the unions were finally joined into the single Local 47.

At this point we'll have to backtrack to pick up a few threads in our narrative. In 1948 both Dexter Gordon and Wardell Gray had left Los Angeles, largely because of reduced playing opportunities due to the recording ban. Dexter spent the next few years freelancing in New York, while Wardell joined one of the biggest names in the business, Benny Goodman. Benny had heard Wardell in concert while visiting the Coast, and was sufficiently impressed to hire the young tenor man for his new septet. Wardell went east with Goodman and spent most of 1948 in New York, first with the Goodman septet and then with the small bands of Count Basie and Tadd Dameron at the Royal Roost, NYC's premier jazz club. In September there was a clandestine recording session for Blue Note with Tadd Dameron's sextet that produced the lovely 'Lady Bird', and in November Wardell rejoined Benny Goodman in the latter's newly-formed big band. He recorded several times with the band, but his best sides with Goodman were those recorded in a septet format, 'Stealin' Apples', 'Bedlam' and 'Blue Lou'. All were cut in LA and are fascinating blends of Goodman's swing style and the more adventurous styles of the younger bop-influenced musicians in the band, including Wardell, trumpeters Doug Mettome or Fats Navarro, and drummer Sonny Igoe. Benny himself was never especially comfortable with modern jazz, but he was a strong admirer of Wardell's. 'If Wardell Gray plays bop,' Benny told one interviewer, 'it is great. Because he's wonderful.'[23]

In December of 1949, while still with Goodman, Wardell made some records for Prestige using Charlie Parker's rhythm section of the time – Al Haig, Tommy Potter and Roy Haynes. One of these sides, an original blues line named 'Twisted', featured a solo that quickly became a favourite of other musicians. (Singer Annie Ross later put words to Gray's solo and came up with a hit vocal.) Shortly thereafter, Benny Goodman broke up his band and Wardell went with Count Basie, who was then touring with an octet.

In August of 1950 the Count Basie octet came through LA and Wardell had the opportunity to renew old acquaintances. A Sunday jam session at the Hula Hut, a club on Sunset Boulevard, was the site of a reunion with Dexter Gordon, and this time recording equipment was present to catch the event 'live'. The two tenors were joined by Clark Terry, the trumpet player with the Basie octet, and altoist Sonny Criss, one of LA's brightest stars. Central Avenue regulars Jimmy Bunn, Bill Hadnott and Chuck Thompson comprised the rhythm section. Two extended performances on bop standards, 'Move' and 'Scrapple from the Apple', were recorded and released by Prestige. Each tune took up four sides of two 78s. Wardell's style by this time had changed; he was no longer a single-minded devotee of Lester Young. 'Scrapple from the Apple' (originally released as 'Kiddo') finds Wardell in a relaxed mood. His tone has a harder edge to it than had been the case on previous records, but his indebtedness to Prez is still evident in his phrasing. Dexter lays out on 'Scrapple', but his absence is more than made up for by the fiery alto work of Sonny Criss. On 'Move' (released as 'Jazz on Sunset'), Dexter and Wardell engage once again in a heated chase, both negotiating the rapid tempo with ease. Clark Terry adds much to the proceedings on both tunes with his fluid, fluent trumpet lines.

Wardell also recorded several times during this period with the Basie octet, but his best solo work with Basie came the following year with the leader's newly reorganized big band. Perhaps because he was holding down the chair once held by Lester Young in the band, Wardell's style on 'Little Pony', recorded in April of 1951, once again reverts to a pure Lestorian mode. Shortly after the big-band sessions, however, Wardell gave Basie his notice and returned to the West Coast to freelance. He was to spend the remainder of his tragically shortened life based in Los Angeles.

Wardell's move was a popular one with the younger Los Angeles jazzmen. Hampton Hawes, in his frank autobiography *Raise Up Off Me*, spoke glowingly of Gray:

Of the regular players along Central Avenue, Wardell Gray,

Dexter Gordon and Teddy Edwards (and Bird when he was in town) were the keepers of the flame, the ones the younger players held in esteem for their ideas and experience and consistency. Wardell was like a big brother to me... He carried books by Sartre with him and talked about Henry Wallace and the NAACP. When white fans in the clubs came up to speak to us, Wardell would do the talking while the rest of us clammed up and looked funny... Aside from Bird he was the player we looked up to most, one of the few of the older, experienced cats who wasn't strung, and when he'd now and then counsel those of us who were starting to fuck with dope to get ourselves together and straighten up, we may not have accepted the advice, but neither did we resent it.[24]

Hawes and several other up-and-coming LA musicians were featured on Wardell's recording date for Prestige in January 1952. Art Farmer, the trumpet player on the date, had moved to Los Angeles from Phoenix in 1945. Since then he and his twin brother Addison, a bassist, had played with many top jazzmen, including Charlie Parker. Hampton Hawes was a native Angeleno as was drummer Lawrence Marable. Bassist Harper Crosby and conga drummer Robert Collier rounded out the rhythm section. The group recorded six tunes in all. Buddy Collette's 'April Skies' (based on 'I Remember April') and Kendall Bright's 'Bright Boy' are medium-tempo swingers; they are matched by a pair of ballad performances that feature Wardell all the way, 'Sweet and Lovely' and 'Lover Man'. The two remaining tunes are both blues: Hampton Hawes' 'Jackie' and Art Farmer's 'Farmer's Market'. The latter was something of a hit for Prestige, and once again Annie Ross paid Wardell the compliment of penning words to his (and Art's) solo and recording the tune as a vocal.

The following year found Wardell in another recording session for Prestige, his last for that company. The session was under the leadership of vibraphonist Teddy Charles, a visitor to the Coast, but the other musicians were all resident Angelenos. Wardell and Lawrence Marable were hold-overs from the 'Farmer's Market' date. Dick Nivison played bass, and a recent arrival, Sonny Clark, sat in on piano. This session also marked the recording debut of Frank Morgan – aged nineteen but already an altoist of surpassing ability. Born 23 December 1933 in Minneapolis, Morgan moved to Los Angeles when he was fourteen. His father, guitarist Stanley Morgan, ran an after-hours club named the Casablanca at the time; Charlie Parker was a frequent attraction. Like Hampton Hawes, Frank Morgan was playing professionally while still in high school, and his playing on this session exhibits an authority that belies his youth.

Four tunes were cut on the Charles date. 'The Man I Love', the only standard recorded at the session, starts out as a ballad vehicle for Wardell, but the tempo soon doubles. Then Teddy Charles jumps in and doubles the tempo again, and it stays at a breakneck pace for solos by Frank Morgan and Wardell. Sonny Clark's 'Lavonne' is an up-tempo blues, paced by an agile Clark and soulful Morgan. The two remaining tunes are both Teddy Charles originals. 'So Long Broadway' is an up-tempo minor piece with adventurous chord progressions, while 'Paul's Cause' bounces along in a relaxed, happy groove.

For some reason, Wardell's work here is something of a let-down; his solos seem a bit perfunctory, and they suffer in comparison with Frank Morgan's spirited lines. Of course this was Teddy Charles's session, but Wardell had previously managed more than to hold his own with leaders as disparate and forceful as Charlie Parker, Dexter Gordon and Benny Goodman. Perhaps the experimental character of some of the compositions put him off; Wardell's forte had always been straight-ahead swinging. Perhaps he just had an off day. In any case, he does not reach the heights he had gained in previous recordings.

With the benefit of hindsight, we can see that Wardell's career was in slight but irreversible decline by this time anyway. For one thing, jazz had turned a corner by early 1953. Bebop was no longer the only, nor even the dominant, form of modern jazz. 'Cool' jazz was in the ascendancy, and men like Wardell Gray and Dexter Gordon were in danger of becoming passé with the new generation of listeners. Certainly bebop was still being played – as for instance by Charlie Parker, Dizzy Gillespie and Bud Powell at their reunion in Toronto's Massey Hall of that same year – but musical styles were changing radically, especially on the West Coast. Then too, some time during this period Wardell ensnared himself in the trap that took such a toll among the jazz masters of the forties and fifties. The man who had been admired by Hampton Hawes as a clean influence finally succumbed to drugs. The habit may well have cost Wardell his life.

Wardell's last recording date came early in 1955 as a sideman for Frank Morgan. At the time Morgan was recording for the Gene Norman Presents (GNP) label. Norman had already recorded the altoist in the company of an Afro-Cuban rhythm section, augmented by organist Wild Bill Davis. The results of that session are hardly memorable, but the date with Wardell is quite a different matter. Trumpeter Conte Candoli joins Frank and Wardell in the front line, and the three horns are supported by the powerful rhythm section of pianist Carl Perkins, guitarist Howard Roberts, bassist Leroy Vinnegar, and Lawrence Marable. Two ballad performances from the session feature Morgan and the rhythm section: 'My Old Flame' and 'The Nearness of You'. Carl Perkins has a tender solo on 'Flame', while Howard Roberts works closely with the altoist and contributes a fine solo on 'Nearness'. Four other tunes feature the entire septet. There are two blues: Morgan's own 'Neil's Blues', a mid-tempo walker, and Dizzy Gillespie's up-tempo 'The Champ'. Wardell, who is in fine fettle throughout the session, contributes commanding solos on both. The two remaining tunes are both up-tempo swingers. 'Milt's Tune' turns out to be 'The Theme', the traditional set-closer used by Miles Davis and Art Blakey during this period. Everybody has a ball on this one. 'Get Happy', taken at a very rapid pace, features a burning Frank Morgan all the way, although he does trade fours with Lawrence Marable at the exciting climax.

The critical acclaim that greeted these sides boosted Frank Morgan's already fast-rising reputation and should have guaranteed him a place in the front ranks of jazz altoists, but sadly he was soon sidetracked by personal problems. Shortly following the recording session Morgan was busted for drug violations and spent a year in jail. His faltering career never quite righted itself and he spent several decades either behind bars or devoting his free time to extra-musical distractions. At that, he was luckier than Wardell Gray. The tenor saxophonist, whose work contributed so much to the Frank Morgan sides, was dead before the album was even released.

Wardell had landed a job with the Benny Carter big band, which had been hired to play for the opening of a new hotel in Las Vegas. The Moulin Rouge hotel and casino had been built specifically to cater to the city's black visitors and gamblers. Two days following the hotel's opening, Wardell Gray's body was found in the Nevada desert, his neck broken. The official report claimed that he had died of a drug overdose, although no autopsy seems to have been performed. There were rumours at the time that Wardell had been the victim of a gang-style execution over gambling debts. In any event, the investigation was not pursued; the Nevada officials didn't seem overly concerned about the cause of death of a visiting black musician.

Wardell Gray's death came a scant three months after Charlie Parker's passing, and the proximity of the two deaths underscores the similar fates that had overtaken the two men. These two giants of the bebop era both died neglected figures, bypassed by the winds of fashion. Parker – due to the lack of job opportunities caused by his reputation as an unreliable performer – had very nearly been relegated to the 'whatever happened to?' category by many of the younger fans. And while Gray seems to have been working fairly steadily during his final years, more often than not the jobs came in the form of casuals or as sideman on recording dates for smaller labels, a roll ill befitting his stature as an artist. Not one but two revolutions had changed the course of jazz since the two had come to prominence in the mid-forties. In 1949, a series of recordings by Miles Davis and by Lennie Tristano had ushered in a style known as cool jazz. This style was to dominate jazz during the early fifties, and both Parker and Gray were thought in some quarters to be passé. And although a counter-revolution had been launched in 1954 (once again led by Miles Davis) its popularity would come too late to help the careers of either Bird or Wardell. Both had to suffer the all too common fate of great artists in any field: re-evaluation and belated recognition of their accomplishments only following their deaths.

In the meantime, the music being given the widest attention in Los Angeles the year of Wardell's death was a variant of the cool style known as West Coast jazz. It was a style that had been developed, and was largely played, by white studio musicians based in Hollywood. At the height of its popularity in the mid-fifties, West Coast jazz spawned an acrimonious debate that rivalled that of the boppers and the Moldy Figs a decade earlier. In truth, this new style was neither as fresh and innovative as its partisans claimed, nor as anonymous and reactionary as its detractors held. To trace its beginnings we have to turn our attention to certain events that followed the 1948 recording ban in New York City.

3.

shorty rogers and his giants

If the recording ban of 1948 did not mark the demise of bebop, it did herald the birth of a new phase of modern jazz. In September of that year a nine-piece band led by Miles Davis played a short engagement at New York's popular jazz club, the Royal Roost. The group differed markedly from the typical bebop combos of the day in both size and instrumentation. Six horns (trumpet, trombone, French horn, tuba, alto and baritone saxophones) gave the band's arrangers a broad palette of orchestral colours to work with. And basically the Miles Davis nonet was an arranger's band. It had been formed as a vehicle for the ideas of a group of young musicians who gravitated around Miles and Gil Evans, the arranger for the Claude Thornhill orchestra. Although the band was not to prove a popular success (it would make only two brief public appearances), the Miles Davis nonet would exert an influence over the subsequent development of jazz entirely out of proportion to its brief moment on stage.

In 1947 Gil Evans had caused quite a stir with a series of adventurous arrangements for Claude Thornhill – notably 'Robbin's Nest', 'Anthropology', 'Yardbird Suite' and 'Donna Lee'. These in turn led to a fruitful and longstanding friendship between Evans and Miles Davis. The two met when Evans approached Davis to obtain recording clearance for the latter's tune 'Donna Lee'. Miles, who had been favourably impressed with Evans's writing, gladly gave his consent in return for instructions in arranging. Thus the trumpeter joined a group of musicians who met often at the New York apartment of Evans to discuss theory and share discoveries. Arranger/baritone saxophonist Gerry Mulligan and trumpeter John Carisi of the Thornhill band were regular participants, as were pianist John Lewis and composers George Russell and John Benson Brooks. When the Thornhill band broke up temporarily in 1948 (largely due to the recording ban), these informal seminars took on an added importance. Miles, who was working fairly steadily with various pick-up groups at the Royal Roost, suggested forming a rehearsal band as an outlet for the group's creative energies. The instrumentation that was finally settled upon came about, Evans would later recall, because nine pieces represented 'the smallest number of instruments that could get the sound and still express all the harmonies the Thornhill band used. Miles wanted to play his idiom with that kind of sound.'[1]

Once rehearsals were under way, Miles began looking for a job for the band. He succeeded in talking the owners of the Roost into booking the nonet as relief band for the Count Basie unit during a two-week stand in September. The engagement was hardly a smashing success, however. Recently-issued recordings, taken from airchecks of a broadcast from the Roost, reveal a great deal of crowd noise and general inattention during the band's performance. More to the point, Miles wasn't offered a return engagement. But if the bulk of the crowd missed the significance of the band's offerings, a few astute listeners were quick to grasp the innovative character of the music. Among these was Pete Rugolo, Stan Kenton's chief arranger. Kenton recorded for Capitol records, and Capitol executives had already decided to jump heavily into modern jazz as soon as the ban was lifted. Rugolo had the ears of the Capitol brass and managed to land Miles a contract with the label. The resulting twelve recorded performances proved to be the true legacy of the Miles Davis nonet.

There were three Capitol sessions in all; two were held shortly after the ban was lifted in January and April of 1949, with a third following almost a year later in March 1950. Each produced four tunes. The bulk of the arrangements were penned by Gerry Mulligan ('Godchild', 'Jeru', 'Venus de Milo', 'Rocker', 'Darn that Dream') and John Lewis ('Move', 'Budo', 'Rouge'). Gil Evans contributed two charts ('Boplicity' and 'Moondreams') and Miles and John Carisi a chart apiece ('Deception' and 'Israel'). Initial sales of the recordings must have disappointed Capitol officials, as witness the lengthy gap between the second and third sessions, but the sides quickly caught on among fellow musicians, and critical reaction was quite favourable: French writer André Hodeir examined the performances at length in his book *Jazz: Its Evolution and Essence.* The Miles Davis sides remain milestones in the jazz discography.

Years later, when Capitol issued these performances on a long-playing record, the album was titled *Birth of the Cool,* and so the collective performances have been referred to ever since. If some question remains whether the Miles Davis sides or the contemporaneous recordings of Lennie Tristano were the true progenitors of cool jazz, there is no doubt that the Davis recordings heavily influenced the musicians who came to be associated with that school. The differences that set the nonet apart from the mainline bop combos of the day went far beyond the obvious points of size and instrumentation. The focus of any bebop performance was the individual solos, and any theme was given cursory treatment – its sole function was to set up a harmonic framework for the soloists to build upon during their flights. Nor was a theme indispensable: many of Charlie Parker's most memorable records feature Parker soloing over an agreed-upon chord sequence, start to finish.

The focus of the Davis nonet performances, on the other hand, was the arrangement – and not just because the three-minute time limit of the era's 78 rpm records tended to emphasize arrangements at the expense of soloists. Even in the band's live performances at the Roost, where soloists were allowed room to stretch out, the arrangements took precedence. And on the best of the studio recordings, the soloists are tightly integrated into the total performance. In the Gil Evans arrangement of 'Boplicity', for example, Miles alternates between lead voice and soloist in such a seamless manner that one must listen carefully to determine just which role he is filling at any given moment.

Another batch of recordings, cut at the same time (and coincidentally also for the Capitol label), may have had more to do with the development of cool jazz than the Miles Davis sides. These were the recordings of pianist Lennie Tristano and a coterie of followers that included saxophonists Lee Konitz and Warne Marsh and guitarist Billy Bauer. Tristano has been called a 'conservative revolutionary', and the oxymoron is quite apt. Although he came to prominence at the height of the bebop era, Tristano steadfastly followed his own path, influenced at least as much by his studies in European concert forms as by the jazz tradition as reinterpreted by Gillespie and Parker. When playing one of their infrequent New York nightclub dates, Tristano and his men were likely to open with a two-part Bach invention, a practice that underscored the pianist's focus on linear invention.

Tristano eschewed easy excitement and his music was deliberately unemotional – some would say to the point of being cold-blooded. His rhythm sections were reduced to the role of timekeepers; the drummer was expected to play an even pulse on brushes, and neither he nor the bassist was allowed to add rhythmic accents. Thus the listener was forced to concentrate on the melodic or contrapuntal lines of the soloists. It was a demanding music which tended to exasperate casual listeners and clubowners alike. 'People have to listen,' Lennie once explained. 'That bothers them. They only want music they can feel like the warmth in a heated room.'[2] Still, for a listener willing to make the effort, it was a music which paid intellectual dividends.

The series of performances Tristano and his men recorded for Capitol in the spring of 1949 are outstanding examples of his style. 'Wow', 'Crosscurrent', 'Marionette' and 'Sax of a Kind' offer technical difficulties such as constantly shifting metres and keys that the soloists thread with ease. But perhaps the most fascinating performances came almost as afterthoughts at the end of one of the sessions. When they had finished recording the more conventional tunes, Tristano asked that the tapes be left running, and the musicians proceeded to record two impromptu group improvisations. There were no themes, no given key signatures or tempi, no guidelines whatever; the musicians simply began improvising, blending their lines as best they could into the collective group effort. (The engineers reportedly threw their hands up in horror and left the control booth, but the tapes were left running.) These performances were later released – albeit reluctantly on the part of the Capitol brass – under the titles 'Intuition' and 'Digression', but while they enjoyed a certain in-group reputation, they had no immediate influence upon developments of the day. They would later be recognized, however, as forerunners of the free jazz of the 1960s.

The two 'free' performances aside, the influence of the other Tristano recordings and of the Miles Davis sides was pervasive. It would seem a remarkable coincidence that two unrelated groups of musicians (that Lee Konitz appeared in both groups was happenstance), working independently, would record the definitive statements of a new style of jazz almost simultaneously. Actually, it's now apparent that the cool approach to jazz was one of those ideas 'in the air' as the forties drew to a close. Other manifestations of the style could be found in a number of widely scattered sources. A youngster named Stan Getz vaulted to prominence in 1948 with an exquisite solo on Woody Herman's recording of 'Early Autumn', and set a standard for a legion of similarly-minded, Lester Young-inspired tenor saxophonists. Tadd Dameron's composition 'Lady Bird', recorded the same year, emphasized flowing, legato lines – as opposed to the jagged leaps and twists of a typical bebop melody – and also featured the Prez-inspired tenors of Allen Eager and Wardell Gray. And a host of young arrangers attempted, with varying degrees of success, to apply their knowledge of twentieth-century classical music theory to their jazz writing. The title of George Russell's 'A Bird in Igor's Yard', the best of these syntheses, clearly delineates the composer's intentions. Not that cool jazz immediately shouldered bebop aside; these developments seemed at the time merely advances in the parent style. Indeed, most of the records we've been discussing would undoubtedly have been thought of as bebop at the time they were released. As so often happens, it's only in retrospect that we can discern that a corner had been turned.

With the advantage of hindsight, we can also see why certain traits of cool jazz would appeal to a group of white musicians who would make their home in the Los Angeles area the following decade. Many were casualties of the break-up of one or another of the big bands; almost all were alumni of those bands. They came lured by the congenial climate and by the possibility of landing a lucrative job in the movie and recording studios. These musicians had, for the most part, received more formal musical training than had their black counterparts, and it's not surprising that the theoretical and disciplined approach to jazz of the Miles Davis and Lennie Tristano groups would appeal to them. When they in turn began recording, their performances would reflect a similar approach. Thus grew the offspring of the cool idiom that came to be called West Coast jazz.

Which brings us to Shorty Rogers.

If any one musician was identified in the public's mind with the term West Coast jazz it was certainly Shorty Rogers, and this fact more than amply illustrates the many paradoxes that stem from the use of such labels. Rogers – whose given name was Milton Michael Rajonsky – was born in Lee, Massachusetts on 14 April 1924, and was raised in New York City, where he

attended the High School of Music and Arts, of 'Fame' fame. His
first professional job came at the age of eighteen, when he joined
Will Bradley's band. Six months later he moved on to the Red
Norvo sextet, staying with Norvo until called by the draft in
1943. While billeted with the Army Port of Embarkation band at
Newport News, Virginia, Rogers first tried his hand at arranging: 'simple things', he remembers, 'like a sustained whole-note
background with somebody else playing the melody'.[3] He also
became a close friend of bassist Arnold Fishkin, who had
travelled to California with Les Brown and who spoke glowingly
of life out on the Coast.

Shortly after he was mustered out in 1945, Shorty joined the
high-powered trumpet section of Woody Herman's First Herd.
He began to attract attention the following year with his playing
and writing for Woody's band-within-a-band, the Woodchop-
pers, on numbers like 'Fan It' and 'Nero's Conception'. He also
added a big-band chart, 'Back Talk', to the Herman book. In the
summer of 1946 Herman and his crew headed for Hollywood for
an extended stay, and when the band returned to New York in
the autumn Rogers and his wife Michele (Red Norvo's sister)
chose to stay behind. Shorty played briefly with Charlie Barnet
and then hired on with Butch Stone's band, which featured such
players as Stan Getz, Herbie Steward, Arnold Fishkin and
drummer Don Lamond. The move to California became
permanent around this time when Michele returned from a
mysterious shopping-trip one day and announced that she had
placed a down payment on a house. The Butch Stone job was by
no means steady, and for a while Fishkin and fellow bassist Joe
Mondragon had to move in with Shorty and Michele to help
defray expenses.

In the autumn of 1947 Shorty rejoined Woody Herman in the
latter's Second Herd, the famed 'Four Brothers' band. Stan Getz
and Herbie Steward, in addition to their gig with Butch Stone,
had been playing a job at Pontrelli's (a Spanish-style ballroom in
LA) in a unique band that featured four tenors – Getz, Steward,
Zoot Sims and Jimmy Giuffre – using charts by Giuffre and Gene
Roland. Herman dropped by one night, was impressed by the
sound, and hired the four en masse for his new Herd. He also
hired Rogers, Fishkin and Lamond, effectively wiping out the
Butch Stone band. Giuffre then penned an arrangement featuring three tenors (Getz, Steward, Sims) and the baritone sax of
Serge Chaloff, using the voicings he and Gene Roland had

worked out for the four tenors. The chart, entitled 'Four Brothers', made Giuffre's reputation and supplied a sound and a tag for this edition of the Herman band. Shorty also came into his own with a series of exciting charts for this band: 'Keen and Peachy' (a collaboration with Ralph Burns), 'I've Got News for You', 'That's Right', 'Lemon Drop', 'Keeper of the Flame' and 'More Moon'. For a break from Woody's vocal on 'I've Got News', Rogers scored a portion of Charlie Parker's solo from the record 'Dark Shadows' for the sax section, thus anticipating the unit called Supersax by some twenty years. When Shorty finally left Herman in December of 1948, it was to join the 'Innovations in Modern Music' orchestra that Stan Kenton was then forming.

By the time Shorty Rogers joined Kenton, his arranging style had fully matured. It was, however, a style somewhat at odds with Kenton's. Whatever one thinks of Stan Kenton – and there seems to be precious little middle ground between his ardent fans and vehement detractors – he was always recognized as a man absolutely determined to go his own way. A largely self-taught pianist and arranger, Kenton had formed his first big band in 1940, writing the bulk of the band's library himself. The band hit it big with the youthful crowds at the Rendezvous ballroom in Balboa, a beach resort some forty miles south of LA, the following year. Kenton struggled to keep the band together through the war years, and by 1946 his was one of the most popular bands in America. Although by this time Kenton had hired other arrangers, notably Pete Rugolo and Gene Roland, he still had definite ideas about the band's musical direction. In a phrase, that would be 'Bigger is Better'. By 1948 the band's line-up included five trumpets, five trombones and five saxes. The Innovations orchestra would take the next inevitable step and add a string section. At full strength, the Innovations unit would number forty players.

Kenton was a bit hesitant about hiring Shorty, feeling that the trumpeter's name was identified too closely in the public's mind with Woody Herman, but did so anyway at the insistence of his lead trumpeter, Buddy Childers. It's possible that Shorty had reservations of his own. It was well known in jazz circles that Kenton's was not a hard-swinging band. Kenton himself simply wasn't that interested in swinging – his focus lay elsewhere – and left such matters in the hands of leaders like Herman and Basie. Shorty set out to prove that Kenton's band *could* swing, given the proper arrangements. Less than a month after he had joined

Kenton, the band – sans strings – recorded Shorty's 'Jolly Rogers', the first in a series of infectious swinging charts that would include 'Round Robin', 'Sambo', and the Latin-tinged 'Viva Prado'. In the meantime, Shorty was gaining on-the-job experience writing for instruments like French horn, tuba and strings; experience that would prove invaluable when he would later come to write scores for movie soundtracks. At this time Shorty also forged friendships with musicians who would form the nucleus of the West Coast school: Milt Bernhart, Bud Shank, Bob Cooper, Art Pepper and Shelly Manne.

Art Pepper's case was special. Art, a native Angeleno, was a white youngster who had learned to play alto by sitting in with the black bands in Central Avenue clubs. He was a natural jazzman whose earthy playing impressed any musician who heard him. The affinity between Shorty's writing and Art's playing quickly became apparent. Kenton had wanted a series of scores featuring various stars and facets of the Innovations orchestra, and Shorty responded with several charts, the best of which was simply titled 'Art Pepper'. As recorded in May 1950, it showed both Shorty's quick mastery of writing for the expanded orchestra and Art's ability quickly to set a mood and at the same time be able to swing like hell on the up-tempo sections. Time and again over the years, Shorty's writing would stir Art Pepper to some of his greatest improvisations.

The first Innovations tour ran until June 1950, when Kenton disbanded for a six-month rest. (There were a couple of recording sessions later in the year.) The second Innovations concert tour was scheduled for early 1951, but by this time Shorty decided he'd had enough of the road. He continued to write and occasionally play for Kenton, but wanted no part of touring. It was time to settle and put down roots. For a time it was the old story of casuals and one-nighters, the usual scuffle to survive. Then, late in 1951, two breaks came his way and Shorty's decision to settle in Hollywood began to pay dividends.

The first break came in October. Gene Norman, an independent record producer and entrepreneur, called Shorty with plans for a record session featuring some Los Angeles musicians. Would Shorty be interested? Shorty agreed and immediately began working on scores and rounding up sidemen. Most of the musicians had been working with Shorty in the Kenton band. Art Pepper and Jimmy Giuffre, along with bassist Don Bagley and Shelly Manne, came directly from Kenton, as did John

Graas and Gene Englund, the French horn and tuba players of the Innovations orchestra. Shorty had enjoyed writing for the latter two instruments, and wanted to try for a sound reminiscent of the Miles Davis Birth of the Cool band. The final musician called was Hampton Hawes, the youthful veteran of Charlie Parker's band and the Central Avenue clubs. Hamp's presence ensured that the rhythm section would swing especially hard.

The session was held on 8 October 1951, and the performances turned out to be gems of modern jazz small-band writing and playing. The first tune recorded set the mood – a sprightly blues called 'Popo' that was destined to become Shorty's theme. The tune itself is only a simple blues riff, with a four-bar intro for the soloists, but the melody is the infectious kind that is hard to put aside, once heard. Pepper, Giuffre, Rogers and Hawes all contribute well-constructed solos. Two other performances from the session are especially noteworthy. The first is Art Pepper's soulful rendering of 'Over the Rainbow'. The melody itself is never overtly stated; Pepper simply soars over the varied phrasings of the other horns, which sketch the ballad's harmonic framework. The other classic performance, a Rogers original called 'Sam and the Lady', features an ongoing conversation between Shorty and Art throughout. Of the remaining three tunes, Shorty wrote two – 'Didi' and 'Apropos' – and Jimmy Giuffre contributed another in his quartet series: 'Four Mothers'. The session was very loose, and the musicians can be heard shouting encouragement to one another as if in a nightclub. Shorty says that this was not affected; the musicians simply felt especially exuberant at the way the proceedings were going.

Comparisons between these recordings (released in a Capitol album entitled *Modern Sounds*) and the Birth of the Cool recordings are inevitable, if only because both sessions featured intermediate-sized bands using a French horn and tuba. But the intentions of the musicians involved were really quite dissimilar. The Miles Davis nonet was formed primarily to allow its arrangers to experiment with new concepts; the Rogers band was formed simply to produce some records. In the Davis band the arrangements were paramount; Shorty's and Giuffre's charts were meant to set off the soloists. Finally, the Rogers recording session was a one-shot affair, although it would lead to many other opportunities, as we shall see. The Shorty Rogers recordings have been disparaged – by those who dislike the style

– as the forerunners of West Coast jazz. While this is no doubt true, it's also true that they avoid the pitfalls (such as over-arranging, bland solos and lifeless rhythm sections) that would come to plague some later examples of the style. Certainly they were far from slavish copies of the Miles Davis recordings.

The records were not immediately released, but shortly after the session a second break came Shorty's way. In December he got a call from Howard Rumsey, who was leading a band at the Lighthouse Cafe, a waterfront bar in the nearby community of Hermosa Beach. Rumsey, despite a cool demeanour that resembles that of a New York hipster, is a native Californian, born in the desert community of Brawley on 7 November 1917. After first studying both piano and drums, he took up bass while attending Los Angeles City College. One of his first professional jobs was with Vido Musso's band, where he met a young pianist named Stan Kenton. Rumsey was a charter member of the original Kenton band, which he left in 1943. He spent some time with the bands of Freddie Slack and Charlie Barnet, but declined all opportunities to go back on the road. Finally, between jobs in the post-war years, he found himself in the town of Hermosa Beach, which he remembered as having had a thriving nightlife during the boom years of the war. The town was now dead, but one club with a Polynesian decor at least had a bandstand. It was called the Lighthouse. Rumsey approached the owner, John Levine, and suggested some live music:

> I asked him, 'How about putting on a Sunday jam session?'
> 'Kid, are you gonna try to tell me what to do with this place? Everybody else has.'
> I talked some more. Finally he said, 'OK, let's try it out.' The next Sunday I put together a fine combo, opened the front doors – there was no PA system, but we kept the music loud enough to roar out into the street – and within an hour Levine had more people in the room than he'd seen in a month. That was Sunday afternoon, 29 May 1949.[4]

So began the jazz policy that would turn the Lighthouse into a name known throughout the world. The musicians for that historic first gig, by the way, were Don Dennis, trumpet, Dick Swink, tenor, Arnold Kopitch, piano, Bobby White, drums and of course Rumsey on bass.

During the next couple of years Levine and Rumsey began to

expand musical operations. At first there was live music only at the weekend; Tuesdays through to Thursdays Rumsey played records for the patrons, 'a DJ without a radio', he remembers. But gradually the live music expanded to six nights a week. The band consisted of whoever was available on a given night, but the calibre of the musicians steadily grew: Teddy Edwards, Sonny Criss and Hampton Hawes were soon regulars, and Wardell Gray a frequent visitor. Finally in 1951 Rumsey decided to go with a permanent group, and the Lighthouse All-Stars were born. The first 'official' Lighthouse band consisted of Shorty Rogers, Jimmy Giuffre, pianist Frank Patchen, Rumsey and Shelly Manne. Other musicians (Teddy, Hamp, Bob Cooper) were added at the weekend or on special occasions.

One of the famous – the musicians say infamous – Lighthouse traditions began around this time: the gruelling Sunday marathon sessions, which lasted from two in the afternoon until two the following morning. Musicians remember those sessions with a mixture of fond memories and awe. 'You look back, and the physical accomplishment – aside from the creative accomplishment – is amazing,' says Shorty. 'All those hours!' Some aspects could be quite amusing. 'We'd start at two,' Shorty recalls, 'and I'd look out and there'd be people sitting in bathing-suits, listening to the music. And then, just as I'd be about ready to collapse at two in the morning, I'd look again and they were still there – two in the morning in their bathing-suits!' Yet despite the physically demanding aspects of the job, it was a steady gig, and Shorty remembers those days with affection. 'Just a wonderful time, a family feeling. A lot of personal friendships and relationships were started then. It was just great.'

Two recordings done 'live' during that period serve as a permanent reminder of the ambience that was a Lighthouse concert in the early fifties. The first, recently issued on the Xanadu label, finds Art Pepper sitting in for Giuffre with the basic quintet of 1951. It's hard to remember, listening to the exuberant playing on the record, that these musicians were often denigrated as founders of the West Coast school. Shorty and Art both had an affinity for bop standards, and they wail their way through tunes like 'Scrapple from the Apple', 'Tin Tin Deo', 'Lullaby in Rhythm', and a blistering 'Cherokee'. As usual, Pepper shines on the ballads, especially 'Body and Soul' and 'Over the Rainbow'. There are also happy romps through

'Robbin's Nest', 'Jive at Five' and of course 'Popo'. The warmth of all the musicians comes through even though the concert was taped on a home recorder.

The other recording was a more professional undertaking by the fledgling Contemporary record company. Recorded over a year later in February 1953, it was an attempt to capture a typical Sunday marathon session 'live'. Rogers, Giuffre, Patchen, Rumsey and Manne are augmented by guests Bob Cooper, Milt Bernhart, Hampton Hawes and Stan Kenton's amazing young lead trumpet, Maynard Ferguson, although not all of these musicians play on every number. One of the numbers recorded that day, a Teddy Edwards original titled 'Sunset Eyes', would become something of a hit for the All-Stars. 'Bernie's Tune' was an almost obligatory selection, having become famous through a recent recording by the fledgling Gerry Mulligan Quartet. Hampton Hawes, subbing for Frank Patchen on several tunes, turned in an especially memorable performance on 'All the Things You are' in a quartet format with Shorty as the sole horn. Shorty contributed several tunes for the proceedings – 'Morgan Davis', 'Creme de Menthe' and 'Comin' Thru the Rye Bread'. There were also performances of Jimmy Giuffre's 'Four Others' and the traditional 'La Soncailli'. The recordings were eventually issued on Contemporary's first long-playing album, *Sunday Jazz a la Lighthouse*.

The first records to be released under the Lighthouse All-Stars banner, however, were studio performances cut the previous summer. Shorty, Milt Bernhart, Jimmy Giuffre, Bob Cooper, Frank Patchen, Rumsey and Shelly Manne recorded four tunes, two each by Rogers and Giuffre. The performances are quite varied. 'Swing Shift', Shorty's up-tempo swinger, is balanced by Giuffre's ballad 'Out of Somewhere'. 'Viva Zapata!' (the title was no doubt inspired by the Brando movie then playing) is out of Shorty's Latin bag. It features sparkling solos by Shorty and Frank Patchen, with a marvellous interlude by conga drummer Carlos Vidal and Shelly Manne. The remaining tune, 'Big Girl', is Jimmy Giuffre's take-off on a rhythm and blues number, complete with a honking solo by the composer. Although it was meant to be tongue-in-cheek, the record seems to have made quite a few sales to the youth audience. These selections were initially released as 78 rpm singles on the Lighthouse label, and later reissued on a Contemporary LP.

The year 1952 indeed seems to have been a turning-point for

the West Coast musicians. That summer Capitol records finally released the six tunes from the 'Popo' session of the previous October, and Gene Norman made sure they received plenty of airplay on his local jazz show. Later that fall, the Gerry Mulligan Quartet recording of 'Bernie's Tune' also became a hit. All of these recordings spread the word that new things were happening on the Coast.

In January 1953 Shorty got an even bigger break when he was asked to record for the RCA label. Jack Marshall, the producer who had midwifed the *Modern Sounds* session for Gene Norman, joined RCA and promptly invited Shorty to record. The line-up for this session remained much as it had for the earlier Capitol recordings. Milt Bernhart was added on trombone, and bassist Joe Mondragon replaced Don Bagley, but the remaining personnel (Art Pepper, Jimmy Giuffre, John Graas, Gene Englund, Hampton Hawes and Shelly Manne) were all hold-overs. The RCA session produced eight tunes, and several invite comparison with those of the earlier Capitol session. 'Morpo', Shorty's up-tempo blues line, is reminiscent of 'Popo', although it doesn't have the infectious lilt of the original. 'Bunny', on the other hand, is a truly memorable ballad, and proved that Rogers could write thoughtful slow pieces as well as up-tempo swingers. Naturally enough, 'Bunny' serves as a showcase for Art Pepper, and recalls the altoist's success on the earlier 'Over the Rainbow'. 'I just loved Art's playing so much,' Shorty remembers. 'I thought, hey, I've got an album to do and Art Pepper's gonna be there, and what a waste not to feature him on a number.' Hampton Hawes is spotlighted on 'Diablo's Dance', a sprightly Rogers original. None of the other tunes is especially memorable. 'Pirouette' is a graceful ballad borrowed from a film score Shorty had been working on. 'Mambo del Crow' is the album's Latin number, and its relationship to the popular 'Viva Zapata!' is obvious. 'The Pesky Serpent' and 'Indian Club' are both Jimmy Giuffre originals, and while the former is a nice enough tune, the latter features a rather embarrassing tom-tom and minor-key melody line that echoes Hollywood's idea of American Indian music. Shelly Manne does supply a good, Latin-tinged original in 'Powder Puff'.

All in all, the level of inspiration of both writers and soloists seems to have flagged somewhat from the earlier Capitol session. Perhaps the staid atmosphere of the Victor studios was intimidating; whatever the reason, the RCA album (titled simply *Shorty*

63

Rogers and His Giants) did not reach the creative levels of the Capitol sides. But the association with RCA definitely had its advantages. The prestige of being recorded by a major label certainly helped open some doors, and the larger company's marketing strengths could obviously help record sales. Still, the thought processes of the RCA executives must have been perplexing to the jazz musicians. Soon after the original album had been recorded, RCA officials approached Jack Marshall with an idea.

'Hey, we have a title for an album, but we need someone to do it.'

'What's the title?' Jack asked.

'*Cool and Crazy*. Can Shorty do it?'

'Sure,' Marshall replied, and so an album was born.

The *Cool and Crazy* album was to be a big-band session, and Shorty remembers its gestation like this. 'I got a chance to do this album, and I wanted to do it with a big band. And although it's been done many times since ... at that time it either hadn't been done or had been done only a few times ... for a band that wasn't an established travelling band to go in and cut a big-band album. So I got a chance to do the gig, and the majority of players I wanted to use were in Kenton's band. So I called Stan and said I wanted to come over ... and I said, "I have a chance to do this album, and I want to use this guy and that guy," and about seventy or eighty per cent of them were in his band, and I told Stan I didn't want to be raiding his band, and I said, "Stan, how do you feel about it?"

'"Go for it," he said, "whatever I can do to help, you have my blessings." And it was just that kind of a wonderful attitude – a giving attitude – that he had that helped me, and made feel right about using all the guys.'

Actually, seventy or eighty per cent might be a little low. The personnel for the two sessions (26 March and 2 April 1953) were: Maynard Ferguson, Conrad Gozzo, John Howell, Tom Reeves and Rogers, trumpets; Milt Bernhart, Harry Betts and John Halliburton, trombones; John Graas, horn; Gene Englund, tuba; Art Pepper, Bud Shank, Bob Cooper and Jimmy Giuffre, saxes; Marty Paich, piano; Curtis Counce, bass; and Shelly Manne, drums. Only Gozzo, Paich and Counce were neither Kenton sidemen nor alumni.

The album turned out to be a great success, and indeed the original ten-inch LP version of *Cool and Crazy* is a prized collector's item, traded for astronomical sums on the second-hand market. Every performance is memorable. 'Coop de Graas' features, as might be expected, a running conversation between Bob Cooper and John Graas. The title of 'Infinity Promenade' also suggests its principal soloist, Maynard Ferguson. Maynard, a young man from Montreal, Canada, had wowed Kenton's audiences with his stratospheric flights. For this number Shorty had written an impressively high unison line for the trumpets, but Maynard thought he could improve upon it. 'Hey Shorts,' he called between takes. 'Would it be OK on the repeat if I did it an octave higher?' 'Be my guest!' Shorty replied. The results, as captured on record, can send chills down the spine of the most jaded listener.

'Short Stop' is another in a long line of swinging up-tempo blues lines from Shorty's pen, and features a melody line that clings resolutely to a single note while the harmonies move on below. 'Boar-Jibu' uses the Four Brothers sound of three tenors and a baritone. It is taken at a tempo just on the up side of medium and has solos by Art Pepper on tenor and Jimmy Giuffre on baritone. Milt Bernhart is featured on 'Tale of an African Lobster', a ballad that also shows Maynard and the trumpet section to advantage. Both 'Contours' and 'Chiquito Loco' are Latin-flavoured. Milt Bernhart once again solos on the former, while Shorty and Art Pepper share the spotlight on the latter. Finally there is the fascinating 'Sweetheart of Sigmund Freud' (marvellous title), wherein Art Pepper on tenor leads a rumbly sax section with Shank, Cooper and Giuffre on baritones, a sort of inverted Four Brothers sound.

Seldom have big bands swung so hard or produced such a joyous sound. Some twenty years later Rogers was invited to tour England and play a series of concerts with a big band comprised of British musicians. He was to bring his own charts. The few arrangements his hosts specifically asked for were, sure enough, those recorded at the *Cool and Crazy* session.

The success of the *Cool and Crazy* LP led directly to another RCA big-band album, this one honouring the bandleader most admired by Shorty and his musicians, Count Basie. The album, *Shorty Rogers Courts the Count,* was quite on par with *Cool and Crazy.* It is by now a commonplace of jazz criticism that Shorty and many of the West Coast musicians were inspired more by Count Basie and Lester Young than by Charlie Parker; that is, they were essentially swing-era musicians rather than boppers.

And of course that's true. The white musicians of Shorty's
generation had grown up in the big-band era and most had
launched their careers in one of those bands. Many would have
been content to have remained big-band sidemen had not the
sharp decline of the bands in the post-war years made it
impossible to do so. There was certainly no lack of competent
and eager musicians from which to choose when it came time to
gather a band for the new recording. The word quickly spread
when Shorty began working on the arrangements, and when the
time arrived, as Shorty said, 'Everybody was ready for the
session.'

The instrumentation was strengthened somewhat for this
session: an additional trombone and sax were added. Many of the
same musicians returned, but there were some important new
additions. Shorty's boyhood idol, Harry 'Sweets' Edison, was on
hand for this go-round, and Zoot Sims (a native Angeleno) added
his highly original solo voice to the band. Other newcomers
included valve trombonist Bob Enevoldsen and altoist Herb
Geller (who replaced Art Pepper). In addition to penning new
arrangements of nine Basie classics, Shorty also contributed
three originals in the Basie mode. None of the Basie charts
slavishly follows the original, but all achieve the feeling and
relaxed swing of the Basie orchestra. 'It's our tribute to Basie and
that's the whole reason we did it,' Shorty would later explain. 'It
expresses the way myself and all the guys feel about him.'

Typical of the Rogers treatments on the album is 'Swingin' the
Blues'. The tune is taken at a much slower tempo than the
original (there are more than enough flag-wavers on the album)
and the saxes get into a relaxed groove that still manages to swing
mightily. Their blending here is marvellous, and the texture can
only be described as creamy. A tune-by-tune exposition of the
numbers isn't necessary here; every jazz fan is (or ought to be)
familiar with the Basie library. The tunes chosen are the cream of
the crop: 'Jump for Me', 'Topsy', 'It's Sand, Man', 'Doggin'
Around', 'H & J', 'Taps Miller' and 'Tickletoe'. Shorty's
originals, very much in the same vein, manage to fit in well.
'Basie Eyes' is second cousin to 'A Smooth One'. 'Over and Out'
is the obligatory flag-waver, an up-tempo blues. And 'Walk,
Don't Run' spotlights Shorty in cup mute and Jimmy Giuffre's
Prez-inspired sub-tone clarinet. But what an opportunity was
missed when Sweets Edison was – for some unfathomable reason
– not allowed any solo space. It is just this touch that keeps the

album from being the perfect gem it might have been.

At this point we must leave Rogers and company for a while. In 1954, when the Basie album was recorded, Shorty Rogers – and for that matter the Los Angeles jazz scene in general – was flying high; national and even international attention was focused on the music being produced in the Hollywood studios, and much of this attention was the result of Shorty's own labours. There was, however, one other major influence at work in the southland at the time, and to pick up that thread in the narrative we have to return to 1952, the year Gerry Mulligan arrived in Los Angeles.

RCA VICTOR

"HIS MASTER'S VOICE"

COOL AND CRAZY

LPM 3138
Non-Breakable

SIDE 1

1—COOP DE GRAAS
2—INFINITY PROMENADE
3—SHORT STOP
4—BOAR—JIBU
(Shorty Rogers)

Shorty Rogers and his Orchestra
featuring The Giants
E3VL-4823

LONG PLAY

33⅓

RCA VICTOR DIVISION, RADIO CORPORATION OF AMERICA, CAMDEN, N.J. MADE IN U.S.A.

"HIS MASTER'S VOICE"

RCA VICTOR
REG. U.S. PAT. OFF. MARCAS REGISTRADAS

For best results use
RCA Victor Needles

20-5503
(E3VB-0060)

INFINITY PROMENADE
(Shorty Rogers)

Shorty Rogers and his Orchestra
Featuring The Giants

RCA VICTOR DIVISION OF RADIO CORPORATION OF AMERICA, CAMDEN, N.J. MADE IN U.S.A.

4.
the gerry mulligan quartet

In 1952 and 1953, as both began to attract national attention, the names of Shorty Rogers and Gerry Mulligan were often linked – primarily because both were headquartered in southern California. Actually, the pair presented striking contrasts, both in their personalities and in appearance. Whereas Shorty was diminutive and stocky, with dark curly hair, Gerry Mulligan was tall and thin (just this side of emaciated at the time), with an unruly shock of red hair. Both men had a ready sense of humour, but Shorty's was the puckish sort of a schoolboy in a chemistry lab – let's mix the green and yellow liquids and see what happens – while Gerry's humour tended to be dry and, at times, acerbic. Both, however, were extroverted soloists, and they shared an impatience with those who would over-intellectualize the music. 'Jazz music is fun to me,' is the way Mulligan began the liner notes to one of his own albums. And Shorty's favourite explanation for the genesis of his musical experiments has always been: 'Why did I do it? Because I thought it would be fun.'

Gerry was born Gerald Joseph Mulligan on 6 April 1927 in the New York City borough of Queens. His father was an industrial engineer and the family was constantly on the move; at one time or another they lived in Marion, Ohio; Chicago; Kalamazoo; Detroit; and Reading, Pennsylvania. Gerry received a strict Irish-Catholic upbringing, and it may have been his rebellion from this that set him on the way to becoming a jazz musician. He would later remember the time in Marion when the idea first occurred to him.

I was on my way to school, when I saw the Red Nichols bus sitting in front of a hotel. I was in the second or third grade, and that was probably when I first wanted to become a band musician and go on the road. It was a small old Greyhound bus with a canopied observation platform, and on the bus was printed 'RED NICHOLS AND HIS FIVE PENNIES'. It all symbolized travel and adventure. I was never the same after that.[1]

Gerry received the usual childhood piano lessons and later was given instructions on clarinet and arranging by Sammy Correnti, a former dance-band musician. By the time his formal schooling ended at the age of seventeen the family had moved to Philadelphia, where Mulligan joined the society band of Tommy Tucker as arranger. Gerry hit the road with Tucker, but his arrangements proved to be a bit too adventurous for the conservative bandleader, and he soon returned to Philly. Here he landed a job as staff arranger for radio station WCAU, whose band was led by Elliot Lawrence. During this period Gerry made frequent trips to New York, where he was offered encouragement by none other than Charlie Parker. In 1946 Gerry moved permanently to the Apple, where he was hired by Gene Krupa. Krupa's recording of the Mulligan original 'Disc Jockey Jump' became a hit, and Gerry's reputation among fellow musicians began to grow. The following year Gerry landed a job as arranger for Claude Thornhill, which led to a friendship with Gil Evans and eventually to the Birth of the Cool recordings.

As has been pointed out, Mulligan penned five of the twelve Capitol sides: 'Jeru', 'Godchild', 'Venus de Milo', 'Rocker', and 'Darn that Dream'. André Hodeir, in his book *Jazz: Its Evolution and Essence,* has painstakingly analysed the scores of the best of the Miles Davis recordings and found the rhythmic complexities of two of Mulligan's scores especially fascinating:

The exposition of 'Godchild' drastically 'reconsiders' the traditional structure of this classical thirty-two-bar theme with bridge. The addition of first two beats and then four to the initial phrase makes the first period cover seventeen and a half bars instead of sixteen. The bridge, on the other hand, is half a bar shorter than customary ... 'Jeru' is still more revolutionary. It includes four choruses in all. The exposition begins in the traditional way with a double eight-bar phrase.

The fact that the bridge has twelve bars would not be surprising in itself if five of them – from the fourth to the eighth – were not in ¾ time. The reprise covers nine bars. Here, then, is an exposition with an uneven number of bars and beats. The same is true of the final re-exposition.[2]

With the artistic (if not financial) success of the Birth of the Cool recordings, Mulligan's reputation – at least among fellow musicians – was assured. As is so often the case though, this in-group reputation did not lead to an equivalent financial security. The next few years found Mulligan scuffling simply to get by. He continued to supply arrangements for Claude Thornhill, Elliot Lawrence and others ('Elevation' was something of a hit for Lawrence in 1949) and worked such gigs as he could find. As we have seen, the years around the turn of the decade were hard on working musicians. The frustrations inevitably took their toll, and some time during this period Gerry became ensnared in a drug habit, the occupational disease that wrecked the lives and careers of so many musicians in those years. Although he eventually was able to break free (several years later in California) the habit simply made Gerry's situation worse. There is little to show for the period except for a recording session for Prestige in the summer of 1951. Gerry's arrangements for a ten-piece band for this session show the influence of the Miles Davis nonet and at the same time anticipate the writing he would do for a similar group in Los Angeles.

Shortly following the Prestige session Gerry left New York for California, hitch-hiking on an odyssey that would take almost a year, with stop-overs in Reading and Albuquerque. Once in Los Angeles Mulligan quickly sold some arrangements to Stan Kenton ('Youngblood' and 'Swing House') and played some weekend marathon sessions at the Lighthouse. His fortunes began to turn when he landed a job on the Monday-night session at The Haig, a small club (actually, a converted bungalow) on Wilshire Boulevard. These sessions featured a rotating group of musicians that included altoist Sonny Criss, trumpeter Ernie Royal, pianists Jimmy Rowles or Fred Otis, bassists Joe Comfort, Red Mitchell or Joe Mondragon, drummers Alvin Stoller or Chico Hamilton, and assorted visitors. One of the musicians who chanced to sit in that summer of 1952 was a young trumpeter named Chet Baker, who had gained local fame when he was chosen by Charlie Parker for a quintet Parker was fronting during a visit to the Coast.

Chesney Baker was born in Yale, Oklahoma on 23 December 1929, and moved to California in 1940. He began instrumental training at Glendale Junior High, first on trombone, then on trumpet. He remembers that he had some difficulties because: 'I would rely too much on my ear instead of the notes.'[3] Nevertheless Chet progressed rapidly on his instrument. In 1946 he was drafted and wound up playing with the 298th Army Band in Berlin. Discharged in 1948, he found the Los Angeles scene a little slow and re-enlisted to play with the Presidio Army Band in San Francisco, where he spent most of his off-duty hours jamming in local clubs. He was discharged once again in 1952 and began playing local jobs around LA. The turning-point came when he heard that Charlie Parker was auditioning for a trumpet player. 'When I got to his club every trumpet player in LA was there. I got up and played two tunes and he stopped the audition and hired me on the spot. I was twenty-two at the time.'[4] The job with Parker lasted several months before the altoist returned to New York. 'When Bird went east,' Chet remembers, 'he told Dizzy and Miles, "You better look out, there's a little white cat out on the West Coast who's gonna eat you up."'[5]

Shortly after that Chet was introduced to Gerry Mulligan at one of the concerts at The Haig. It wouldn't be correct to say that the two found instant rapport with one another, but over a period of time – playing together weekly at the Monday-night sessions – Mulligan and Baker began to realize that each had an affinity for the other's playing. The Gerry Mulligan Quartet was not formed instantly; it evolved over a period of months. Richard Bock, who served as publicity man for The Haig and who had been an A & R man and producer for Discovery records, thought that Mulligan ought to be recorded and suggested a few trial tapings. On 10 June 1952, Bock and a few of The Haig's regulars met at the Laurel Canyon bungalow of Phil Turetsky, a recording engineer. It was to have been a quartet date, but Jimmy Rowles missed the session for some reason. A trio comprised of Mulligan, Red Mitchell and Chico Hamilton nevertheless taped three selections on Turetsky's Ampex recorder. In July they tried again. This time Chet Baker was invited, but although Rowles made this session, Chico Hamilton was absent. The drumless quartet (with Joe Mondragon on bass) taped two more pieces.

In the meantime, Mulligan and his crew were working on a new concept during the regular concerts at The Haig. Bock recounts what happened next:

In mid-July of 1952, The Haig booked the Red Norvo Trio for an engagement of indefinite length. The trio at that time consisted of Red Mitchell on bass and Tal Farlow on guitar. Inasmuch as the trio did not use a piano, and since Gerry had insisted that he would rather play the Monday-night sessions without the piano, Haig owner John Bennett decided to put the piano in storage. It was this decision that brought Chet Baker, Chico Hamilton and a young bass player from Long Beach by the name of Bob Whitlock to form the first Mulligan pianoless quartet.[6]

Gerry and the others experimented with the format before the live audiences until things began to gel. In the meantime, Bock was so impressed with the group sound that he borrowed some money and set up a new record company specially to record the quartet. Thus was born the Pacific Jazz label. Bock continues the story:

After five Monday nights, Gerry felt the quartet was ready to record. On the afternoon of 16 August 1952, at the Turetsky bungalow again, we recorded the memorable 'Bernie's Tune' and 'Lullaby of the Leaves'. That record, released as a single in the autumn of 1952, put Pacific Jazz in business. The quartet rapidly became a West Coast sensation.[7]

It did indeed, and not only in Los Angeles. Less than a month after the initial Pacific Jazz session the quartet travelled up the coast for an engagement at the Blackhawk in San Francisco. Because of prior commitments, Bob Whitlock couldn't make the trip, and Carson Smith filled in on bass. In San Francisco the group was invited to record (on the recommendation of Dave Brubeck) for the independent Fantasy label. The four tunes recorded at that session helped to spread the quartet's fame. There were two Mulligan originals, 'Line for Lyons' (Jimmy Lyons, who would later produce the Monterey Jazz Festivals) and 'Bark for Barksdale', and two standards, the Latin-flavoured 'Carioca' and the classic Rodgers and Hart ballad 'My Funny Valentine'. This last tune became an even bigger hit than

'Bernie's Tune'. It features Chet Baker, accompanied at first only by a walking bass, then by the other members of the quartet singing *a capella,* and finally by some exquisite counterpoint by Mulligan's baritone sax.

The following month found the quartet back in LA and once again recording for Pacific Jazz. With Bob Whitlock back on bass, the group recorded six more tunes, enough – with the addition of 'Bernie's Tune' and 'Lullaby of the Leaves' – to fill a ten-inch LP. Mulligan contributed three originals: 'Nights at the Turntable', 'Soft Shoe' and 'Walkin' Shoes'. All are taken at easy middle tempos and highlight the comfortable interplay between the musicians – especially Mulligan and Baker. Chet Baker also contributed an original for the session, an up-tempo piece aptly called 'Freeway'. Two standards, 'Frenesi' and a jaunty 'Aren't You Glad You're You', complete the bill.

With this nucleus of twelve sides (eight for Pacific Jazz and four for Fantasy) the Gerry Mulligan Quartet had provided a sampling of their wares for the record-buying public. Not surprisingly, most of these tunes are taken at a medium tempo, where the interplay between the horns of Baker and Mulligan is shown to best advantage. One of the highlights of a Mulligan quartet performance, whether on record or in concert, is the improvised weaving of contrapuntal lines of the horns and bass. The influence here is at least as much King Oliver as J.S. Bach, and the comment has often been made that the quartet was at times playing a sort of neo-Dixieland. Although this was meant as a put-down, it is an observation to which Mulligan – who has always felt respect and admiration for his jazz elders – would readily assent. Gerry knew just where his quartet stood in relation to the evolution of jazz. 'The idea of a band without a piano is not new,' he wrote, in the liner notes introducing his first Pacific Jazz album. 'The very first jazz bands didn't use them (how could they? They were either marching or riding in wagons.') In fact, it would be useful to reprint here Mulligan's comments from the same liner notes, explaining the concept on which his quartet was based:

I consider the string bass to be the basis of the sound of the group; the foundation on which the soloist builds his line, the main thread around which the two horns weave their contrapuntal interplay. It is possible with two voices to imply the sound of or impart the feeling of any chord or series of chords as Bach shows us so thoroughly and enjoyably in his inventions.

When a piano is used in a group it necessarily plays the dominant role; the horns and bass must tune to it as it cannot tune to them, making it the dominant tonality. The piano's accepted function of constantly stating the chords of the progression makes the solo horn a slave to the whims of the piano player. The soloist is forced to adapt his line to the changes and alterations made by the pianist in the chords of the progression.

It is obvious that the bass does not possess as wide a range of volume and dynamic possibilities as the drums and horns. It is therefore necessary to keep the overall volume in proportion to that of the bass in order to achieve an integrated group sound.[8]

These notes were in response to the controversy over the pianoless group then raging in the press, and they clearly show Mulligan as an articulate and knowledgeable musician. But they also tend to leave an impression of Mulligan as a solemn intellectual, preoccupied with the theories behind his music, and this is wide of the mark. Actually, Gerry is quite impatient with

those who would scrutinize, rather than enjoy, the music. Some
seven years after he wrote the notes above, he would write (in the
album notes for a later edition of the quartet):

> Jazz music is fun to me. All music can be fun for that matter,
> but what I mean is we usually have a hell of a good time
> playing and listening to each other.
>   But some of the people who do the most talking about jazz
> (that may even be the basic problem right there!) don't seem to
> get any real fun out of listening to it. It seems to me that all the
> super-intellectualizing on the technique of jazz and the lack of
> response to the emotion and meaning of jazz is spoiling the fun
> for listeners and players alike.[9]

Certainly the quartet offered the crowds at The Haig
enjoyment as well as intellectual stimulation. Soon after the
initial Pacific Jazz single was released the quartet became The
Haig's star attraction, moving from the off-night slot to the
weekends. Throughout a tenure that lasted from the autumn of
1952 to the summer of 1953, Mulligan and his crew consistently
drew overflow crowds. The Haig was a small room (capacity
about eighty-five), and as Bock remembers it, 'on weekends
more people could be found outside waiting in line to get in than
were actually inside'.[10] An article in *Time* magazine (2 February
1953) helped to spread the group's fame. That fame edged into
notoriety when Mulligan stopped the quartet in mid-
performance one night to chew out the audience for talking while
the band was playing, an occasion that was duly noted by the jazz
press. Mulligan answered his critics in an interview in *Down
Beat* magazine – and incidentally proved that he could be as
tactless with fellow musicians as he was with an audience.

> Most of The Haig's customers are there to listen to the music
> – those who aren't don't matter. It's a small place, and when
> anyone starts talking it not only annoys those who are trying to
> listen, but disturbs the continuity of our collective musical
> thinking. I know the people talk, laugh and carry on down
> there at the Lighthouse all the time when Rumsey's band is
> playing – but they blast all night long anyway, so it doesn't
> matter.[11]

The first five months of 1953 found the quartet at the height of its popularity, and Mulligan took advantage of the situation to record heavily. In January there was another trip north to San Francisco, where the group cut four more sides for Fantasy records: 'The Lady is a Tramp', 'Moonlight in Vermont', 'Limelight' and 'Turnstile'. By this time Carson Smith had permanently replaced Bob Whitlock as the group's bassist. An even more important change in personnel took place when Chico Hamilton left the group. Chico had proved to be the perfect drummer for the quartet, displaying an ability to swing like hell while keeping his volume to a level compatible with the group sound. However, The Haig's small size made it impossible for Gerry to pay his sidemen much more than union scale. When Hamilton was offered a lucrative job as accompanist for Lena Horne, he felt he couldn't refuse. His replacement was Larry Bunker, a versatile musician who also played vibes, and who was one of the few drummers capable of adequately filling in behind Chico Hamilton.

At the end of January Mulligan once again entered the recording studios, but not with the quartet. This time it was with a much larger group: a ten-piece band that would be dubbed a tentette. Gerry would later remember its genesis as follows: 'When we were first playing at The Haig with the quartet, I started the tentette as a rehearsal band to have something to write for. After a time, Gene Norman, a Los Angeles promoter and disc jockey, came to me and said he'd like to record the band. Since no one else had suggested recording us, I said yes.'[12] Mulligan came to regret that snap decision. Norman did not have a union recording licence of his own and planned to offer the date to Capitol records if he could use their licence, the same arrangement he had used to record the initial Shorty Rogers session. Neither Gene Norman nor Mulligan was aware that Capitol officials had already planned to approach Gerry with an offer of their own, but once Norman had made his offer to Capitol, they felt it would be unethical to proceed. The session was eventually recorded for Gene Norman and released by Capitol. Gerry later felt that had he recorded directly for the label he might have had 'more albums to show for our work'.[13]

The tentette, as Gerry has pointed out, was essentially the quartet 'combined with the ensemble instrumentation of the Miles Davis nonet'. That is, there were two trumpets, a (valve) trombone, French horn, tuba, an alto and two baritone saxophones, bass and drums. Comparisons are inevitable between the tentette and both the Miles Davis and Shorty Rogers mid-sized bands, but the similarities with the Davis nonet are necessarily more pronounced, simply because Mulligan wrote and played for both groups. Three of the tentette performances relate directly to the Miles Davis sides. 'Rocker' was recorded by both groups, and Gerry's arrangement stays basically the same, although he does drop a variation on the theme that was included at the close of the earlier version. 'Ontet', on the other hand, is Gerry's expansion of the out-chorus on his earlier chart of 'Godchild'. And Gerry's 'A Ballad' clearly reflects the influence of Gil Evans's writing on 'Moondreams'.

Of the remaining five performances, four are Mulligan originals. 'Walkin' Shoes' is the only piece that appears in the repertoire of both the quartet and tentette. 'Westwood Walk', taken at a brighter pace, features Chico Hamilton booting the band along. (Chico was replaced by Larry Bunker on the second of the tentette's two recording sessions, however.) 'Simbah' is taken at the fastest tempo of all, while 'Flash' features Mulligan's aggressive piano and the Konitz-like alto of Bud Shank. Finally, 'Takin' a Chance on Love' showcases Gerry's piano all the way.

Unfortunately, the tentette sides were somewhat buried under all the hoopla surrounding the quartet. They enjoyed a certain in-group reputation among musicians, but this was not enough to get the tentette back into the studios. The experience Mulligan gained writing for the group undoubtedly paid dividends later in his writing for the Concert Jazz Band of the sixties, but that is beyond the scope of this narrative. Perhaps the most important achievement of the performances at the time was to show that Chet Baker could play a more forceful and aggressive horn than he had previously exhibited on the quartet sides.

One other group of performances recorded early in 1953 found Mulligan and company straying from the quartet format. Lee Konitz came through California with Stan Kenton's band and sat in at various times with the quartet. Several of these collaborations – caught live at The Haig as well as in the recording studio – were taped by Richard Bock and released for Pacific Jazz. These sides are fascinating studies of the effect Konitz had on the quartet and vice versa.

There is, it might be added, considerable confusion about the dates of these meetings. For that matter, the entire Pacific Jazz catalogue is a discographical quagmire. Apparently few files were kept documenting the label's recording sessions. The liner notes to the twelve-inch album *Lee Konitz Plays with the Gerry Mulligan Quartet* give 25 January 1953 as the date for the live recordings, and Bock himself – on another album – gives 10 June as the date for one of the 'studio' (actually Turetsky's bungalow) sessions. But other sources show that Lee Konitz was out of town with the Kenton band on 10 June. The standard discography, Jorgen Jepsen's *Jazz Records* (currently under revision), lists 25 and 30 January and 1 February as the dates for all of the Konitz recordings, but in each case indiscriminately mixes live performances with those obviously taped in a studio or other controlled environment. Without going into too much detail, a good 'guesstimate' is as follows. The most likely date for the live performances seems to be 25 January (a Sunday evening). At least three of the studio cuts – 'I Can't Believe that You're in Love with Me', 'Lady be Good' and 'Sextet' – had to have been recorded at about the same time. (All three were issued on a ten-inch LP, PJLP-2, which was reviewed in the 20 May issue of *Down Beat*.) The remaining studio cuts, 'Broadway' and 'Almost Like being in Love', may have been recorded at some later date.

Whenever they were recorded, the performances from The Haig show a less introspective, more fiery Konitz than was usually the case in these early years. On the up-tempo numbers, 'Too Marvelous for Words', 'I'll Remember April', 'All the Things You are' and a recently discovered 'Bernie's Tune', Lee reels off chorus after chorus of effortless improvisation. Perhaps the lack of a piano freed his imagination. The two ballads, 'Lover Man' and 'These Foolish Things', find Konitz closer to his usual relaxed and lyrical style. Gerry selflessly allows the altoist the bulk of the solo space on all these sides and is content mainly to provide sympathetic counter-lines and riffs. Baker, for some reason, sounds tentative and even intimidated in his few solos from this session.

The studio recordings, on the other hand, are something of a let-down. The solos are kept short, since the sides are limited to the three-minute format of a 78 rpm single, and this in turn gives too much prominence to the opening and closing themes, making the records sound over-arranged. Still, the musicians get into a nice relaxed groove on several of the sides, and on an alternate take of 'Lady be Good' Lee Konitz momentarily regains some of the fire he had shown on the live performances.

As interesting as the Konitz and tentette sessions are, however, it is still the quartet that holds our attention, and the basic group was far from idle in the early months of 1953. In February the quartet, with its new rhythm section of Carson Smith and Larry Bunker, returned to the studios and recorded four tunes, 'Makin' Whoopee', 'Cherry', 'Motel' and 'Carson City Stage'. These were released with four of the Lee Konitz collaborations on the album mentioned above. The group recorded three more tunes in March, 'Festive Minor', 'All the Things You are' and 'My Old Flame', although the latter tune was the only one released at the time.

A month later the group recorded a series of tunes that would be released on PJLP-5, the second album devoted strictly to the quartet. 'Love Me or Leave Me', 'Swing House' and 'Jeru' were cut on 27 April, while 'Darn that Dream', 'I May be Wrong', 'I'm Beginning to See the Light', 'The Nearness of You' and 'Tea for Two' were done at additional sessions on 29 and 30 April. Mulligan's originals, 'Swing House' and 'Jeru', are especially interesting. The first is based on 'Sweet Georgia Brown' changes and features some delicious 'French horn' harmonies in the chase chorus. This version of 'Jeru' (Gerry's nickname) is fascinating simply because it does away with the unorthodox metres and structure that Gerry had used on the

Birth of the Cool arrangement of the tune. Here we have a conventional thirty-two-bar, AABA framework. (The change is not unlike that which Duke Ellington's 'Concerto for Cootie' underwent in being transformed into the pop song 'Do Nothing till You Hear from Me'.) 'Tea for Two', incidentally, was entitled 'Tea or Two' on some earlier issues of the original ten-inch LP, and although Mulligan's version is obviously based on the Youmens and Caesar standard, the melody line is delightfully altered. The new title could well represent an insider's joke.

Finally, the quartet was recorded live at The Haig one more time on 20 May 1953. Only two of the performances, 'Five Brothers' and 'I Can't Get Started', were originally released, but seven additional performances have recently been issued on a five-record Mosaic album that offers all of the quartet (including the Konitz) sides and tentette performances we've been discussing. The additional tunes taped at this final live session are 'Ide's Side', 'Haig and Haig', 'My Funny Valentine', and – with a visiting Chico Hamilton sitting in for Larry Bunker – 'Aren't You Glad You're You', 'Get Happy', 'Poinciana' and 'Godchild'. The musicians all seem to be having a ball on these sides, and it's a shame the tapes were buried for so long.

These were the final recorded performances of the original Gerry Mulligan Quartet – with the possible exception of the previously mentioned Lee Konitz session in June. Shortly thereafter Gerry was arrested on a narcotics charge and was sentenced to a ninety-day stay on the California Honor Farm. When he was released, Gerry felt that he had had enough of California for a while. Chet Baker no doubt helped to confirm Gerry's decision. As one of Mulligan's friends remembers it, 'Chet met Gerry when he got out of jail and said, "I want four hundred dollars a week." This to a guy who'd just taken a bust and didn't have a job.'[14] Chet's own version is a little different. Both he and Mulligan had won the *Down Beat* polls during Gerry's confinement, and Baker says it was Mulligan who brought up the subject of re-establishing the group.

All I wanted was $300 a week and he started laughing like I was asking for something outrageous. Up to this point all I was making was $120 a week, six nights a week. So that was the end of the group. Our original band never went on tour. Three hundred dollars a week was nothing! And that's what really pissed me off. I worked for him for eleven months without asking for a raise, but after we both won the polls I figured, Jesus, it's time to get a little more bread.[15]

In any event, the quartet did not get together again and Mulligan left for New York. There have been reunions of Mulligan and Baker; once in 1957 for a Pacific Jazz album (cut in New York), and again in 1974 for a Carnegie Hall concert, which was recorded by CTI Records. If the two aren't close friends, they nevertheless still respect each other's playing, and the 1974 recordings show that there is still an uncanny empathy when the two play together.

Meanwhile, back in the summer of 1953, Richard Bock found himself with a struggling young record company and his star artist temporarily unavailable. Naturally he turned to Chet Baker, who had formed a quartet of his own. The results were a series of records that made Chet a star in his own right. Chet cut his first solo side ('Isn't It Romantic') on 24 July, with a quartet consisting of Russ Freeman, piano, Red Mitchell, bass and Bobby White, drums. A few days later he recorded three additional numbers; then on 29 and 30 July he recorded fourteen pieces with a quartet that featured Russ Freeman and his stablemates from the Mulligan quartet, Carson Smith and Larry Bunker. All told there were enough tunes for two ten-inch LPs and a number of singles.

In Russ Freeman, Chet had found an ideal collaborator. Freeman was born 28 May 1926 in Chicago and moved to Los Angeles in the 1930s, where he studied classical piano. He was one of the first of the white pianists on the Coast to adapt to the post-war modern-jazz styles, and was soon in demand whenever there was need of a hard-swinging rhythm section. Russ backed Charlie Parker for a time during the altoist's first stay in California, and later made jazz time with Howard McGhee and Dexter Gordon. In the early fifties he was with Art Pepper and Wardell Gray, and briefly filled the piano chair with the Lighthouse All-Stars. His is a sparse style, with no unnecessary notes, and perhaps because of this his reputation is much higher among fellow musicians than with the general public. He is also a jazz composer whose lines are truly original, rather than merely new melodies grafted on to standard chord progressions. Several of Freeman's originals were featured in these early Chet Baker sessions, including 'Maid in Mexico', 'Russ Job', 'Batter Up', 'No Ties', 'Band Aid', 'Bea's Flat' and 'Happy Little Sunbeam'.

If the empathy between Chet Baker and Russ Freeman was not quite as complete as that between Baker and Mulligan, it was none the less striking. More than any other musician, Russ could break Chet free of his introspective shell, and the bland quality that marred much of the trumpeter's work was usually kept to a minimum whenever Russ Freeman was present. Baker returned the favour by being an especially sensitive interpreter of the pianist's compositions. 'He's the only one who could play my songs the way I hear them. He had such an innate feeling for them,' Freeman would later tell an interviewer.[16] These two facets of the collaboration are best illustrated by two tunes cut in the July sessions. Baker romps through 'All the Things You are' with an abandon that puts to rest any doubts about his ability to generate a fire; while his jaunty interpretation of Freeman's 'Happy Little Sunbeam' strikes the perfect evocation of the mood suggested by the tune's title.

Pacific Jazz continued to record its new star, but unfortunately Richard Bock seemed to get sidetracked by a bid for mass popularity. This resulted in an album entitled *Chet Baker Sings,* which is, from a jazz standpoint, an unmitigated disaster. The very worst faults of Baker's trumpet style – a tendency towards introspection, a limited emotional and dynamic range – are multiplied tenfold by his soft, quavering voice. No doubt the singer's small-boyish vocals brought out the mothering instinct in some of the females of his audience, but hard-core jazz enthusiasts were and remain turned off. On the other hand, the popularity of the album probably helped underwrite many other more worthy jazz offerings.

With one exception (a seven-piece ensemble album which we'll examine in the next chapter) there is little that needs to be said of the remaining records produced by Chet Baker during this period. They featured him in a variety of contexts: there was a *Chet Baker and Strings* album for Columbia which was almost as innocuous as the vocal album; a live recording by the quartet (with Bob Neel in for Larry Bunker) at a concert at the University of Michigan; a sextet session with Bob Brookmeyer and Bud Shank that has some nice arrangements by Johnny Mandel and Jack Montrose; and another 'strings' album for Pacific Jazz. None of these is outstanding, and the strings albums are not even of average interest. The next year in which Chet Baker recorded albums of importance was 1956, and we'll return to him then.

In the meantime, Gerry Mulligan had gone his own way. His next record was taped in concert at the Salle Pleyel in Paris, during a European tour, and is thus somewhat out of our purview. The new quartet consisted of Bob Brookmeyer on valve-trombone, Red Mitchell, bass and Frank Isola, drums. The recordings are of interest if only because of the new personnel, but they suffer in comparison with the Mulligan–Baker sides. Although Bob Brookmeyer has a definite affinity for Gerry's music, the range and timbre of the valve-trombone is so similar to that of the baritone sax there is little effective contrast between the two horns. The formation of a quartet with a trumpet as the lead voice had to wait until Mulligan returned to California.

Gerry did return in December of 1954 for a concert tour that introduced his new trumpet player, Jon Eardley. Red Mitchell remained the quartet's bassist, and Chico Hamilton rejoined Mulligan for this tour. Pacific Jazz's first twelve-inch LP captured the quartet – and a sextet – at two stops along the tour, Stockton and San Diego. The concert at Stockton, on 3 December, opens with an impromptu blues. Gerry's comments to late arrivals, 'I think maybe I'll play some blues while you get seated,' gives the number its title, 'Blues Going Up'. Jon Eardley proves to be a more than adequate replacement for Chet Baker, displaying a fat tone that at times suggests an updated Bix Beiderbecke. Eardley is also featured on the Rodgers and Hart ballad 'Little Girl Blue'. 'Piano Blues' finds Gerry at the keyboard, playing in a traditional, down-home style. Gerry returns to the baritone sax for the closing number, Charlie Parker's 'Yardbird Suite', taken at a relaxed yet swinging up tempo. There is also a brief taste of the quartet's theme, 'Utter Chaos'.

The San Diego concert on the fourteenth introduced Gerry's new sextet. Larry Bunker replaced Chico Hamilton, and Mulligan, Eardley and Mitchell were joined by Bob Brookmeyer and tenor saxophonist Zoot Sims on three numbers. The first, 'Western Reunion', is a straight-ahead swinger on the familiar 'I Got Rhythm' foundations. The four horns combine timbres nicely and afford Mulligan the opportunity to produce a full band sound. 'I Know, Don't Know How' is an original ballad of Gerry's, while 'The Red Door' is a composition of Zoot's. On the latter number, Jon Eardley lays out, and Bob Brookmeyer plays piano. These three numbers were the only sextet performances released on the original twelve-inch LP, but several additional numbers from both concerts were later issued on various Pacific Jazz anthologies. These were, according to Jepsen, 'Bark for Barksdale', 'Soft Shoe' and 'Blues for Tiny' by the quartet and 'There'll Never be Another You', 'Polkadots and Moonbeams' and 'Flamingo' by the sextet. However, at least one of the quartet performances, 'Soft Shoe', is quite obviously a studio recording. It's tempting to hope that other studio performances of the short-lived quartet with Eardley may some day be unearthed, for it is a well balanced band, quite on a par with the Mulligan–Baker quartet.

These concerts marked Mulligan's last appearance in California for some time. He spent the next several years in New York, working with the sextet format and recording a series of albums for the Emarcy label. When Gerry Mulligan returned to New York at the close of 1954, he left a musical scene far different from the one he had found upon his arrival in Los Angeles a short two years earlier. The catchphrase West Coast jazz was being bandied about in the jazz press and, much to his irritation, Gerry's name was often linked with the music. Gerry was quite right in rejecting the linkage; his quartet was *sui generis* and belonged to no school save that of Mulligan himself. At the same time, though, the national popularity of the quartet did much to draw attention to jazz in southern California and helped smooth the way for other musicians who were trying to be heard. As we have seen, Pacific Jazz owed its very existence to the Mulligan quartet, and that label and the other independent companies that sprang up in its wake were largely responsible for launching the careers of many southland musicians who had been anonymous before Gerry had arrived. Gerry Mulligan's help may have been inadvertent, but it was indispensable nevertheless.

5.

the west coast sound

Chief among Pacific Jazz's competitors in the southland's independent record derby was Lester Koenig's Contemporary records. Koenig had founded Good Time Jazz records in the post-war years to record traditional Dixieland and New Orleans revivalist groups, and the Contemporary label was a natural outgrowth of the parent company. As we have seen, the first Lighthouse All-Stars recordings were released on Contemporary. (Actually, the 78 singles were issued on the Lighthouse label, and that trademark and logo was then used for Contemporary's Lighthouse series of 45s and long-playing albums.) In addition to Howard Rumsey and the Lighthouse crew, Koenig signed Shelly Manne (the All-Stars' drummer at the time) to a long-term contract. Shelly was given *carte blanche* with regards to recording sessions and sidemen, and the liberty he enjoyed paid dividends for Koenig and the Contemporary label.

The first session under Shelly's own name was held on 6 April 1953, shortly following the Shorty Rogers *Cool and Crazy* sessions, and featured a number of the same sidemen. The band was a septet, and the instrumentation was slightly unusual: the front line consisted of three saxes and a valve-trombone. Art Pepper's alto, Bob Cooper's tenor and Jimmy Giuffre's baritone were joined by Bob Enevoldsen's trombone and the rhythm section of Marty Paich, Curtis Counce and of course Shelly. However, in both this and a second session held later in July, the featured artists were really the writers. For the initial session Shorty Rogers contributed two arrangements, an original entitled 'Mallets' and a chart on a traditional Mexican folk theme,

'La Mucura'. Both are Latin-tinged. 'Mallets', as the title suggests, features Shelly using mallets throughout. The remaining two arrangements were by Bill Russo, a trombonist and writer then with Stan Kenton. 'You and the Night and the Music' has lovely alto work by Art Pepper (recording under the name Art Salt for contractual reasons) on both section lead and solo. Russo's second piece, 'Gazelle', is aptly named, for the difficult theme runs and leaps at a brisk pace.

There were two changes in personnel at the second session, held on 20 July. Altoist Bud Shank replaced Art Pepper, who was away on the first of numerous absences from the scene, and Joe Mondragon replaced Curtis Counce. Shorty Rogers and Bill Russo each contributed an additional chart for this date. Shorty's ballad 'Afrodesia' was written with Art Pepper in mind, but Bud Shank fills in admirably; Russ's minor-key number is named 'Sweets'. Pianist Marty Paich contributed an arrangement of 'You're My Thrill' which seems influenced by Russo's writing on 'You and the Night and the Music'. Finally, there is Jimmy Giuffre's 'Fugue', an attempt to stretch the boundaries of jazz writing. 'Fugue' is atonal, and the rhythm section plays melodies or counter-lines rather than time. There is, however, a repeated figure – as old as a Kansas City riff – that ties the arrangement together.

When these eight numbers were first released on a long-playing record, the album was entitled *The West Coast Sound*, and indeed these arrangements – much more than the Shorty Rogers Capitol sides – set the style for much of what came to be called West Coast jazz. The valve-trombone is used here not as the ensemble lead, but is treated as a member of the sax section. The inner voices – trombone and tenor sax – are given the most dissonant notes (they are often voiced in minor seconds), thus thickening the ensemble sound. There are many contrapuntal passages, even aside from the formal 'Fugue'. Perhaps most importantly, the writing definitely takes precedence over the solos: often each horn gets only half a chorus to blow in. Moreover, Shelly confines himself to brushes (or mallets) for the most part, and there are few 'bombs' dropped. The result is an intellectual music that exhibits a great deal of craftsmanship but little warmth or swing. At the time it was recorded it was certainly a new and fresh sound, and that may have had much to do with the music's initial acceptance. But it palled rather quickly and made one long for some uninhibited, straight-ahead blowing.

Several months later the Lighthouse All-Stars once again recorded for Contemporary. By this time the key members of the original All-Stars – Shorty Rogers, Jimmy Giuffre and Shelly Manne – had left to form Shorty's working group, the Giants. The second-generation members who met in the studio on 20 October included the Swedish trumpet star Rolf Ericson, saxophonists Herb Geller, Bud Shank and Bob Cooper, pianist Claude Williamson, and a most important new addition, Max Roach. In retrospect, it might seem strange that the fiery drummer of Charlie Parker's quintet and the acknowledged father of modern jazz drumming would take a job on the Coast, which was already gaining a reputation for a laid-back style, but the All-Stars – especially in concert at the club – were always exponents of straight-ahead blowing. Max was with the All-Stars six months, starting in September 1953. Shelly Manne had recommended Max as his replacement, and Howard Rumsey phoned New York to see if the drummer was interested. He was. 'I called him – he needed work,' Rumsey recalls. 'When he finished he told me it was the only job he ever had for a six-month period.'[1] Max seemed to enjoy working with the All-Stars, although it may be significant that he left as soon as his contract expired. Bob Cooper remembers Max telling him that he liked working in a 'clean' atmosphere; the always professional Rumsey saw to it that drugs were off-limits at the club. In any case, the California musicians certainly enjoyed working with Max Roach.

Four tunes were recorded at the October session, Shorty Rogers's 'Mambo Los Feliz', Jimmy Giuffre's beautiful arrangement of the Victor Young standard 'Love Letters' and two originals by Bob Cooper, 'Witch Doctor' and 'Jazz Invention'. Jack Costanzo was added on bongos for 'Mambo Los Feliz' and 'Witch Doctor', and Milt Bernhart's trombone was added on the latter tune. 'Love Letters' features a contrapuntal arrangement that has the four horns passing the melody from player to player, as well as a haunting piano solo by Claude Williamson. Bob Cooper's 'Jazz Invention', which also features contrapuntal lines throughout, shows that the saxophonist had come into his own as a jazz composer. Coop's arrangement is thoughtful yet genial, which, come to think of it, is quite accurate as a sketch of Cooper himself.

An even more ambitious attempt at showcasing the West Coast composers came with Shelly Manne's second album. Where the first album had featured an ensemble dominated by reeds, the ensemble on the new LP was composed of a brass choir (two trumpets, valve-trombone and tuba) plus rhythm. Again, the recording was done in two sessions. The first, held on 18 December 1953, had Ollie Mitchell and Shorty Rogers on trumpets, Bob Enevoldsen back on trombone, Paul Sarmento on tuba, and the rhythm section of Russ Freeman, Joe Mondragon and Shelly. All of the album's pieces, incidentally, were original compositions. Shorty Rogers must have enjoyed the challenge of working with the unorthodox instrumentation; his 'Shapes, Motions, and Colors' shows that he was capable of much more than the swinging big-band riffs that had become his trademark. Each composer was invited to comment on his own work for the album's liner notes, and Shorty's personality comes through clearly in his statement.

> I didn't consciously try for any specific overall form, prefer-ring free forms in my own thinking. I did however use many devices within this free form, but as ends in themselves and not as means to an end. I realized, after I finished this work, that it had taken the shape of a first rondo, but the form was really a result of an instinct for balance ... This is a reflection of my likes in music. I tried only to write what I like, not con-cerning myself with such thoughts as: Is it Jazz? or: Is it legiti-mate? or: Will anyone like it?[2]

'Dimension in Thirds', by Marty Paich, is fairly conventional, yet clearly shows the talent that the youthful Paich was developing. Jimmy Giuffre once again offers an atonal composi-tion, 'Alternation', and once again the rhythm section plays melodies or counter-lines, rather than time. The resulting piece is much closer to the Third Stream experiments that would take place later in the decade than to any works of the other West Coast writers. By the same token, 'Alternation' is further removed from jazz than any other piece on this album.

The outstanding composition to come out of the second session, which was held on 17 March 1954, was 'Etude de Concert' by Jack Montrose. The piece features a number of different moods, instrumental combinations and tempi, high-lighted by Shorty Rogers's swinging trumpet. Montrose com-bines classical techniques with jazz feeling better than any of the other composers, and 'Etude' remains an important work. Its secret is found in Montrose's own comments: '"Etude de Concert" is first and last a jazz composition. The main objective I had in mind was that it must swing.'[3] Bob Cooper's 'Divertimento for Brass and Rhythm' is more conventional, but Coop also remembers the necessity to swing. The sixth selection, Bill Holman's 'Lullaby', is so named for the childlike directness and simplicity of the theme. On this second session Don Fagerquist and Marty Paich replaced Ollie Mitchell and Russ Freeman on trumpet and piano.

Another Lighthouse All-Stars album cut the same year had the participants experimenting with forms and instruments not usually (at the time) associated with jazz. Saxophonists Bud Shank and Bob Cooper had originally begun doubling on flute and oboe, respectively, while members of the Kenton Innovations orchestra. Cooper, born on 6 December 1925 in Pittsburgh, Pennsylvania, had joined Kenton in 1945 and was a mainstay of the sax section in the post-war years. In 1946 he married Kenton's popular vocalist, June Christy. Although he is adept on just about any of the woodwinds, he gained special recognition as being one of the very few jazzmen to have mastered the difficult oboe. Bud Shank was born Clifford Everett Shank Jr, in Dayton,

Ohio on 27 May 1926. He had played with the bands of Charlie Barnet, Alvino Rey and Art Mooney before joining Kenton in 1951, and had taken up the flute as a double expressly to audition for the Innovations orchestra.

In 1953, as members of the Lighthouse All-Stars, Shank and Cooper began experimenting with duets featuring their alternate woodwinds. The audience enjoyed the fresh sounds of the duets and asked for more, and their burgeoning popularity suggested a recording date. By February 1954 everyone felt ready, and the quintet entered the Contemporary studios to record eight tunes. In addition to 'head' arrangements of two jazz standards, 'Night in Tunisia' and 'Bag's Groove', the musicians had written six originals specifically for the flute and oboe combination. Bob Cooper contributed three of the tunes, 'Warm Winds', 'Still Life' and 'Hermosa Summer'. Bud Shank's offering was a bright number called 'Happy Town'; Claude Williamson wrote 'Aquarium'; and Max Roach penned a number entitled 'Albatross'. Shank and Cooper also play alto flute and English horn on several of the numbers, achieving a darker coloration with the lower-pitched instruments. The flute and oboe combination works well on the slower mood numbers, but is less effective on the up-tempo pieces, which tend to sound anaemic. The group sound begins to pall over the length of a full album, but the experiments did help to legitimize the use of such 'exotic' instruments in the jazz arsenal.

The culmination of the Contemporary/Shelly Manne experimental series came on 10 September 1954 when Shorty Rogers, Jimmy Giuffre and Shelly met in the studios to tape an album entitled simply *The Three*. Rogers, Giuffre and Manne had been playing together for over five years: in various editions of the Herman and Kenton bands, with the Lighthouse All-Stars, and in Shorty's own group, the Giants. They had in that time developed, in Giuffre's words, 'a mutual instinct which enables us to work together in volume, motion and sound'.[4] As was the case with the flute and oboe duets, the trio first experimented with the combination on the job, informally, as the mood struck them. Again, a recording date was suggested, and again, several tunes were composed specifically for the instrumentation. Two of the tunes, 'Autumn in New York' and Charlie Parker's 'Steeplechase', were in the Giants' regular book. Two more tunes were composed especially for the date, Shorty's 'Three on a Row' and Jimmy's 'Pas de Trois'. As the name suggests, 'Three on a Row' is based on a twelve-tone row. Finally, two of the numbers were worked out in the studio. Shelly Manne's 'Flip' (Shelly's wife's nickname) is a head arrangement featuring the horns in two-part canon. The sixth piece, 'Abstract No. 1', is a completely free improvisation.

The trio sounds somewhat empty on first hearing; the lack of the jazz pulse usually supplied by the bass is especially disconcerting. But the versatility of the musicians helps matters greatly. Shelly Manne, as has often been noted, is an extremely melodic drummer, and here he often functions as a third voice. Jimmy Giuffre divides his playing time almost equally between three horns – clarinet, tenor and baritone saxes – which significantly extends the range of colours available to the trio. Most importantly, the three can and do swing. One method Shorty uses to avoid excessive repetition in 'Three on a Row' is to vary the tempi and accents in the various statements and permutations of the tone row. He succeeds admirably, and the performance is far from the rigid and sterile statement one might expect from such a premise. 'Steeplechase' turns out to be a straight-ahead swinger, with Giuffre starting out on tenor and switching to the more assertive baritone for a surging solo. The album's capstone is 'Abstract No. 1', which recalls Lennie Tristano's 'Intuition' and anticipates the free jazz of the sixties as well. The lack of a piano is an advantage here, as there is no implied tonal centre. The two horns listen closely to each other and respond quickly to changes in direction. Moreover, 'Abstract' breaks into swing, something the Tristano free pieces never managed to do.

A short four days later, a sequel to *The Three* was recorded. This time the participants were Shelly Manne and Russ Freeman, so the album was naturally enough entitled *The Two*. Russ and Shelly had worked together both at the Lighthouse and in the original edition of the Giants, and had developed an empathy that went beyond the usual partnership expected of two rhythm-section instruments. As Russ Freeman remembered it,

Playing on the job, Shelly and I used to do things together in the rhythm section, not just counterpoint to the horns, but between us. Instead of playing a drum solo or a piano solo, in some spots, we'd play a solo at the same time, trying to feel each other out, with an awareness of each other being there.

And Shelly would add, 'We enjoyed playing together so much that we kept talking about making an album, just the two of us, because of the freedom we'd have ... We have a lot of confidence in each other, particularly in each other's time. We're not afraid to try unusual things metre-wise.'[5]

'The Sound Effects Manne' is a perfect introduction to the method the two had worked out. A thirty-two-measure tune, Russ carries the melody for the first sixteen, with Shelly playing a counter-line; then the two switch roles for the second sixteen. Throughout the 'solos', Russ and Shelly take turns as lead voice or in offering a supporting role to the other. The fine Matt Dennis tune 'Everything Happens to Me' serves as a ballad vehicle for Russ, with Shelly providing sympathetic accompaniment. The two swing so hard on 'Billie's Bounce' that the absence of a bass is hardly felt, and this is also true for 'With a Song in My Heart', which is taken at a very rapid tempo. The two remaining tunes – 'A Slight Minority' and 'Speak Easy' – are both Russ Freeman originals (as is 'Sound Effects Manne'). 'Minority' is a ballad, while 'Speak Easy' is a thirty-two-bar AABA piece; both showcase the thoughtful yet swinging interplay between Russ and Shelly. The teamwork these two demonstrate throughout the session would pay dividends later in the decade when they would be reunited in Shelly's own working quintet.

The experiments we've been discussing in this chapter suffered the fate that happens to so many similar artistic searches. At first they were lavishly praised as fresh and original; then a reaction set in and they were damned (often by the same critics!) as straying too far from their jazz heritage. André Hodeir, one of the most thoughtful critics ever to write about jazz, had this to say about the West Coast musicians:

Men like Bill Holman, Shorty Rogers and Jimmy Giuffre are certainly excellent musicians; they have proved it on many occasions. Why do they apparently find it necessary to think in terms of two types of works, the 'normal' and the 'experimental'? An attitude as artificial as this cannot help being reflected in an alternation of failures that do not at all make up for each other. The medium-size-group sessions ... under the aegis of Shelly Manne are revealing. They show us what mistakes can be made by estimable jazzmen working without any doctrine except, perhaps, the most detestable – eclecticism. The risks taken here are inversely proportional to the jazz level achieved: the closer one gets to the language of jazz, the more commonplace becomes the performance. That is exactly the opposite of what should have happened; or, to be more precise, a maximum of jazz discipline should have been combined with a maximum of musical risks. Such as they are, the pieces included on the Shelly Manne records suffer from a distressing lack of unity.[6]

Hodeir seems to miss the point here, however. Of course the works are eclectic. There is a wide cross-section of musicians at work here, and certainly no jazz musician is going to sit down and compose a piece hewing to any preconceived strictures of 'doctrine'. In the case of the first two Shelly Manne albums, there were no givens – with the exception of the instrumentation. Each composer or arranger was specifically enjoined to write whatever he wished. Under such conditions it makes no sense to complain about lack of unity.

Nor could the musicians be blamed for dividing their works into 'normal' and 'experimental' modes – the very nature of the recordings assured that. Most of the experimental works were never played outside the recording studios. There seems to have been a picture in the minds of jazz writers at the time of attentive audiences sitting in Hollywood clubs listening to twenty-piece orchestras play the latest atonal scores from the pens of the West Coast musicians. In reality, a typical jazz-club patron would be listening to a quartet or quintet working out on 'Donna Lee' or 'Now's the Time'. The flute and oboe duets, it is true, were originally played before live audiences at the Lighthouse, but they would typically represent only a small portion of an evening's programme.

On the other hand, Hodeir is nearer the mark when he says that 'the closer one gets to the language of jazz, the more commonplace becomes the performance'. Numbers like 'You're My Thrill' and 'You and the Night and the Music' from the first album are little more than scaled-down big-band dance charts with slightly advanced harmonies, the sort of music that Dave Pell would later manufacture in a seemingly endless series of albums.

In any case, the albums we've been discussing sold well and paved the way for additional sessions – both conventional and experimental – on various labels, including Contemporary,

Pacific Jazz, and a host of other independent labels that sprang up in their wake. Not all of the musicians on the Coast were experimenting with exotic forms and instruments, of course, but the atmosphere at the time was very conducive to such experiments. One such experiment, whose significance would not be fully realized until the following decade, was that of joining the samba rhythms of Brazil with those of jazz.

Laurindo Almeida, a Brazilian concert guitarist, first came to prominence in this country as a featured soloist with Stan Kenton in 1947. Laurindo had been born in São Paolo on 2 September 1917 and had taken up the guitar as a youth. By the time Kenton invited him to the States for a concert tour, Almeida had become famous in his native country playing Spanish concert-style acoustic guitar. His extensive musical training – he had played staff radio jobs in Rio de Janeiro and led an orchestra at Casino de Urca in that city – helped land him a job in the movie studios when Kenton disbanded following the 1947 tour. While working on the soundtrack of *A Song is Born*, Almeida would relax between takes playing duets with bassist Harry Babasin, and a fast friendship developed between the two.

In 1952 Almeida and Babasin were reunited when the bassist subbed for another musician on a club date the guitarist was working. As Babasin remembers it, 'During the evening Laurindo would play several sets of solo guitar, and rather than hang around the bar or take a walk, I found myself joining him on bass.'[7] The chemistry between the two was still working, and Babasin began to wonder what would happen if the guitarist were to be backed by a regular jazz combo. The opportunity finally came in 1953, when a quartet composed of Almeida, altoist Bud Shank, Babasin and drummer Roy Harte began to rehearse in the back room of Harte's Drum City, a Hollywood music shop. Roy Harte, a veteran of the Boyd Raeburn and Les Brown bands, takes up the tale.

> We rehearsed for about a month. It was Harry's idea, and his bass parts provided the lead rhythmically. Actually we rehearsed for our own education – to see whether Laurindo would swing. Of course, we all knew how great he was as a formal guitarist, but we wanted to find out if he could swing in jazz.
> Our main purpose was to achieve the light, swinging feel of the baião – combined with jazz blowing. In order to get this, I

played brushes on a conga drum, not a snare drum. This gave it a light feeling. Actually, I was trying to play with my right hand to Bud's jazz blowing, and with my left I was putting in the samba colour with Laurindo's playing.[8]

Things gelled from the first, and the group soon landed an engagement at The Haig. In September the quartet entered the Pacific Jazz studios to record six tunes for a ten-inch LP. Three of the tunes, 'Blue Baião', 'Carinoso' and 'Nonô', were standards of the Brazilian repertoire, and a fourth, 'Tocata', was written especially for the recording by one of Brazil's foremost classical composers, Radamés Gnattali. Harry Babasin contributed an original called 'Noctambulism', and the sixth tune, 'Hazardous', was written by Dick Hazard. The music is instantly appealing; the infectious samba rhythms fit in quite well with the jazz feeling, and Bud Shank's pure alto tone is a perfect complement to Almeida's unamplified guitar. Listeners at The Haig were enthusiastic, and Babasin wanted very much to continue, but Almeida preferred to continue with his classical concert work. A second ten-inch album was cut the following year, but there were no further live performances by the group.

In late 1953 Laurindo Almeida returned to Brazil for a visit and took with him twenty-five copies of the first album. 'I gave copies to many of my friends, and it was given close attention,' he remembers.[9] It is tempting to argue that these experiments linking Brazilian samba rhythms with jazz led to the music called bossa nova, which made such an impact on the popular music of the early 1960s, but there is no positive proof of this. No doubt there was some influence at work here, but the Brazilian musicians had already been exposed to the Latin–jazz fusion of some Charlie Parker and especially Dizzy Gillespie recordings of the late forties. But whether the Laurindo Almeida sides were the progenitors of bossa nova or not, they certainly exhibited characteristics of that style some nine years before bossa nova became a national craze.

The Laurindo Almeida–Bud Shank quartet sides were not the only recordings on which Harry Babasin and Roy Harte collaborated. In fact Roy Harte had formed his own label, Nocturne, prior to the Almeida session. The label was short-lived, but Harte did record some interesting albums while it was in existence. The first Nocturne album introduced two rising young jazzmen, Herbie Harper and Bob Gordon. Trombonist

Harper, whose album this was, was a veteran of the big bands, having played with Johnny 'Scat' Davis, Gene Krupa, Charlie Spivak, Benny Goodman and Charlie Barnet. Herbie was born in Salina, Kansas on 2 July 1920 and was raised in Amarillo, Texas. Bob Gordon (no relation to the author) was a baritone saxophonist who, at the time the album was cut, was rapidly developing an individual voice on the large instrument. Gordon was born in St Louis on 11 June 1928 and had been a California resident since the forties. He had played with the bands of Shorty Sherock, Alvino Rey and Billy May. The rhythm section for the recording date was Jimmy Rowles on piano, Harry Babasin and Roy Harte on bass and drums. Both of the hornsmen favour a straight-ahead blowing style, which results in relaxed yet swinging versions of 'Jeepers Leapers', Gerry Mulligan's 'Five Brothers', 'Herbstone' (A Harper original) and 'Jive at Five'. There are also ballad performances of 'Dinah' and 'Summertime'. Bob Gordon, despite the inclusion of 'Five Brothers', exhibits an individual style that is not beholden to Gerry Mulligan.

The second Nocturne set marked Bud Shank's first recording as a leader. The Nocturne house rhythm section of Jimmy

Rowles, Harry Babasin and Roy Harte returned, and Bud's ex-boss Shorty Rogers provided the second horn. Shorty, moreover, supplied all six of the album's tunes: 'Shank's Pranks', 'Casa de Luz', 'Lotus Bud', 'Left Bank', 'Jasmine' and 'Just a Few'. Two of the tunes, 'Shank's Pranks' and 'Lotus Bud', were minor hits at the time; 'Shank's Pranks' features a bright, catchy tune based on diverging lines, while 'Lotus Bud' is a beautiful ballad with an engaging alto flute solo by Shank. Rogers, by the way, plays flugelhorn on all numbers, imparting a dusky coloration that blends well with both alto sax and alto flute.

As national interest began to focus on the Los Angeles jazz scene, sparked by the growing controversy over 'West Coast jazz' in the trade press, recording activity in the area grew apace. By 1954, a seemingly endless stream of albums issued by both independent and major labels gushed forth from the Coast. Some of the artists represented certainly would not have considered themselves West Coast jazzmen, but were recorded under the banner none the less. Stan Getz, for example, formed a quintet with Bob Brookmeyer in 1953 which, although often on tour, was headquartered in Los Angeles and recorded prolifically there for Norman Granz's Norgran label. Two tunes from their first Norgran album, 'Crazy Rhythm' and 'Willow Weep for Me', became jazz equivalents of hits. 'Crazy Rhythm' is highlighted by some improvised contrapuntal lines by Getz and Brookmeyer of the type that would become the group's trademark. 'Willow' features Stan in his most lovely ballad style. Whether or not they were true West Coast jazzmen, Getz's cool, Lestorian tenor and Brookmeyer's genial valve-trombone certainly fit in well with the West Coast sound. An album taped at a pair of concerts held in LA's Shrine Auditorium in November 1954 (but unfortunately long out-of-print) gives the best idea of the alchemy that existed between the two. Getz and Brookmeyer, backed by pianist Johnny Willams, bassist Bill Anthony and drummer Art Mardigan or Frank Isola, romp through up-tempo numbers like 'Open Country', 'It Don't Mean a Thing' and 'Feather Merchant', and play at their lyrical best on ballads like 'Polkadots and Moonbeams' and 'We'll be Together Again'.

Earlier that year Maynard Ferguson recorded the first of many albums for Mercury records' subsidiary label, Emarcy. This was an octet session with Maynard on trumpet or valve-trombone; Herbie Harper on trombone; Bud Shank, Bob Cooper and Bob

Gordon on alto, tenor and bari saxes; and a rhythm section of Russ Freeman, Curtis Counce and Shelly Manne. The arrangements by Willie Maiden were in the by now familiar West Coast style, and so Maynard – whose trumpet style is anything but cool – became allied in the public's mind with the West Coast jazzmen. A contrapuntal version of 'The Way You Look Tonight' is the album's up-tempo swinger, while both 'Over the Rainbow' and 'All God's Children Got Rhythm' feature Ferguson's patented stratospheric trumpet range.

Another West Coast musician to come into prominence at the time was altoist Lennie Niehaus. Niehaus, born in St Louis on 11 June 1929, moved to LA at the age of seven. He had a very thorough grounding in music theory, including a BA in music from Los Angeles State, and had played for Jerry Wald and Stan Kenton before being drafted. Discharged in 1954, he returned to LA and began playing casuals around town. Niehaus happened to sit in with Shorty Rogers one night at The Haig. Shelly Manne was so impressed he mentioned the altoist to Les Koenig, and Niehaus was promptly signed to a contract with Contemporary records. He recorded his first album less than a month later, in July 1954.

The first of many Lennie Niehaus albums for Contemporary

featured a quintet composed of Niehaus, Jack Montrose and Bob Gordon on alto, tenor and baritone saxes, Monty Budwig on bass, and Shelly Manne on drums. Four standards ('I'll Take Romance', 'You Stepped Out of a Dream', 'I Remember You', 'Day by Day') and four originals ('Bottoms Up', 'Whose Blues', 'Prime Rib', 'Inside Out') were all scored by Niehaus, and his formal training is quite evident – perhaps too evident. The writing is highly contrapuntal; even the rhythm-section parts are largely written. The altoist also gets the bulk of the solo space – and on a ten-inch LP there isn't that much space to go around. The result is a one-man showcase for the leader, whose talent is large indeed, but not large enough to support such a burden.

CONTEMPORARY RECORDS

HOW ABOUT YOU
BY BURTON LANE & RALPH FREED
FIGURE 8
BY LENNIE NIEHAUS
PATTI-CAKE
BY LENNIE NIEHAUS
THE WAY YOU LOOK TONIGHT
BY JEROME KERN & DOROTHY FIELDS

C 2517
(LKL 81)   Side 1

LENNIE NIEHAUS

Lennie Niehaus, *alto sax*; Jack Montrose, *tenor sax*;
Bob Gordon, *baritone sax*; Stu Williamson, *trumpet*;
Bob Enevoldsen, *valve trombone*; Lou Levy, *piano*;
Monty Budwig, *bass*; Shelly Manne, *drums*

Niehaus is an accomplished altoist, with an awesome technique and a seemingly inexhaustible storehouse of ideas, but his work on the Contemporary albums is somewhat lacking in emotion; a listener soon longs for the earthy, blues-tinged soul of a Parker or Sonny Criss. The one number in which the players let their hair down is the up-tempo 'Whose Blues', which features an exchange between the three saxophonists. Bob Gordon's surging baritone is especially impressive here.

A second album taped a month later expands the instrumentation to an octet by adding trumpeter Stu Williamson, valve-trombonist Bob Enevoldsen, and pianist Lou Levy. The remaining players are all hold-overs from the first session. Again there are eight tunes, including four originals ('Figure 8', 'Patti-Cake', 'Night Life' and 'Seaside'). No new ground is covered or even attempted, and many of the faults of the first album are exacerbated by the increased instrumentation. Even more than the first, this is a writer's album, as three more potential soloists vie for the same limited space. Again, it's largely Niehaus supported by a seven-piece ensemble, and again his playing is technically adroit and emotionally bland. Shortly after this album was taped Niehaus rejoined Kenton, although he continued to record albums for Contemporary – largely in the same vein as those mentioned above – for several years.

Another composer-arranger whose work was superficially similar to that of Lennie Niehaus was tenor saxophonist Jack Montrose. Montrose's background was very similar to that of Niehaus. Born 30 December 1928 in Detroit, Michigan, Montrose attended high school in Chattanooga, Tennessee, and – like Niehaus – took his BA in music at Los Angeles State. Montrose was with Jerry Gray's band in 1953 and played with Art Pepper in 1954. Like Niehaus, Montrose favoured contra-puntal rather than vertical writing, but Montrose usually managed to breathe a little more individuality into his scores; there is less of the arid feel of the classroom in his writing.

Jack Montrose's first major writing assignment was for a Chet Baker ensemble album cut for Pacific Jazz in December 1953. The seven-piece ensemble consisted of Baker, Herb Geller on alto and tenor saxes, Montrose on tenor, Bob Gordon on baritone, and a rhythm section of Russ Freeman, Joe Mondragon and Shelly Manne. Montrose arranged all eight tunes for the session, including three standards ('Moonlight Becomes You', 'Little Old Lady' and 'Goodbye') and five originals ('Ergo', 'Bockhanal', 'Headline', 'A Dandy Line' and 'Prodefunctus'). Although the writing does tend to get over-elaborate at times, Montrose allows plenty of room for blowing (given the space limitations of a ten-inch LP). Chet Baker, of course, gets the majority of the solo space, but none of the other musicians is relegated solely to a supporting role. The two best performances are on the up-tempo 'Bockhanal' and 'A Dandy Line'. 'Bockhanal' is a blues with two equal but complementary melody lines, in the manner of Charlie Parker's 'Chasin' the Bird'.

Montrose quickly became house arranger for Pacific Jazz, writing for a variety of artists and instrumentations in the next few years. He supplied the arrangements and played for Bob Gordon's debut album, *Meet Mr Gordon*, recorded in June 1954. In fact Montrose and Gordon were close friends as well as extremely compatible players, and the baritone saxophonist appeared on all of the albums which Montrose arranged until Gordon's tragic death in a car accident in 1955. We'll examine three of these albums in upcoming chapters, including one that featured trumpeter Clifford Brown supported by a contingent of West Coast jazzmen.

The years 1953 and 1954 were pivotal ones for jazz in Los Angeles. As 1953 opened, the Gerry Mulligan Quartet and the Lighthouse All-Stars were just beginning to attract national attention, and Shorty Rogers had yet to record his second album. By December 1954, the Los Angeles jazz scene had received international scrutiny, and musicians who had been obscure sidemen a short two years before had achieved national reputations and lucrative recording contracts. For good or ill – and in retrospect it seems largely ill – West Coast jazz had become a catchphrase in the jazz press. And as is so often the case, writers who had initially heralded the new style quickly became satiated and switched to being vehement detractors. When the Gerry Mulligan Quartet made their first trip north to San Francisco in late 1952, Ralph J. Gleason – at the time West Coast editor of *Down Beat* – wrote, 'The Gerry Mulligan Quartet is certainly the freshest and most interesting sound to come out of jazz in a long time.'[10] But by September 1953, some critics were having second thoughts. Nat Hentoff, in his 'Counterpoint' column in *Down Beat*, was moved to ask:

But was the quartet really that brilliantly original? Weren't the chords more barbershop harmony than anyone except a few musicians publicly noted? Was the counterpoint that contra-puntal or was that revived praiseword used quite loosely at times? And don't the records – some of them – sound kind of dull on rehearing? As one who lauded the group loudly at initial hearings, I'm just wondering. Anyone for reflection?[11]

Many of the critics seemed annoyed at the attention given the West Coast musicians. Chet Baker won the *Down Beat* readers' poll for best trumpet in 1953 and 1954, which particularly incensed some writers, although he had won the critics' own New Star Award in the same magazine in 1953. Nat Hentoff observed (with some justification) that '... Baker certainly is a rewarding soloist. But I cannot get particularly excited about [his] present work. When there are giants in the land like Dizzy Gillespie, I marvel at Chet winning polls.'[12] But of course Chet Baker could hardly be blamed for the voting preferences of *Down Beat* readers. Years later, a bemused Baker would look back on the vagaries of his youthful popularity with irony:

I feel right now [1977] I can play twice as good as I could play when I won the *Down Beat* poll. And right now I'm twenty-second or something. I'm twice as good now as I was then, so the whole thing is kind of dumb. Yeah I played some nice things on that first Gerry Mulligan album. It was a different style – soft, melodic. I think people were wanting and needing something like that and it just happened that at the time I came along with it and it caught on. But I don't think I was one-half the trumpet player that Dizzy was, or Kenny Dorham. Clifford was around then, Jesus Christ! So it just didn't make sense to me that I should have won the poll. It was kind of a temporary fad kind of thing that was bound to work itself out.[13]

In the meantime, as the critics were arguing the respective merits of the white upstarts from the West Coast versus the established black jazz stars of New York City, a group of Los Angeles-based musicians were serving up a harder style of jazz in relative obscurity. Most of their achievements would not be recognized until years later, but the foundations were firmly laid in 1954.

6.

california hard (i)

Early in 1954, shortly before Max Roach's contract with the Lighthouse was due to expire, promoter Gene Norman approached the drummer with the offer of a concert tour if Max would form a band. Max readily agreed and his first step was to call New York City. He reached the man he was looking for, a talented young trumpet player named Clifford Brown, and offered him a spot as co-leader of a quintet. Clifford jumped at the opportunity and flew out to Los Angeles as soon as he could wrap things up in New York. Thus was formed one of the most rewarding partnerships in jazz and one of the strongest jazz combos in the history of the music.

Clifford Brown was just beginning to come into his own when he got the call from Max. He was born 30 October 1930 in Wilmington, Delaware, and received his first trumpet at the age of thirteen from his father, a non-professional musician. While in high school, Clifford studied piano and arranging, in addition to playing trumpet in the school band. Following high school Brown first majored in mathematics at Delaware State College, but soon transferred to Maryland State on a music scholarship. There he played and arranged for the fifteen-piece jazz ensemble. While still in his teens Clifford jammed with such major stars as Miles Davis, Fats Navarro and J. J. Johnson in nearby Philadelphia; it was at one of these sessions that he first met and played with Max Roach. Fats Navarro in particular encouraged and influenced the youngster. During this same period, Brown played a one-week gig with Charlie Parker, who was favourably impressed. Things came to an abrupt halt, however, when

Clifford was seriously hurt in an automobile accident in June 1950. He was hospitalized for almost a year.

In 1952 and 1953 Brownie (as he was affectionately called by fellow musicians) toured with the rhythm-and-blues outfit of Chris Powell's Blue Flames. He played and recorded with Tadd Dameron in the summer of 1953, then joined Lionel Hampton's big band that August. During a European tour the same autumn, Clifford recorded with some French musicians and fellow members of the Hampton band. Brownie left Hampton in December and was almost immediately hired by Art Blakey (on Charlie Parker's recommendation) for a new group the drummer was forming. Shortly after, on the evening of 21 February 1954, this group recorded an evening's performance at Birdland, and the resulting albums (*A Night at Birdland, Volumes 1 & 2*, for Blue Note) marked Clifford's arrival as a soloist of the first rank. These same albums convinced Max Roach out on the Coast that Brownie would be the perfect trumpeter for his new group.

The Max Roach–Clifford Brown quintet suffered a few growing pains at first. Sonny Stitt, Roach's first choice as saxophonist, flew out to LA with Clifford, but left the group six weeks later, to be replaced by Teddy Edwards. Pianist Carl Perkins and bassist George Bledsoe filled out the original edition of the quintet. These were the musicians recorded at one of the Gene Norman concerts in April 1954. Despite poor recording quality and some heavy-handed editing of the tenor-sax and piano solos, these sides give a clear indication of the excitement that the team of Brown and Roach could spark. 'All God's Chillun Got Rhythm' showcases Brownie's seemingly inexhaustible stream of ideas at a rapid tempo, and features one of Max Roach's fiery yet melodic drum solos. Unfortunately the solos of both Teddy Edwards and Carl Perkins have been edited to a chorus each. 'Tenderly' is Clifford's solo vehicle, and the mood is very similar to his already famous treatment of 'Once in a While' on the earlier Birdland albums. 'Sunset Eyes' is an original composition of Teddy Edwards, and the tenor saxophonist finally gets a chance to stretch out a little. The final cut from this concert is 'Clifford's Axe', a medium-tempo swinger based on 'The Man I Love' changes. This one is Clifford all the way, sparked by Max's sympathetic yet forceful support. 'Clifford's Axe' gives notice of exciting things to come. These sides were eventually released on a 'Gene Norman Presents' LP.

Between this concert and the group's next recording session,

some important personnel changes were to take place. Teddy
Edwards left the group, to be replaced by an almost unknown
tenor saxophonist named Harold Land. Land, who had been
born in Texas and raised in San Diego, brought to the quintet a
big-toned tenor sound which complemented Brownie's silvery
trumpet lines. Land's induction into the quintet was pure
serendipity. He had moved to LA from San Diego earlier the
same year and was scuffling between occasional gigs in the
time-honoured manner. Harold spent much of his all too copious
spare time jamming at informal sessions held at the house of
another saxophonist, Eric Dolphy. Dolphy, a native Angeleno,
was the same age as Land (twenty-five) and the practice and jam
sessions held at his home were already the stuff of legend among
the black Los Angeles musicians. Harold Land remembers what
happened next:

> Eric Dolphy and I were very close friends, even before I
> moved to Los Angeles. He'd come down to San Diego and
> we'd play together, and when I moved up here, we'd go over
> to his house and have sessions that would last from morning
> until night, practically – everybody loved to play so
> much ... one day I was over there playing and Max Roach
> came by – he'd heard about our all-day sessions. And the
> next day Max came by with Brownie; they heard me play and
> asked me if I'd like to be part of their group. And naturally I
> was just ... I thought it was the best opportunity I'd ever had
> to that point in my career.[1]

About the same time, a new pianist and bassist were added to
the group. Richie Powell, the new pianist, was the younger
brother of Bud Powell and a family friend of Max Roach.
Initially Richie had wanted to take up drums, and as a youth he
prevailed upon Roach for help, often dropping by Max's house,
before Max was even awake, for lessons. Max finally suggested
that Richie take up piano, since an obvious talent for keyboards
ran in the family. Richie took the suggestion and soon proved
Max right. When the young pianist came through LA with the
Johnny Hodges band, he was invited to join Max and Brownie
and gladly accepted. The new bassist, George Morrow, was – like
Harold Land – a veteran of the Eric Dolphy marathon sessions.
With the addition of Land, Powell and Morrow, the classic
edition of the Max Roach–Clifford Brown band was realized.

But before the group got the chance to record on its own, Clifford took part in a fascinating collaboration with some of the West Coast musicians. Dick Bock of Pacific Jazz wanted to record the new trumpet star with some of his players, and asked Jack Montrose to write the arrangements for a seven-piece ensemble. Tenor saxophonist Zoot Sims – a native Angeleno who had long made his residence in New York City – was on one of his occasional leaves of absence from the Apple and added his distinctive voice to the proceedings. The remaining personnel were all West Coast regulars: Stu Williamson on valve-trombone, Bob Gordon on baritone sax, and the rhythm section of Russ Freeman, Joe Mondragon and Shelly Manne.

Of the three tunes recorded at this session, two – 'Daahoud' and 'Joy Spring' – were originals of Brownie that would soon be recorded by his own quintet. The up-tempo 'Daahoud' features a potent yet relaxed solo by Clifford, who seems to fit in very comfortably with the westerners. Zoot Sims, Stu Williamson and Russ Freeman all have fine solos, no doubt inspired by Brownie's presence. 'Joy Spring', on the other hand, suffers somewhat in comparison with the Roach–Brown version, which would be recorded less than a month later. The tune's line is rather complex, and Jack Montrose's arrangement – with numerous counter-lines – is simply too busy to let the classic purity of Clifford's tune come through. If this bothered Brownie, he didn't let it show in his solo. The third tune recorded at the session was a Jack Montrose composition, 'Finders Keepers'. It sounds more typically West Coastish, and perhaps for that reason the solos by Brown and Zoot Sims are quite laid-back.

The second Pacific Jazz session took place just a month later, on 13 August, with but one personnel change: Carson Smith in on bass. Again, Brownie contributed two originals, but this time there were also two standards. 'Gone with the Wind' features driving solos by Bob Gordon, Zoot Sims and Brownie. Montrose's arrangement of 'Blueberry Hill' moves between 3/4 and 4/4 time, but has straight-ahead blowing on the solos by Clifford, Stu Williamson and Gordon. Brownie's two originals – neither of which was ever recorded by the quintet – are 'Bones for Jones' and 'Tiny Capers'. Both feature solos by Brownie, Zoot Sims and Russ Freeman. The arrangement and solos on 'Tiny Capers' are especially impressive (it has often been anthologized on Pacific Jazz collections) and 'Capers' vies with 'Daahoud' as the best side of the collaboration.

Between the two Pacific Jazz sessions, however, came the momentous first studio recordings of the Max Roach–Clifford Brown quintet. These recordings announced the arrival of one of the decade's outstanding jazz units and are basic to any library of modern jazz. Brownie and Max had signed with Emarcy, a jazz subsidiary of the Mercury label, and their first recording session took place on 2 August 1954. It would be a hectic month, with seven recording sessions (including the second Pacific Jazz date) taking place in less than two weeks. The band recorded three tunes on 2 August. 'Delilah', a Victor Young composition from the score of the movie *Samson and Delilah*, has Max supporting the group with mallets, in keeping with the Middle Eastern flavour of the tune. The solos, however, are straight jazz. 'Darn that Dream' is a solo vehicle for Harold Land. 'Parisian Thoroughfare', written by Richie Powell's older brother Bud, features an 'American in Paris' introduction and coda, but again the solos are hard-swinging jazz.

Three more recording sessions followed hard on the heels of the first. On 3 August, the group recorded Duke Jordan's 'Jordu', a version of 'Sweet Georgia Brown' entitled 'Sweet Clifford' and 'Ghost of a Chance', a solo feature for Brownie.

'Jordu' proved to be especially popular, and soon became a staple in jam sessions. The next session, on 6 August, finally saw the quintet recording the definitive versions of Brownie's 'Joy Spring' and 'Daahoud'; both show Clifford at his lyrical best. The third tune, 'Milama', features an awe-inspiring flight by Brownie and an intense drum solo by Max. Finally, on 10 August, the quintet recorded swinging versions of 'Stompin' at the Savoy' and 'I Get a Kick Out of You', and the rhythm section taped a trio version of 'I'll String Along'.

With enough numbers on tape to fill two LPs, the quintet could afford a rest, but the Emarcy officials – no doubt impressed by the group's productivity – scheduled two addition-al informal sessions. The first, held the following day (11 August), was a collaboration between the two co-leaders and some impressive local talent. Altoists Herb Geller and Joe Maini and tenor saxophonist Walter Benton joined forces with Clifford and a rhythm section of pianist Kenny Drew, bassist Curtis Counce and Max. Four extended performances were recorded; each would fill one entire side of a twelve-inch album. There were two up-tempo numbers ('Caravan' and 'Coronado') and two ballads ('Autumn in New York' and 'You Go to My Head'). 'Caravan', taken at an especially breakneck speed, shows off the chops of the locals (Clifford's and Max's are taken for granted). Herb Geller is particularly impressive in a Birdlike flight, and Walter Benton and Joe Maini negotiate the flying changes with ease. There are equally strong strong solos on 'Coronado' and the two ballads. These four performances, recorded at the height of the West Coast jazz craze, gave clear notice that LA had its share of more aggressive musicians as well.

The second Emarcy date was a true jam session. It came one day after the second Pacific Jazz session (on 14 August) and featured – in addition to all five members of the Brown–Roach quintet – trumpeters Maynard Ferguson and Clark Terry, Herb Geller, pianist Junior Mance, bassist Keter Betts and singer Dinah Washington. Not all of the musicians were featured on each tune, of course. Enough numbers were recorded to fill two LPs, *Jam Session* and *Dinah Jams*. Particularly impressive is the trumpet duel featuring all three trumpeters on a blistering 'Move'. Dinah Washington more than holds her own in the fast company and manages to invest ballads such as 'Darn that Dream' with more than a hint of the blues.

Finally, on 30 August, the quintet capped off a hectic month by recording one more Gene Norman concert. The group recorded four tunes from their working repertoire, 'Jordu', 'Parisian Thoroughfare', 'I Get a Kick Out of You' and 'I Can't Get Started'. By this time the personnel of the quintet was firmly fixed, and the performances show the confidence that comes from working together night after night. As had been the case with the earlier concert tapes, there is some editing of solos, but Harold Land's gutsy solo on 'Parisian Thoroughfare' is here in full. All of Brownie's solos are left intact, of course, and again one can only wonder at the endless stream of ideas that flow from his horn.

Shortly following this second Gene Norman live date, the quintet moved permanently back to the East Coast. They were headquartered in Philadelphia, near Brownie's Wilmington home, although they were on the road much of the time. There were numerous additional recordings for Emarcy, but all took place in New York and so are beyond the scope of this book. Two major events in the group's short-lived history need to be noted, though. In November 1955 during an engagement in Chicago, Harold Land was called home to Los Angeles on family business. Sonny Rollins happened to be in Chicago at the time, on one of his sabbaticals from the jazz scene, and Max invited him to fill the vacant tenor chair. This resulted in an even stronger unit, for although Harold Land was a major voice, he was still growing at the time, and Sonny Rollins was quite simply the best tenor sax in jazz in the mid-fifties. Tragically, the revamped group had only a short time left in its existence. On 27 June 1956 the car carrying Clifford Brown, Richie Powell and Richie's wife skidded off a rain-slick portion of the Pennsylvania Turnpike, killing all three. Max Roach carried on – Kenny Dorham filled in for Brownie for a time, to be followed by another rising young trumpet star, Booker Little – but it was years before Max could bring himself to play any of Clifford's tunes. Brownie's voice was stilled just as he was reaching full maturity, and we will never know what he – or the quintet – could have accomplished if he had been given the time.

The Max Roach–Clifford Brown group was, while it lasted, one of the finest examples of a style that came to be called post-bop or hard bop. As the names imply, this style was a successor to bebop, and its practitioners favoured a harder, more aggressive approach to jazz. In large part, hard bop was a reaction to the excesses of the cool and West Coast styles, a deliberate attempt to regain some of the fire and emotion that had been lost in the more esoteric experiments. The year 1954 proved to be seminal for this approach. As had been the case with the first statements of cool jazz in 1948 and 1949, the idea seemed to be 'in the air', and several groups, working independently, came up with similar ideas. There were the Art Blakey recordings at Birdland in February, of course, and the subsequent formation of the Roach–Brown quintet. In April (the month of the first Roach–Brown recordings) Miles Davis led a group into the Prestige recording studios in New York for an historic session. There the musicians (Miles, J. J. Johnson, Lucky Thompson, Horace Silver, Percy Heath and Kenny Clarke) recorded extended performances of 'Walkin'' and 'Blue 'n' Boogie'. And late in the year Art Blakey recorded some equally important performances for Blue Note with his new group, the first edition of the Jazz Messengers. The group had Kenny Dorham on trumpet, Hank Mobley on tenor, Horace Silver on piano and Doug Watkins on bass, and the recordings they made in November 1954 and February of the following year – including 'Doodlin'', 'The Preacher', 'Stop Time' and 'Hippy' – quickly gained stature as prototypes of the new style. By the beginning of 1955 the battle lines were firmly drawn, and for the remainder of the decade it became a staple (if not cliché) of jazz criticism to contrast the East Coast hard boppers with the more laid-back West Coast jazz musicians.

There were, however, players on both coasts who stubbornly refused to be so conveniently pigeonholed. The years 1955 to 1957 saw an explosion (albeit a rather muffled one) of harder-swinging music in California, although there was little recognition of this at the time. The musicians who favoured this approach were, for the most part, poorly received by clubowners and recording executives, and their jobs were few and far between. When they did get a chance to record, their albums were largely ignored by the influential East Coast critics. Despite all these handicaps, these Underground musicians (as Leonard Feather would later so aptly tag them) produced a body of work whose importance is only now coming to be fully recognized.

It would of course be wrong to think of this Underground as a monolithic body. Many of the musicians discussed here recorded with representatives of the West Coast style, and often the difference between a 'hard' or 'cool' approach to jazz was a matter of degree, not kind. Herb Geller, to cite one instance, was a member of the Lighthouse All-Stars for a time, and had played variously with such 'West Coasters' as Shorty Rogers and Chet Baker. Nevertheless, his alto work was basically more impassioned (especially during this period) than that of players like Lennie Niehaus or Bud Shank, as his work on the Clifford Brown session mentioned above shows.

Herb Geller was a rarity among West Coast musicians: a native Los Angeleno. He was born 2 November 1928, and started out on saxophone at age eight, later adding clarinet and piano to his studies. At an early age he heard and was influenced by Benny Carter, although Charlie Parker later cast his spell on the youngster, as he did with most saxophonists coming of musical age in the forties. Geller's first professional job was with violinist Joe Venuti in 1946, and he later played in the bands of Jimmy Zito, Jack Fina, Lucky Millinder, Jerry Wald and Claude Thornhill. While with Thornhill in 1950, Geller settled briefly in New York, where he met and married pianist Lorraine Walsh. The Gellers returned to California in 1951, where Herb worked briefly with Billy May and then joined Howard Rumsey's Lighthouse crew in 1952.

Lorraine Walsh Geller was also an important musician, born in Portland, Oregon on 11 September 1928. Her first professional job was with Anna Mae Winburn's Sweethearts of Rhythm. Later she settled in New York, where she worked briefly with Jerry Wald and in a duo with bassist Bonnie Wetzel. Moving to Los Angeles with Herb, she played occasional gigs with Shorty Rogers, Maynard Ferguson and Zoot Sims. In 1954 the Gellers formed their own quartet, which they managed to keep together on an intermittent basis until Lorraine's tragically early death in 1958.

Two albums cut by the Gellers for Emarcy in late 1954 and early 1955 showcase their styles. On the first, Herb and Lorraine are joined by card-carrying members of the LA Underground, Curtis Counce and Lawrence Marable. Counce, born in Kansas City, Missouri on 23 January 1926, took up bass at an early age and started touring with the Nat Towles band at the age of fifteen. In 1954 he settled in Los Angeles, where he studied composition with Lyle (Spud) Murphy and worked with Edgar Hayes. In his early years in California Counce played briefly with Benny Carter, Wardell Gray, Billy Eckstine and a visiting Powell. Counce was one of the first black musicians to break the ranks of the largely white studio musicians, and from

1956 he was the bassist in Shorty Rogers's Giants. Lawrence Marable, another Los Angeles native, was born on 21 May 1929. A distant relative of the legendary bandleader Fate Marable, Lawrence was largely self-taught on drums. From 1947 on, Marable was a mainstay of Central Avenue rhythm sections, making jazz time with Charlie Parker, Dexter Gordon, Wardell Gray, Stan Getz, Hampton Hawes and Zoot Sims, among others.

The first album of the Gellers, a ten-inch LP, stands in marked contrast to the contemporaneous albums of altoist Lennie Niehaus. This is a blowing session, plain and simple, and everyone gets a chance to stretch out. Herb Geller exhibits a penchant for picking tunes that are surprising but welcome additions to the jazz library. Leroy Anderson's 'Sleigh Ride', taken at a breakneck pace, is one such vehicle, and Noël Coward's ballad 'A Room with a View' is another. Lorraine Geller would later name her solo on the album's 'Alone Together' as a personal favourite, and everybody shines on an up-tempo version of 'You Stepped out of a Dream'.

In May 1955 the Gellers returned to the Emarcy studios with a new rhythm section. Red Mitchell and Mel Lewis were just beginning to make names for themselves at this time. Keith Mitchell was born on 20 September 1927 in New York City. His first instruments were piano and alto sax, but he soon switched to bass. He began playing professionally in the late forties, gigging around town with Jackie Paris and Charlie Ventura. In 1949 he joined Woody Herman and toured with the Herd until 1951. Hospitalized for over a year with tuberculosis in 1951, he returned to the scene with Red Norvo in 1952 and later played with Gerry Mulligan, staying behind in California when Mulligan left for New York. Mel Lewis was born Melvin Sokoloff in Buffalo, New York on 10 May 1929. He was trained by his father, a professional drummer, and like Lawrence Marable, made his professional debut at the age of fifteen. He honed his trade in the big bands of Boyd Raeburn, Alvino Rey, Ray Anthony and Tex Beneke. Lewis joined Stan Kenton in 1954, touring with him until 1956, when he settled in Los Angeles to freelance.

This second Herb Geller album is every bit as swinging as the first, and the added space made available on a twelve-inch LP allows plenty of room for stretching out. Highlights include Geller's slashing Birdlike alto on 'Arapahoe' (as one would suspect, a workout on 'Cherokee' changes) and his blues-drenched work on 'Come Rain or Come Shine'. Lorraine is particularly impressive on 'Love', a *tour de force* for unaccompanied piano. Herb Geller's compositional abilities are evident on 'The Answer Man', 'Patterns' and 'Two of a Kind'. Each of these tunes is a true original; none uses 'standard' chord changes. All of the performances display a rhythmic thrust that is a far cry from the blandness of some of the West Coast studio recordings.

Joe Maini, the altoist who appeared with Herb Geller on the Clifford Brown All-Stars date, was also an exponent of the Charlie Parker school. Maini in fact was one of those jazzmen who came up in the forties and patterned not only his music but, unfortunately, his whole lifestyle on Parker. Born 8 February 1930 in Providence, Rhode Island, Maini was playing professionally by the time he was fourteen. At the age of nineteen he left home for the Apple with his close friend trombonist Jimmy Knepper. The pair led a chaotic life, scuffling between occasional jobs. Busted on a narcotic charge, Maini spent a year and a half in the Federal Hospital in Lexington, Kentucky, then moved west to Los Angeles. There, while gigging in a strip joint, he met a struggling comedian named Lenny Bruce, whose brand of improvisational humour quite naturally appealed to jazzmen. The two hit it off immediately. For years thereafter Joe Maini and Lenny Bruce were at the centre of an in-group of musicians who shared an existential outlook deliberately at odds with the smug complacency that marked the 1950s. The group included drummers Gary Frommer, Lawrence Marable and (for a time) Philly Joe Jones, bassist Don Payne, trumpeter Jack Sheldon, and Herb and Lorraine Geller. Many of their intermittent jobs were in strip joints and third-rate nightclubs, where Lenny Bruce served as MC and stand-up comedian.

In late 1955 Jack Sheldon somehow managed to land a recording date for a quintet with Pacific Jazz – an unlikely label for the brand of music these musicians favoured. Whether or not Richard Bock meant to do an entire album with the group remains unclear, but in any event only two selections were ever released, and these on separate anthologies. The personnel for the session, which was held on 18 November 1955, were Sheldon, Maini, pianist Kenny Drew, bassist Leroy Vinnegar and Lawrence Marable. The two tunes, 'It's Only a Paper Moon' and Kenny Drew's boppish line 'Contour', show a definite post-bop influence. 'Paper Moon' suffers somewhat in retrospect, since it can't help but be compared with the storming arrangement by the Jazz Messengers of a few years later, but 'Contour' is given a satisfying, swinging performance. Neither tune can be accused of sounding remotely West Coastish.

In the meantime, even as these manifestations of a harder approach to jazz began to surface in LA, two veterans of the Central Avenue scene returned to the jazz wars following lengthy absences. Hampton Hawes and Dexter Gordon had grown up in the same Los Angeles neighbourhood, and although Dexter was almost five years older, the two had often worked together from their teens on. Their careers took similar detours in the early fifties: both were sidetracked for several years by drug-related problems, and both gained national attention with comeback albums recorded in 1955.

Hampton Hawes was born 13 November 1928. His father was a Presbyterian minister and his mother played piano for the church choir, so Hawes grew up steeped in the music of the black church. He took up piano at an early age, teaching himself to play by listening to pianists like Freddy Slack, Fats Waller and Earl Hines on the radio, picking out melodies on the parlour piano. By the time he was in high school, Hawes was playing professionally. He recalled:

In 1947 I graduated from Polytechnic High School, split out the back of the auditorium (thinking, *Damn, I'm free, got my diploma and didn't fuck up, can sleep till twelve tomorrow*), threw my cap and gown in the back of the Ford and made it only fifteen minutes late to the Last Word where I was working with the Jay McNeely band. A few months later I joined Howard McGhee's quintet at the Hi-De-Ho. Bird had worked his way back from the East Coast and joined us.[2]

In the next several years Hawes made jazz time with just about all the regulars on Central Avenue – often in the company of Wardell Gray or Sonny Criss – and began to acquire a growing, if local, reputation. He moved to New York for a short time, then went on the road with Wild Bill Moore's band, and later worked with Red Norvo in San Francisco and Happy Johnson in Las Vegas. By the early fifties he was back in Los Angeles, playing Sunday sessions at the Lighthouse. In 1951 he was pianist on the Shorty Rogers 'Popo' session, and the following year he recorded with Art Farmer and Wardell Gray ('Farmer's Market') for Prestige and Art Pepper ('Surf Ride') for Discovery. In

Charlie Parker with Miles Davis, late forties (photo: Ray Avery's Jazz Archives)

Conte Candoli, Frank Morgan and Wardell Gray (left to right) at GNP recording session, 1955 (photo: Ray Avery)

Original Lighthouse All-Stars in concert at the Lighthouse, 1952: (left to right) Milt Bernhart, Shorty Rogers, Jimmy Giuffre, Bob Cooper, Howard Rumsey (photo: Ray Avery)

Gerry Mulligan at The Haig, c. 1953 (photo: Ray Avery)

'The Three': Shelly Manne, Shorty
Rogers, Jimmy Giuffre (left to right)
recording for Contemporary, 1954
(photo: Ray Avery)

Zoot Sims (left) and Clifford Brown at
Pacific Jazz recording session, 1954
(photo: Ray Avery)

Bob Gordon, Buddy Collette and Frank Morgan (left to right) recording for Contemporary, 1955 (photo: Ray Avery)

Red Mitchell (left) and Hampton Hawes, c. 1955 (photo: Ray Avery)

The Curtis Counce Group at their first recording session, 1956: (left to right)
Carl Perkins, Curtis Counce, Harold Land, Frank Butler, Jack Sheldon
(photo: Ray Avery)

'Chet Baker and Crew', c. 1956: (left to right) Chet Baker, Phil Urso,
Bobby Timmons, Peter Littman (photo: Ray Avery)

The Chico Hamilton Quintet, c. 1957: (left to right) Fred Katz, Chico Hamilton,
Carson Smith, Paul Horn, John Pisano (photo: Ray Avery)

Lighthouse All-Stars in concert, mid-fifties: (left to right) Frank Rosolino, Bud Shank,
Bob Cooper, Howard Rumsey, guest soloist Barney Kessel (photo: Ray Avery)

Red Mitchell Quartet, 1957: (left to right) James Clay, Lorraine Geller, Red Mitchell,
Billy Higgins (photo: Ray Avery)

Art Pepper (right) and Carl Perkins,
c. 1958 (photo: Ray Avery)

Don Cherry (left) and Ornette Coleman, early sixties (photo: Ray Avery)

Teddy Edwards (photo: Ray Avery)

Sonny Criss (photo: Ray Avery)

September 1952 Hawes got his own session for Discovery, recording 'Jumpin' Jacque', 'Don't Get Around Much Anymore', 'It's You or No One' and 'Thou Swell' backed by Joe Mondragon and Shelly Manne. Then, just as things were moving into high gear, he got his notice from Uncle Sam.

Hampton Hawes was not really suited for army life. He had by this time acquired a drug habit, a fact that should have kept him out of the service, but which was initially overlooked. When the army discovered its error it followed its usual practice, however, and promptly punished Hawes for being inducted by mistake. Nor did Hamp help any by going AWOL several times to play jazz gigs. The upshot was that Hawes spent a great deal of his army time in various stockades, both in the States and in Japan, where he was later transferred. One happy result of his trip to Japan was his meeting with a young girl who played piano with as much soul as if she'd been raised in Harlem. Hawes encouraged the pianist, whose name was Toshiko Akiyoshi, and the two remained lifelong friends. Toshiko of course later moved to the States and became an international celebrity.

When he was finally released from the army in 1955, Hawes returned to LA to re-establish his credentials as a musician. His luck finally turned for the better. First, Shelly Manne introduced Hawes to Lester Koenig, who was anxious to record the pianist on his Contemporary label. Then, by sheer serendipity, the Hampton Hawes Trio was formed. As Hamp remembered it:

Next day John Bennett, owner of The Haig on Wilshire Boulevard, phoned and said if I'm available he wanted me to come in with a trio and there was a bass player standing right next to him who would be perfect for me. Things were happening; I wasn't forgotten. I drove down there and the bass player said, 'I'm Red Mitchell and I think we might have fun playing together.' I said, 'Well let's go in and see.' Four bars into 'All the Things You are' I turned to him and said, 'I think we're going to have fun playing together.' With Mel Lewis on drums, and then Chuck Thompson who had played in the Happy Johnson band with me, we began a two-week engagement that stretched to eight months. I can't remember a happier time.[3]

A few months later Hamp felt ready to record. The session was held in the gymnasium/auditorium of the Los Angeles Police

Academy in Chavez Ravine, an isolated (in those pre-Dodger days) setting several miles from downtown Los Angeles, and lasted from midnight to dawn on 28 June 1955. 'They had a good Steinway there that Artur Rubinstein used,' Hawes explained, 'and Lester [Koenig] wanted to get away from the cold studio atmosphere, experiment with a more natural sound. It was a relaxed session, the lights were low, Jackie [Hamp's wife] and Red's wife Doe sipping beer at a table behind the piano while we played ...'[4] Lester Koenig expanded on this in the liner notes of the resulting album:

It was agreed Hamp would just play sets as he did on the job, letting the tunes run as long as he pleased. We got a balance while he warmed up, and when he was in the mood, the recording machines were turned on. Between sets we listened to a few playbacks, had a few drinks, made additional takes on a couple of tunes, and so the pre-dawn hours passed quickly and pleasantly.[5]

The album, *Hampton Hawes Trio, Vol. 1*, was a best-seller for Contemporary, and established Hawes's credentials on a national level. The album opens with a blazing 'I Got Rhythm', in which Hamp sounds like a perpetual-swinging machine. On 'All the Things You are' Hawes remembers and briefly reprises his solo from the Lighthouse All-Stars Sunday session of a few years earlier. 'So in Love' is a vehicle for solo piano, and proves that Hawes is no right-hand-only pianist. There are no less than three blues on the album: slow ('Blues the Most'), medium ('Hamp's Blues') and up-tempo ('Feelin' Fine'). 'Hamp's Blues' has a line closely akin to Horace Silver's 'Opus de Funk', while 'Feelin' Fine' has a 'cycle of fifths' blues progression. In addition, there is a ballad performance of 'Easy Living', a ballad-*cum*-swinger, 'What is this Thing Called Love', and the Latin 'Carioca'.

In the next year Hampton Hawes recorded two more trio albums for Contemporary and went on a nationwide tour which included an extended stay in New York. The new trio albums kept up the high standards of the first, but covered no new ground. Then late in 1956 came another session as good, if not better, than the original date. On the night of 12 November Hawes entered the Contemporary studios with a quartet: guitarist Jim Hall was the added starter. On this session Bruz Freeman replaced Chuck Thompson. This was the famous

'All-night Session', and even more than the initial trio date, this was an impromptu event. Once again a balance was set and the tapes allowed to roll, but this time there were no second takes.

CONTEMPORARY RECORDS

1. HAMP'S BLUES
BY HAMPTON HAWES
2. EASY LIVING
BY LEO ROBIN & RALPH RAINGER
3. ALL THE THINGS YOU ARE
BY JEROME KERN & OSCAR HAMMERSTEIN 2ND
4. THESE FOOLISH THINGS
BY HOLT MARVELL, JACK STRACHEY & HARRY LINK
5. CARIOCA
BY VINCENT YOUMANS, EDWARD ELISCU & GUS KAHN

C3505   Side 2
(LKL 12-30)

Hampton Hawes
Vol. 1, The Trio

Hampton Hawes, *piano*; Red Mitchell, *bass*;
Chuck Thompson, *drums*

The quartet recorded sixteen numbers in all, and the tunes were issued on three LPs – with no editing – in the same order in which they were recorded. (As with the Miles Davis Quintet sides for Prestige cut the same year, mistakes and fluffs were left in.) The tunes were a mixture of improvised blues; bebop classics ('Jordu', 'Groovin' High', 'Woody 'n' You', 'Two Bass Hit' and 'Blue 'n' Boogie'); and standards ('Broadway', 'I Should Care', 'I'll Remember April'). As usual, Hamp is at his best on the medium- to up-tempos, but tends to over-embellish the slower ballads ('I Should Care'). Jim Hall's guitar adds much to the proceedings, both in his solo work and rhythm accompaniment. Bruz Freeman's drumming is adequate, but he lacks the total empathy with Hawes that Chuck Thompson had.

With the release of *All Night Session, Vols. 1–3*, Hawes's national reputation was assured. As the decade wore on, and the terms 'funky' and 'soul' became the new catchwords of jazz, Hamp found himself lionized; the music he had been playing all his life had become the in thing, and the popularizers were soon running the fad into the ground. Through it all, Hawes remained himself, playing the mixture of bebop and church music that he had learned growing up in south-central LA. In 1958, however, at the height of his popularity, Hawes was once again arrested on a narcotics charge, and this time he drew a ten-year sentence. Although he was released five years early (on an order of executive clemency by President Kennedy), Hamp was removed from the jazz scene for the remainder of the decade.

But back to 1955. Several months after Hampton Hawes cut his first album for Contemporary, another native Angeleno returned to jazz. Dexter Gordon had also spent several years in confinement during the early fifties on drugs charges. When he was released in 1955, one of his first moves was to look up his friend and partner in the tenor-sax chases of yore, Wardell Gray. Unfortunately, Gray had just left town for Las Vegas with Benny Carter's band, on what would be his final job. Several days later Gordon heard about Wardell's death and resignedly set about working as a single.

In September Dexter was invited to record with drummer Stan Levey on a date for Bethlehem records. Levey, who had been the drummer with Diz and Bird at Billy Berg's, had come to California with Stan Kenton's band in 1952 and later replaced Max Roach at the Lighthouse. For his Bethlehem date, Levey chose a group of like-minded swingers. Trumpeter Conte Candoli and trombonist Frank Rosolino were working with the drummer at the Lighthouse; both were veterans of the bebop wars and of the same edition of the Kenton band in which Levey had worked. Pianist Lou Levy and bassist Leroy Vinnegar were two of LA's strongest rhythm players. The sextet thus formed was a powerful neo-bop unit.

The Stan Levey Sextet recorded seven tunes for the album on 27 and 28 September 1955. Two of the tunes are bebop standards. 'Diggin' for Diz' was first recorded by Diz and Bird at Ross Russell's first Dial session back in 1946; Stan of course was the drummer on that one. 'This Time the Drum's on Me' is Oscar Pettiford's 'Max is Makin' Wax' under a new title. Both tunes feature some fiery playing by all hands; Levey is particularly impressive in a drum solo on the latter tune that owes much to Max Roach's melodic approach to jazz drumming. There are also performances of two later additions to the jazz library, Miles Davis's 'Tune Up' and Thelonious Monk's 'Ruby, My Dear'. The latter is a solo vehicle for Conte Candoli's sympathetic trumpet. 'Tune Up' has strong solos by all the hornsmen, although Frank Rosolino is especially impressive in his agile trombone work. Bob Cooper contributed an arrangement of Offenbach's 'La Chaloupée' (From *The Tales of Hoffman*) that swings hard and avoids the cutesy tricks that one might suspect of such a borrowing. 'Day In, Day Out' is taken at a medium-up tempo and has several rhythmic twists in the arrangement. Finally, there is 'Stanley the Steamer', Dexter's own blues line that features a steaming six-minute tenor solo at a walking blues pace. Gordon has lost none of the fire from his earlier days, and shows a growing maturity of style that acknowledges the contributions of some of his juniors, especially Sonny Rollins.

Dexter's work on the Stan Levey album led to an album of his own for Bethlehem, which was released under the title *Daddy Plays the Horn*. (At least that's the way Dexter remembers it; the album gives the recording date as 18 September, a week earlier than the Stan Levey session.) On this album Gordon is joined by the strong rhythm section of Kenny Drew, Leroy Vinnegar and Lawrence Marable. Dexter of course gets to stretch out much more in the quartet setting. 'Daddy Plays the Horn' is another extended blues performance, and it is matched by the faster 'Number Four'. 'Confirmation' has Dexter acknowledging his debt to Charlie Parker. The remaining three tunes are all standards: 'Darn that Dream', 'Autumn in New York' and 'You Can Depend on Me'. Dexter's playing here is authoritative and swinging, but one misses the contrast that another horn would add. Kenny Drew adds just the right touch both in a supporting role and in his solos – it's a shame his tenure on the Coast was of such a short duration.

The following year Gordon recorded for an even smaller local label, Dootone records. The rhythm section this time consisted of Leroy Vinnegar (once again), Chuck Thompson and the fast-rising pianist Carl Perkins. Perkins, who was attracting quite a bit of attention at the time, contributes substantially to the proceedings, and his blues-oriented style fits perfectly with Dexter's conception. On three numbers, trumpeter Jimmy Robinson is an added starter. Robinson's style is very much hard-bop, with staccato tonguing and a hard edge to his tone, but there is little originality to his improvisations. (He was quite young at the time.) The tunes are the usual mixture of standards and 'heads' based on the blues or AABA changes. All of the originals are simple riffs designed as launching-pads for the soloists, and Dexter does give us some meaty blowing. He is at his best on the medium blues 'Blowin' for Dootsie'.

These three albums should have been enough to have revived Dexter's waning popularity, but such was not the case. Gordon spent the remainder of the fifties playing in smaller clubs around LA, and there was no further recording until the sixties. Much the same fate befell players like Teddy Edwards and Sonny Criss. Their harder-edged styles just didn't find favour with the bulk of the LA jazz audience. By the same token, however, there were signs by 1956 that the wheel was beginning to turn, and that things were looking up for those West Coast musicians who favoured a harder approach. Two significant groups were formed that year. Chet Baker, to the surprise of those who thought of him as an introverted miniaturist, formed a neo-bop quintet with tenor saxophonist Phil Urso that included a young pianist named Bobby Timmons. And bassist Curtis Counce teamed with Harold Land in a quintet that would soon prove to be a truly big-league outfit. Both of these bands will be more fully discussed in a later chapter; it is enough at this point to say that the forming of such units refutes many commonplaces about the LA jazz scene of the fifties. Certainly there were other indications as well. Shelly Manne, besides his inexhaustible work on a seemingly endless succession of studio records, formed his own working quintet – another neo-bop unit with Stu Williamson, Charlie Mariano, Russ Freeman and Leroy Vinnegar. And musicians like Dexter Gordon, Sonny Criss and Teddy Edwards, although unable to land recording contracts at this time, were at least keeping the flame lit in southside clubs.

In the meantime, of course, the popularity of so-called West Coast jazz continued unabated, although in retrospect it can be seen that 1955 and 1956 were the peak years for the style. As a flock of independent labels – Jazz West, Mode, Tampa, Intro, to name a few – followed down the path blazed by Pacific Jazz and Contemporary, a mind-boggling array of albums were made available. There was much dross, to be sure, but there were also many worthwhile LPs issued at this time. Today the original albums fetch astronomical prices among collectors, and many of these sides are being reissued. The next chapter will examine a representative sampling of these albums.

7.

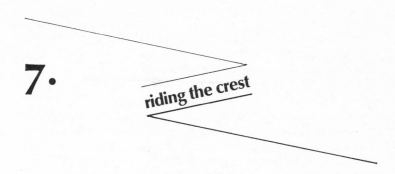

riding the crest

Not the least of factors contributing to the jazz boom of the mid-fifties was the recording industry's adoption of the 33⅓ rpm long-playing record. Its predecessor, the ten-inch 78 rpm disc (long the industry standard) had many drawbacks. The 78s were heavy and extremely fragile; moreover, they offered only a very limited playing time of three minutes per side. (Twelve-inch 78 singles offered up to five minutes of playing time per side, but were even heavier and more likely to crack or chip.) Because of this, even the skimpiest record collection took up an inordinate amount of room. The new microgroove records, on the other hand, were significantly lighter as well as practically unbreakable (although they did warp fairly easily if exposed to heat). Best of all, they allowed a significant increase in playing time. The new ten-inch LPs, which came into common use in the early fifties, offered a playing time equivalent to four 78 singles, and twelve-inch LPs allowed up to twenty or twenty-five minutes of music per side, the equivalent of seven or eight 78 singles.

Moreover, the increased playing time allowed extended jazz performances to become the norm on record. The three-minute time limit of the 78s had been increasingly galling to the musicians, since a jazz performance is by nature an impromptu and loosely structured event. With the advent of the twelve-inch LP, jazz performances on record came increasingly close to what a listener might expect to hear at a club or concert. Improvements in sound reproduction ('high fidelity') also helped to give recorded selections the feel of a 'live' performance. All this meant that a jazz fan could amass a respectable collection of recorded jazz for a relatively insignificant outlay of cash, and many did just that. Record sales rose to new heights as both new and established labels continued to record feverishly. And, for a time, club attendance rose apace.

Some record companies not previously associated with jazz were attracted by the skyrocketing sales and began to move into the field. Among these newcomers was Atlantic records. Long a power in the rhythm-and-blues field – Ruth Brown, Laverne Baker, Joe Turner and Ray Charles were among those on its roster – Atlantic launched its jazz venture by hiring as Artists and Repertoire man Neshui Ertegun, a lecturer in jazz at UCLA and former A & R man for Contemporary. One of the first jazz LPs issued by Atlantic featured Shorty Rogers.

In retrospect it seems strange that Shorty had yet, in 1955, to record an album with his working band, but such was the case. The original *Modern Sounds* album for Capitol had been recorded before Shorty left the Lighthouse to form his own group, of course, and just about all the RCA albums featured expanded personnel. The one exception was the twelve-inch version of the RCA *Giants* album where four cuts ('Joycycle', 'The Lady is a Tramp', 'The Goof and I', 'My Little Suede Shoes') from a 1954 session with the basic quintet were added to fill out the original ten-inch LP.

In May, 1955 Shorty and the Giants (Jimmy Giuffre, Pete Jolly, Curtis Counce and Shelly Manne) entered the Atlantic studios to record numbers from their working repertoire. The resulting tracks were released on an album entitled *The Swinging Mr Rogers*. In the album's liner notes, Neshui Ertegun discussed the growing controversy over West Coast jazz and the increasingly popular perception that the West Coasters couldn't swing. The Rogers album was meant to refute that thesis, and it did so convincingly. It did not, of course, exhibit the unbridled emotions or aggressive swing that could be found on, say, any of the period's Jazz Messengers recordings, but neither did it reflect the emotionless academic flavour of the more extreme West Coast experiments. Shorty credits much of the album's success to Ertegun:

Neshui Ertegun produced it, and Neshui – we were playing at Zardi's and The Haig and at different clubs around town – and he was there every night. He was a fixture and our closest friend; we'd go to eat after work every night. So when we'd run into the studio he knew everything we played, and he'd say, 'Do this tune,' or: 'Last night you did something you hadn't done before – let's record it.' It was a special time, and it was just like coming into the club and doing it live.

There are eight tunes on the album, and the long-playing format gives ample opportunity for stretching out on each piece. Jimmy Giuffre's versatile doubling adds variety to the group's approach. On the two standards, 'Isn't It Romantic' and 'My Heart Stood Still', Giuffre plays a surging, all-stops-out baritone that owes nothing whatsoever to the Mulligan style. Both of the Richard Rodgers tunes are taken at a brisk pace that swings all the way. Johnny Mandel's 'Not Really the Blues', a flag-waver from the Woody Herman book, recalls the days when Rogers, Giuffre and Manne were all in the Herman band. The tempo is way up, and Giuffre switches back to his original instrument, tenor sax. The tenor is also featured on 'Trickleydidlier', one of Shorty's most engaging compositions, which is taken at a jaunty pace. On three of the remaining numbers Giuffre blows clarinet, which he plays entirely in the lower, or Chalumeau, register. The resulting dark-toned sound – reminiscent of the timbre Lester

Young achieved on the Kansas City Six recordings of the thirties – seems warm yet ethereal. It is undoubtedly this other-worldly quality that led to the inspired christening of 'Martians Go Home', a Basie-like blues line. Shorty plays in cup mute on both 'Martians' and 'Oh Play that Thing', another Rogers original somewhat akin to Benny Goodman's 'A Smooth One'. The album's ballad, a beautiful tribute to Shorty's wife entitled 'Michele's Meditation', has a lovely piano solo by Pete Jolly. The album closes with 'That's what I'm Talkin' About', a blues often used to close sets during nightclub appearances. It features strong performances by Shorty, Giuffre (on tenor) and Shelly Manne.

The album was a definite success – 'Martians Go Home' in particular was the jazz equivalent of a hit – and its sales undoubtedly helped ensure the continuation of the Atlantic jazz policy. A sequel seemed called for, and Shorty soon came up with an album entitled *Martians Come Back!* This album contains eight selections cut at five different sessions held from October through to December 1955. The first two sessions continued the policy of the previous album and featured the working band, albeit with two changes in personnel: Lou Levy had taken over the piano chair from Pete Jolly, and Ralph Peña replaced Curtis Counce on bass. The title tune is an obvious take-off on 'Martians Go Home', with Shorty in tight cup and Giuffre on sub-tone clarinet. On 'Lotus Bud', a tune Shorty had written for Bud Shank's Nocturne album, Rogers switches to flugelhorn; the arrangement is reminiscent of 'Michele's Meditation'. 'Papouche' and 'Planetarium', which feature Giuffre's driving baritone and tenor saxes respectively, round out the selections by the quintet.

On 6 December, Shorty entered the Atlantic studios with a unique instrumentation – a five-man trumpet section with supporting rhythm. The trumpets on the date were Pete and Conte Candoli, Don Fagerquist, Harry Edison and of course Rogers. Shorty, who had been given *carte blanche* by the Atlantic brass, came up with the idea simply because it had long been a dream of his to play in the same section as Sweets Edison. 'It was one of my childhood ambitions, because the first trumpet thing I ever learned, playing along with records, was Harry Edison's solo on the old Basie record "Sent for You Yesterday, Here You Come Today",' Shorty would remember. 'And the thought that I could get him on a date, in the same section, that was a big part of it.' Everyone solos on both 'Astral Alley' and 'Serenade in Sweets' with the exception of Pete Candoli, who plays section lead on both numbers. 'Serenade in Sweets', as the name implies, features Edison, who works in Harmon mute on the ensembles and open horn on his solo.

Each of the album's remaining two numbers features yet another ensemble combination. 'Chant of the Cosmos' recalls the original nine-man Giants, complete with French horn and tuba. Jimmy Giuffre gets the bulk of the solo space on clarinet, and finally achieves the *reductio ad absurdum* of his breathy sub-tone style: a chase chorus finds Giuffre blowing and slap-tonguing his horn without producing a note. In the final session Shorty returns to the Kansas City roots that are never too long absent from his work. Harry Edison once again rejoins Shorty in a seven-piece group that also has Bud Shank on alto, Barney Kessel on guitar, Pete Jolly, Ralph Peña and Shelly Manne. The musicians work out on 'Dickie's Dream', an old Count Basie–Lester Young warhorse. Bud Shank in particular seems more forceful than was his wont in recordings from this period. Several additional tunes from these various sessions were eventually released on another Atlantic LP entitled *Way Up There*.

The following year found Rogers once again recording for RCA. In July 1956 Shorty led a big band into the RCA studios to record four tunes intended to round out the old *Cool and Crazy* selections for a new twelve-inch album. The tunes were 'Blues Express' (the new LP would be entitled *Big Band Express*), 'Pay the Piper', 'Pink Squirrel' and 'Home with Sweets'. As the last title indicates, Harry Edison is among the soloists, which also include Art Pepper, Charlie Mariano, Bill Holman, Milt Bernhart and Lou Levy. Stan Levey was the drummer on the date. The band thunders, especially on the *way* up-tempo 'Blues Express', which is Shorty's reworking of a chart from the old Woody Herman book called 'That's Right'.

Shorty Rogers continued to record for RCA throughout the remainder of the fifties, but a gradual decline in the quality of his recordings began to make itself felt. Jazz writer John S. Wilson has suggested that Rogers 'stretched himself too thin' during this period, and that may have been partly the trouble. Certainly Rogers spent a great deal of his time working on movie scores. All the Victor albums save one (*Wherever the Five Winds Blow*) consist primarily of big-band selections, and all seem hastily-prepared affairs. Shorty's charts are competent, but he begins to rely more and more on certain effects and routines that had become clichés. The musicians on these dates are all first-rate Hollywood studio and jazzmen, but the sloppy playing on some of the sides suggests a lack of rehearsal time. Unhappily, Shorty's reputation fell into a decline as the end of the decade neared.

For a time in the mid-fifties, Jack Montrose's reputation as an arranger threatened to eclipse even that of his former instructor Shorty Rogers. As 'staff arranger' for Pacific Jazz in 1953 and 1954, he had gained favoured attention for his writing on the Chet Baker and Clifford Brown ensemble albums, as well as the initial ten-inch LP of his favourite playing companion, baritonist Bob Gordon. In 1955 Montrose was offered his own album by Dick Bock, and the resulting LP was entitled *The Jack Montrose Sextet*. Joining the tenor saxophonist were Gordon, Conte Candoli and the rhythm section of pianist Paul Moer, bassist Ralph Peña and Shelly Manne. The album's eight tunes were all either written or arranged by Montrose. 'Listen, Hear' is a minor-key fugue that moves to major on the bridge, and Montrose's lines feel more natural than is usually the case in such attempts at cross-pollination. Of the remaining originals, 'Speakeasy' and 'Credo' are similar attempts to stretch the boundaries of jazz writing. Both use a technique that Montrose had introduced in the Chet Baker album: the rhythm-section instruments carry the full weight of the composition's line; they are not used simply as timekeepers (although they do break into time behind the soloists). 'Pretty', a ballad, is indeed – but Montrose keeps things from getting saccharin with a sprinkling of out-of-key chord changes. And 'Some Good Time Blues' are just that also. The theme may have come from Gordon's solo on the Clifford Brown ensemble recording of 'Gone with the Wind'. (Or perhaps Gordon was remembering the Montrose tune when he took the solo.)

There are three standards on the album, and each gets a fresh treatment from Montrose that gives it the flavour of an original composition. 'Bewitched, Bothered and Bewildered' opens, for example, with a statement of the verse by bassist Ralph Peña. It is played as a ballad, while 'Fools Rush In' and 'That Old Feeling' are both taken at rapid clips. The one major failing of the album is that the solos do not live up to the adventurous writing. Gordon is the best soloist, and his booting baritone sax work is amiable yet gutty. The solos of Montrose, Candoli and Moer are good but not exceptional, and they often come as a let-down after the spirited heads. Jack Montrose gives an eloquent statement of his aims in the liner notes. 'I don't believe that progress is ever the result of deliberately trying to further the cause. Progress happens when people express themselves naturally.'[1]

Shortly following the Pacific Jazz session, Montrose was again recorded – this time by Atlantic. The line-up for this date was a quintet with Bob Gordon, Paul Moer, Shelly Manne and bassist Red Mitchell. The quintet format must have felt more congenial to Montrose, for this Atlantic session produced his finest work. Again every tune on the album was either composed or arranged by the leader. There are nine tunes: four standards (if you include the blues line 'I'm Gonna Move to the Outskirts of Town') and five originals. Once again the standards are transformed into original-sounding jazz vehicles. 'Cecilia', for example, is an unexpectedly gutty performance thanks in part to Bob Gordon's sinewy baritone. 'When You Wish Upon a Star' offers a moving ballad performance, and it is matched by Montrose's own 'April's Fool'. Montrose and Gordon both get funky on 'Outskirts of Town', and Gordon especially shines on Montrose's own up-tempo blues 'Paradox'. Red Mitchell's presence seems to prod Shelly into swinging especially hard, and the rhythm section is a joy to hear on 'Dot's Groovy' and 'Have You Met Miss Jones'. The remaining tunes, 'A Little Duet' and 'The News and the Weather', are typically Montrosian compositions, original in chord progressions and feeling as well as melody lines.

With these two albums Jack Montrose seemed about to be recognized as a major jazz writer, but tragedy struck before either album was even released. On the way to an out-of-town concert with Pete Rugolo, Bob Gordon was killed in a car accident. Montrose and Gordon had been close friends offstage as well as in performance, and the loss seems to have hurt Montrose creatively as well as personally. Whatever the reason, Jack Montrose never again produced any recorded work comparable to the Pacific Jazz or especially the Atlantic album.

One other West Coast arranger is worth mentioning at this point, if only for his work on a single Pacific Jazz album recorded in 1955. Long before Johnny Mandel gained an Oscar and fame as a writer for movies and television ('The Shadow of Your Smile', the theme from 'M*A*S*H'), he had won a reputation among jazz musicians as a talented composer and arranger. Born

23 November 1925 in New York City, Mandel was a veteran of the big bands, having played trombone and bass trumpet for Boyd Raeburn, Jimmy Dorsey, Buddy Rich and Count Basie, among others. In 1953 he left Basie and settled in Hollywood as a freelance arranger. For a time he played bass trumpet in a combo with Zoot Sims at The Haig. Mandel's abilities as an arranger brought him to the attention of Richard Bock and Bock's right-hand man at Pacific Jazz, Woody Woodward. Tentative plans for an album featuring Mandel arrangements were made, but the project was put on the backburner for some time due to prior commitments by everybody concerned. The only musician definitely decided upon for the album was trumpeter Harry Edison.

Almost a year passed before another name was added to the roster. In 1954 Bock and Woodward were excited by a new voice they heard in Herman's brash young Herd, bass trumpeter Cy Touff. Richard Bock spoke to Touff and the latter readily agreed to record for Pacific Jazz. The time was still not right, however, and again a year would pass before events came to fruition. Then, in the autumn of 1955, Woody Herman again came through town, this time with an octet. Bock and Woodward dropped by rehearsals to hear and talk to Cy Touff and were particularly impressed with two of the other musicians in the band, tenor saxophonist Richie Kamuca and drummer Chuck Flores. The two were added to the list.

With the instrumentation beginning to firm up, Johnny Mandel was given the go-ahead to start work on the charts. He would be writing for an octet consisting of two trumpets, bass trumpet, tenor and alto or baritone saxes, piano, bass and drums. Mandel had contracted to produce four arrangements; the album would be filled out with a quintet featuring Touff, Kamuca and the rhythm section.

On Sunday 4 December, the musicians gathered in the Forum, a vacated movie theatre, for the octet session. The Forum had been chosen for its natural acoustics, which everyone felt would be warmer than those of a recording studio. The personnel finally settled on included Conrad Gozzo and Harry Edison, trumpets; Touff; Richie Kamuca and Matt Utal, saxes; and Russ Freeman, Leroy Vinnegar and Chuck Flores. John Mandel contributed three charts: an arragement of Tiny Kahn's 'TNT' and two originals, 'Keester Parade' and 'Groover Wailin''. 'Keester Parade', the album's highlight, is an expanded version of a slow blues recorded elsewhere by Sweets Edison as 'Centerpiece'. Edison starts things off with a relaxed yet blues-drenched solo in Harmon mute, and Touff and Kamuca – following a couple of solo choruses each – trade fours as the ensemble builds in a crescendo behind them. Russ Freeman also takes a typically understated solo. 'TNT' is medium up-tempo, and 'Groover Wailin'' is way up; on both Mandel achieves the feeling of big band in full cry despite the limited octet instrumentation. Because he had been swamped with some last-minute writing jobs, Mandel asked his old Basie bandmate Ernie Wilkins to do the fourth octet chart. Wilkins agreed and came up with an arrangement of Duke Ellington's 'What am I Here for?' for the date. The arrangement takes some liberties with Ellington's melody, but it is satisfying none the less.

The quintet session, recorded the following day, featured Touff, Kamuca, pianist Pete Jolly (in for Russ Freeman), Vinnegar and Flores. Five numbers were taped. Neal Hefti's 'Half Past Jumping Time' is a medium-tempo swinger, as is a head arrangement of an original of Touff and Kamuca's titled 'Primitive Cats'. 'Prez-ence' is a line based on Lester Young's solo (recorded for Aladdin) on 'You're Driving Me Crazy'. The two finest performances from the quintet session are a relaxed version of 'A Smooth One' and a steaming up-tempo version of the old Basie favourite, 'It's Sand, Man'.

The resulting album, *Cy Touff, His Octet and Quintet*, was an instant hit among fellow musicians, and seems to have sold well – if not spectacularly – to the jazz public. 'Keester Parade' in particular has been anthologized many times by Pacific Jazz, and was made familiar to a generation of LA jazz fans when it was used as a theme by the late jazz-show host Frank Evans. Unfortunately, the complete octet and quintet sessions were never issued on one album. 'It's Sand, Man' was issued only once, on the anthology *Jazz West Coast, Volume 2*, and never with the other quintet performances. 'Primitive Cats' was also dropped on a later reissue of the album entitled *Having a Ball*. Even worse, the many versions of 'Keester Parade' made available on anthologies were usually heavily edited. Of course the entire Pacific Jazz catalogue has been long out of print, but it is especially sad that this album has never been issued in its entirety and that it is unavailable in any form today.

The year 1955 saw, in addition to a prolific production of albums from the LA studios, the formation of a jazz unit that came to be especially identified in the public's mind with the West Coast. The Chico Hamilton Quintet was formed almost by accident; it was a textbook case of serendipity. Serendipity, of course, has often favoured jazz musicians, if only because they are always ready to take chances. Many of the greatest jazz performances have 'just happened', and some of the finest groups have come together in the same manner. The Chico Hamilton Quintet – certainly one of the most popular products of the West Coast jazz boom – is a case in point.

Chico, as we have seen, was a charter member of the original Gerry Mulligan Quartet, but he left early in 1953 to take a lucrative job with Lena Horne. During his stay with Lena, he formed a lasting friendship with the singer's pianist Fred Katz. Katz was also a classically trained cellist and served as concert master when Lena was accompanied by an orchestra. In 1954 Chico left Lena Horne to freelance around LA, and later that year he cut a trio album for Pacific Jazz, using Lena's bassist George Duvivier and guitarist Howard Roberts. The ten-inch LP was both a crititical and popular success, and Chico began thinking about forming a group of his own.

He began by contacting multi-reedman Buddy Collette, a

long-time friend. By now Buddy had gained a secure foothold in the studios, and his mastery of the woodwinds made him a natural prospect for the versatile sort of group that Chico wanted to form. He played alto and tenor saxes, clarinet and flute equally well, and was a fine composer and arranger to boot. Buddy was more than willing to play in such a group. At about the same time (early 1955) Chico got a call to back singer Jana Mason on a club date. The pianist on the gig was Fred Katz, and Fred soon agreed to join the proposed group. George Duvivier was still with Lena Horne, so Hamilton looked up his old section mate from the Mulligan quartet days, Carson Smith. The new quartet began rehearsing, but somehow things didn't quite gel. Another voice was needed, but which instrument would fill the bill? Johnny Mandel sat in on bass trumpet, but prior commitments kept him from joining permanently. Chico toyed with the idea of adding a French horn and called John Graas, but Graas also had a steady job. However, Graas did recommend Jim Hall, a young guitarist who had been rehearsing with him. Hall, fresh from Cleveland, sat in with the group and immediately excited everyone. The new quintet was set.

In the meantime, Chico had been looking around for a gig. He approached Harry Rubin, who had owned a series of clubs around the Los Angeles area, and Rubin immediately invited the new group to open at the Strollers, his new club in Long Beach, some twenty miles south of LA. The job offer came so suddenly the musicians were caught off guard. Buddy Collette was working with 'Scatman' Cruthers at the time and immediately gave notice, but he was unavailable for the first week, and tenor saxophonist Bob Hardaway filled in. There were few formal arrangements; most of the band's book consisted of heads worked out in rehearsal and on the job. During intermissions, Fred Katz would play solo cello.

At this point, serendipity took a hand. Buddy Collete recalls how things worked out:

We'd been rehearsing, but still the idea was that the cello was only to play solos on the intermission; it wasn't part of the sound ... Bob Hardaway had done some arrangements and we'd play those. And when I came in, I had two or three things that I'd done with my other group, but I still wasn't thinking cello; I just wrote for the piano. So we did that for the first couple of weeks. And Fred would always have the energy to play a lot of cello on the intermission. And the stand was very small, and we'd have to come back on the stand – because Fred wouldn't stop playing – not in a malicious way; he'd be playin' with his eyes closed – so we'd sneak back on the stand, and once we'd do that he couldn't get back to the piano, it was just that tight. So he'd just stay there and play his lines on the cello.

Gradually the cello was incorporated into the group sound; Katz would play the tenor lines Buddy had been using and Buddy would add an additional counter-line. Arrangements were written featuring the cello, and finally the piano was dropped altogether. The Chico Hamilton Quintet was born.

The musicians worked hard to achieve an integrated sound. Several times a week they'd drive down to the club in the afternoon and rehearse for a couple of hours, then take a dinner break before the nine o'clock job. Business was slow at first, but it began to pick up when disc jockey Sleepy Stein began a series of live broadcasts from the club for radio station KFOX. It was now summertime, and southern Californians were out on the road trying to escape the heat. 'People were driving to the beach cities in the car,' Buddy remembers, 'and they'd hear this [broadcast] from the Strollers, and the cars began to zip around. That did it!' Before long the club was packed every evening.

On 4 August 1955 – a Thursday evening – Richard Bock set up recording equipment in the Strollers to capture a live performance by the quintet. Five tunes were eventually issued on a Pacific Jazz LP. 'I Want to be Happy' features Buddy on flute, propelled by Chico's aggressive brush work. 'Spectacular', a Jim Hall original, has Fred Katz playing lead in pizzicato, doubled by Carson Smith, but the blowing choruses are straight-ahead swinging with Buddy's alto and Jim Hall's guitar. 'Free Form' is just that: spontaneous improvising by all hands. This is not Free Jazz – there are tonal centres throughout – but the lead changes from musician to musician in an unpreconceived manner. Everyone listens intently to what the others are doing, and the high calibre of musicianship of each player is especially in evidence here. 'Free Form' is followed by the most basic of jazz vehicles, a B flat blues, titled (after the fact) 'Walking Carson Blues'. Carson Smith does indeed lead off, accompanied at one point by an auto horn from a passing car. Buddy tells a story on the alto, and Jim Hall responds with an equally poignant tale.

The set closes with another blues, Collette's 'Buddy Boo', as unlike the previous tune as two blues can be. 'Buddy Boo' has an infectious tune and features the composer's tenor.

Later the same month, on 23 August, the quintet met in a recording studio to tape enough selections to complete the album. On this occasion Buddy Collette confined himself strictly to flute and clarinet. He plays the latter instrument on his own tune, 'A Nice Day', and on the haunting Freddie Katz folk theme entitled 'The Sage'. On 'My Funny Valentine', 'The Morning After' and 'Blue Sands', Buddy switches to flute. Fred Katz carries the lead on 'Valentine' and counterpoints the flute on 'Morning After', a bouncy little tune. Buddy Collette's 'Blue Sands' is the album's high spot. The minor-mode theme gives the song a near-Eastern flavour, which is emphasized by Buddy's flute work, Jim Hall's flamenco-style guitar, and Chico's empathetic yet driving mallets. As Fran Kelley writes in the album's line notes, 'Blue Sands' 'would make the very famous "Caravan" turn around and go the other way'.

The Pacific Jazz album was issued late in 1955 and immediately thrust the quintet into the national spotlight. The group had a fresh and original sound, and if the flute and cello combination sounded a bit effete on some tunes, Chico's driving brushwork on the up-tempo numbers more than made up for it. A second Pacific Jazz album, recorded in January and February of 1956, seems to go out of its way to feature more of the quintet's straight-ahead swingers. Buddy's tune 'Santa Monica' (retitled 'Sleepy Slept Here' in honour of DJ Sleepy Stein for the album) has some take-charge tenor work by Collette; the performance never lets up. Another Collette original, 'The Ghost', and a swinging rendition of 'Taking a Chance on Love' feature Buddy on alto and tenor, respectively; both have some tasty guitar work by Hall. Fred Katz, usually confining himself to the role of accompanist, has a chance to blow some blues on the up-tempo 'The Ghost'. Then there is a driving arrangement of the old Basie favourite, 'Topsy', which has Buddy on tenor once again, and features a marvellous Charlie Christian-inspired solo by Jim Hall.

The album's remaining tunes fall into the chamber-jazz category. Carson Smith's 'Jonalah' and the quintet's version of 'Sleep' – the old waltz is played in a fast four – both swing, but neither runs much over two minutes. Russ Freeman's 'The Wind' and Freddie Katz's arrangement of 'Gone Lover' ('When

Your Lover has Gone') are both impressionistic; Buddy plays alto on the former and clarinet on the latter. Jim Hall's 'Chrissie' and Fred Katz's 'The Squimp' both have a minimum of improvisation. Finally there is an extended drum solo of Chico's, called 'Drums West'.

These first two albums remain the high point of the Chico Hamilton Quintet's recorded output from the fifties. The group's strengths – first-rate musicianship, remarkable cohesion, and the ability to swing intensely at a low volume of sound – are showcased on these sides. At the same time, faults that were to loom much larger in the ensuing years were already becoming apparent. The cello, which undoubtedly attracted the greatest initial attention to the group, is at times an intrinsic component of the quintet and at others a slightly embarrassing fifth wheel. Fred Katz's one real jazz solo (on 'The Ghost') is competent enough, but hardly first-rate jazz. And some of the band's arrangements are simply cute, a term that translates into 'cloying' on the second or third hearing. A few of the mood pieces – most notably 'Blue Sands' – are memorable jazz experiences; some of the others ('The Squimp', 'Chrissie') are eminently forgettable.

Unfortunately, none of the quintet's subsequent albums lived up to the promise of the first two. The group's instant popularity following the release of the original albums practically guaranteed that the quintet would hew to a formulaic approach in subsequent albums. Looking back on those days from the vantage point of the 1960s, Chico would recount the dangers of such success. 'I realize, perhaps more so than the average musician, that it's easy to be caught in that web. Your agent's happy because he can sell you; your record company is happy because they can sell your records; you become popular, and so on.'[2] The Chico Hamilton Quintet quickly became a package, and was marketed in the manner of today's popular rock acts.

Later in 1956 Buddy Collette and Jim Hall left to pursue independent careers. Their replacements, reedman Paul Horn and guitarist John Pisano, were certainly more than adequate musicians, but neither had – at that time – developed truly original voices. Still, the personnel changes weren't the major cause of the quintet's subsequent artistic decline. It was simply that the group sank ever further into a formulaic approach to jazz, taking fewer and fewer chances. A record cut with the new personnel in October 1956 offered twelve tunes, which just about precluded any stretching out by any of the musicians. The performances are pleasant but bland, and only on 'Satin Doll' do the musicians seem to let down their hair.

But if the Chico Hamilton Quintet eventually lapsed into a predictable mould, the original edition of the group had more than enough successes to make up for that. Buddy Collette says that the essence of the group was revealed on numbers like 'Blue Sands', which depended so heavily on the spontaneous interplay between the musicians.

I don't play it now – I should – but you gotta have the right players, and you gotta have a setting where they see this begin to happen; then they believe in it. But if you just rehearse it, they say, 'There's not that much there.' Well, the 'much there' is what you *put* there – right? – with what you have to work with. It's very simple.

Buddy remembers when the tune worked its magic at the 1956 Newport Jazz Festival:

We were the next to the last group on. Duke Ellington followed us ... And everybody was so worn out at Newport, because after three days of trumpets and tenors, and tenors and trumpets and trombones, most groups begin to sound alike. So finally we get on and it's a bad spot, and we play our stuff and everybody ... [claps desultorily] ... and people begin to leave. We were really bombing! So Chico says, 'What're we gonna do?' And I said, 'Well, we better try "Blue Sands"; that's all we got.' But we were afraid of it because – the crowd is down already, and 'Blue Sands' would sometimes put 'em in a trance – a *good* trance, but we didn't know; this night it might put them to sleep ... so we go into it, and they don't move at all; even the smoke seemed to stop out there! It was just like they were silhouettes. And we played for about ten minutes, giving it our best shot. And at the end, as we'd do, we just tapered off, and everything just stopped. And for eight or ten seconds nobody moved, and then they jumped up and screamed; they went wild, and it went on and on ... Later, as we were moving off stage and Duke's band was setting up, we passed Duke on the stairs and he smiled and said, 'Well, you sure made it hot for me.'

A later edition of the quintet did regain some of the excitement of the original when young reedman Eric Dolphy joined the fold, but that's the subject of another chapter.

In February 1956 Dick Bock recorded an album for Pacific Jazz as unique and special in its own way as the Cy Touff album of a few months earlier. Tenor saxophonist Bill Perkins, a veteran of the Woody Herman and Stan Kenton bands, was one of the label's rising young stars, and Bock wanted to record him in as many settings as possible. An outstanding opportunity developed when the Modern Jazz Quartet visited LA for a local engagement. Bock made arrangements with Atlantic records to 'borrow' pianist John Lewis for a recording with Perkins, and a session was hastily set up. The resulting album was truly a co-operative affair, featuring Lewis and bassist Percy Heath of the MJQ, Jim Hall and Chico Hamilton of the Hamilton quintet, and Perkins.

At the time of the recording (10 February 1956) Bill Perkins had been a professional musician only five years. Born 2 July 1924 in San Francisco, Bill had been raised in Santa Barbara (and, for a time, Chile) and had taken an Electrical Engineering degree from Cal Tech. He had first made a name for himself with Woody Herman's Third Herd, and was a mainstay of the Kenton band during the mid- and late fifties. In this period he was a staunch devotee of the Lester Young *cum* Stan Getz school, and although he was perfectly capable of up-tempo flights, he was at his best in the mid-tempos and especially on ballads, where he achieved a poignantly beautiful tone. The pairing with John Lewis seemed a natural, and the Pacific Jazz recording would prove this to be the case.

There are no fireworks, no flag-wavers, on the album; no tune proceeds at a pace faster than a gentle lope. But there is plenty of relaxed swinging by all hands. John Lewis contributed an original for the recording, a gentle blues called 'Two Degrees East, Three Degrees West', which also supplied the album's title. There is plenty of room for everybody to stretch out on this tune, as well as on 'Almost Like being in Love' and 'Love Me or Leave Me'. 'Skylark' serves as a vehicle for Jim Hall's guitar in a trio setting; Hall is backed by Lewis and Percy Heath. 'I Can't Get Started' also features a trio, in this case Lewis, Heath and Chico Hamilton. Finally there is a languid and beautiful rendition of 'Easy Living' which features Perkins all the way, sympathetically backed by the other four. In fact, there is no shortage of empathy on the album; the musicians sound as if they'd been playing together for years. The album remains a classic, always easy to listen to, as comfortable and familiar as an old sweater.

A little less than a year later Jim Hall got the chance to record an album of his own using the trio format. His companions on the session were bassist Red Mitchell and pianist Carl Perkins, two of the strongest yet most melodic rhythm players around. Carl Perkins was, at this time, the anchor of the Curtis Counce Group – one of the West Coast's hardest-swinging combos – and of course Red Mitchell was an indispensable member of the Hampton Hawes Trio. The trio thus formed certainly had the potential to be an outstanding combo, and the resulting album, *Jazz Guitar*, is proof that they more than lived up to that potential.

The album was cut in two sessions, held 10 and 24 January 1957. There was a minimum of writing and a maximum of improvising, which certainly agreed with the musical philosophy of all hands. All of the songs were standards, either of the Broadway musical tradition or of the jazz repertoire. The album's highlight is probably the old Mercer Ellington standby, 'Things ain't what They Used to be', although the high level of musicianship exhibited on all tracks makes such a choice rather difficult. 'Things ain't' is taken at a relaxed walk, and all three get a chance leisurely to examine the depths of the blues. 'This is Always' and 'Deep in a Dream' are the album's two ballad performances, and in each Jim Hall displays an especially sensitive style. 'Seven Come Eleven' is Hall's respectful nod to the great Charlie Christian, and 'Stomping at the Savoy' and '9:20 Special' continue the tribute to the swing era. The remaining tunes are all standards: 'Thanks for the Memory', 'Tangerine', 'Stella by Starlight' and 'Look for the Silver Lining'. It would be hard to pick any of these performances as significantly superior to the others, although 'Look for the Silver Lining' does exhibit a joyous swing by the three musicians. As with the John Lewis–Bill Perkins album, this is a record that one never tires of listening to.

(A warning. In the 1960s, Richard Bock reissued the album, but for some obscure reason added a drum track by Larry Bunker, expanding the trio to a quartet. Larry Bunker is of course a fine musician, but the addition ruins the ambience of the original album. Bock produced a great many fine albums over the years, but one often wishes he could have resisted the urge to splice and otherwise tamper with his tapes, a temptation to which he all too often succumbed.)

Three additional recordings complete this survey of outstanding albums recorded during the height of the West Coast jazz boom. Two of these albums – both of which feature Shelly Manne in a trio context – were quite popular, and one was definitely a best-seller. This, of course, was the collaboration with pianist André Previn on the score of *My Fair Lady*. The second trio side, *Way Out West*, starred a visiting Sonny Rollins.

As has been mentioned, Shelly Manne formed his own quintet in 1955, a driving neo-bop unit with trumpeter Stu Williamson, altoist Charlie Mariano, pianist Russ Freeman and bassist Leroy Vinnegar. Shelly's working band always went under the name Shelly Manne and His Men. But beginning in 1956, Shelly cut a number of albums with André Previn, and the trio was listed as Shelly Manne and His Friends (if it were Shelly's session) or André Previn and His Pals (if it were the pianist's date). The first of these trio albums, entitled simply *Shelly Manne and His Friends*, was cut in February 1956, and failed to attract much attention. The second, recorded in August of 1957, did.

André Previn, Shelly's partner for the album, was a Hollywood *wunderkind* long before he established his jazz credentials. Born on 6 April 1929 in Berlin, he studied at both the Berlin and Paris Conservatories before his family moved to the US in 1939. He continued his studies in the US and was making money as a pianist and arranger while still in high school. He went from high school directly to the MGM studios as a staff arranger, and was composing and conducting for MGM by 1948. By the early 1950s he was making jazz time with Shorty Rogers and recording with his own trio for Victor. Then, in 1956, he was invited to record for Contemporary by Lester Koenig, and thus began his fruitful association with Shelly Manne.

When it came time to record their second trio album in 1957, Les Koenig suggested to Manne, Previn and bassist Leroy Vinnegar that they do a couple of tunes from *My Fair Lady*, the spectacularly popular musical then running on Broadway. The musicians agreed and obtained some copies of tunes from the show, thinking to pick out one or two for the recording. Shelly tells what happened next:

When André got the book – Les sent down to a music store to

get the score of *My Fair Lady* – we found that there was so much material in there that we could use, and change, and construct to the way that would suit us best, we said, 'Let's go ahead and use this other material.' There was no thought of, 'Hey, we're making a hit record,' it was just the thought of making another good record, but not using the same old standard material but using new material from a new show. And as it worked out, of course, it was a smash! Of course André, with his knowledge of harmony and composition, was fantastic. He'd play something and he'd say, 'Oh, let's do this at *this* tempo,' and we'd play it and I'd say, 'That's great!' And he'd play something else at a fast tempo, and I'd say, 'Why don't we try that as a ballad?' There was a total thing going back and forth ... We were so revved up – we were gonna do a three- or four-hour session and come back the next day and finish it up or whatever – why, we just went on through the night ... We started in the afternoon and broke and had some sandwiches and everything – the juices were flowing so good, and everybody was playing so well, that we said, 'Hell, let's go ahead and do the whole album.' And that's the way *that* thing happened.[3]

It seems hard to believe now that this was the first album based entirely on jazz versions of tunes from a contemporary Broadway show, but the instant popular success of the *My Fair Lady* album ensured that there would be many imitators, and soon the concept became something of a cliché.

The opening number, a rousing version of 'Get Me to the Church on Time', sets the pace. André Previn has suffered over the years at the hand of jazz critics; the rap was that his piano style was unoriginal and excessively eclectic. Though there is truth to the charge, he has never been accused of not swinging, and on 'Get Me to the Church on Time' Previn fairly smokes. Both 'On the Street where You Live' and 'Wouldn't It be Loverly' start out in a funky two and break into a relaxed four on the solos. As Shelly mentions, liberties were taken with tempi and time signatures. 'Show Me', originally a waltz number, swings into a bright four, while 'With a Little Bit of Luck' – an English music-hall number in the play – is played as a romantic ballad. 'I've Grown Accustomed to Her Face' is the album's other ballad; Previn's tender piano is backed sympathetically by Shelly's mallets. Both 'Ascot Gavotte' and 'I Could Have Danced

All Night' are up-tempo swingers. Throughout the proceedings, the three musicians respond to one another with an instant rapport that would be the envy of many working groups.

In March 1957 Sonny Rollins came through LA with the Max Roach Quintet, and Les Koenig jumped at the opportunity to record the premier jazz tenor saxophonist. Rollins expressed interest in being backed only by bass and drums – an unorthodox instrumentation that he would later utilize extensively – and Koenig agreed. Bassist Ray Brown, also in town with the Oscar Peterson Trio, and Shelly Manne rounded out the trio. As all three men were working club dates in the evenings, and Brown and Manne had additional studio calls in the afternoon, the session was called for three in the morning. Shelly Manne remembers feeling a little nervous about playing the first time with Sonny Rollins. 'I went into making that album with a little trepidation. I respected and admired Sonny Rollins so much – I still do – and I knew he hadn't been playing with this kind of set-up – with the bass and drums, just a trio. I was a little worried, but Sonny was so beautiful, and played so great, it was just enjoyable.'

Sonny picked two tunes with a western theme for the album, 'I'm an Old Cowhand' and 'Wagon Wheels', and through his usual alchemy transformed the pieces into swinging jazz vehicles. Ray Brown and Shelly Manne provide Rollins with such firm support the lack of a piano is quickly forgotten. Sonny's treatment of the two ballads, 'There is No Greater Love' and Duke Ellington's 'Solitude', is typical of his work at the time; on both he is brusque yet tender, and at times he lays behind the beat so far he creates a sense of almost unbearable tension, finally resolving the tension with a multi-noted run that ends precisely and unerringly at his appointed rendezvous with the underlying beat. Rollins also brought two originals, 'Way Out West', a typically wry, tongue-in-cheek theme, and 'Come, Gone', an up-tempo scorcher based on 'After You've Gone'. *Way Out West* helped cement Sonny Rollins's position as one of the leading voices in jazz, and coincidentally exploded many of the East Coast–West Coast distinctions that were so prevalent in the jazz press of the day.

One other album cut the same year also focused on a meeting between musicians from East and West. A month before the Sonny Rollins album was recorded, Dizzy Gillespie's big band came through LA. On one of their Sunday afternoons off, several members of the band – trumpeter Lee Morgan, tenor saxophonist Benny Golson, pianist Wynton Kelly and drummer Charlie Persip – dropped by the Lighthouse to catch Howard Rumsey's current group: Conte Candoli, Frank Rosolino, Bob Cooper, pianist Dick Shreve, Rumsey and Stan Levey. Much to the delight of the All-Stars, the visiting musicians sat in with the locals. Everyone in the audience and on stage was enthusiastic about the meeting and later, over dinner, Howard Rumsey suggested that the two groups combine forces for a recording. Two sessions were hastily arranged at Liberty records for 14 and 17 February 1957. The resulting album, *Double or Nothin'*, is one of the lesser-known gems of the 1950s.

Eight tunes in all were recorded during the two sessions, and the instrumentation and personnel varies from number to number. The album opens with the Jazz Statesmen – Morgan, Golson, Kelly, bassist Wilfred Middlebrooks and Persip – playing Golson's tune 'Reggie of Chester'. On 'Stablemates', Lee Morgan and Benny Golson join Frank Rosolino and the All-Stars rhythm section, Dick Shreve, Red Mitchell and Stan Levey. (Mitchell sat in on bass so that Howard Rumsey could stay on top of things in the control booth.) Next comes a lovely ballad of Benny Golson's, 'Celedia', with the All-Stars front line – Candoli, Rosolino and Cooper – backed by the visitors' rhythm section – Kelly, Middlebrooks and Persip. Finally the combined bands join forces on Bob Cooper's 'Moto', an up-tempo swinger. All five horns solo, backed by Shreve, Mitchell and Levey. Side two opens with the Lighthouse crew working out on Dizzy Gillespie's 'The Champ'. Next comes the album's finest performance, Benny Golson's 'Blues after Dark', which features Lee Morgan, Golson, Wynton Kelly, Red Mitchell and Charlie Persip. The full group combines once again on Gigi Gryce's 'Wildwood', backed this time by the visiting rhythm section. A burning version of Horace Silver's 'Quicksilver' by the Lighthouse All-Stars brings the album to a storming conclusion.

As is the case with the Sonny Rollins *Way Out West* album, *Double or Nothin'* presents ample proof that East and West could indeed meet, and produce some swinging and satisfying jazz in doing so. The differing styles of the hornmen complement each other, and it is especially instructive to listen to Benny Golson and Bob Cooper solo back to back, as they do on 'Moto' and 'Wildwood'. Golson comes out of the Coleman Hawkins big-toned school, by way of Don Byas; Cooper is definitely orientated towards the lighter-toned Lester Young school. Yet both are hard swingers, and each blends modern ideas with a profound respect for the jazz tradition. Conte Candoli and Lee Morgan are both squarely in the modernists' camp, but Candoli plainly shows his bebop roots, while the younger Lee Morgan shows his indebtedness to the tone and ideas of Clifford Brown. And Frank Rosolino remains *sui generis*, a trombonist with a truly unique style.

Unfortunately, *Double or Nothin'* never achieved the popularity of some of the other albums we've examined, and it has long been out of print. This is a shame, for the record goes far to refute the standard invidious comparisons of the East Coast and West Coast groups of the fifties. For that matter, there were several West Coast groups at the time whose aims and formats were analogous to such Eastern groups as the Jazz Messengers or the Horace Silver Quintet. One such band is only now, some thirty years after the fact, beginning to achieve its due. This was the Curtis Counce Group, one of LA's finest working bands in the later 1950s.

8.
california hard (ii)

It is hard to understand why the Curtis Counce Group failed to achieve the recognition – either popular or critical – it deserved. Perhaps it's because the group was so difficult to pigeonhole. As a Los Angeles-based group it couldn't remotely be identified with the West Coast school. Stylistically, the Curtis Counce Group fit quite naturally with such groups as the Jazz Messengers or the Horace Silver Quintet, but such a comparison tended to upset the East Coast–West Coast dichotomy that then figured so prominently in jazz criticism. So, stuck as they were thousands of miles from the centres of editorial power, the musicians in the group turned out their own brand of hard-swinging jazz in relative obscurity. It wouldn't be fair to say they were totally ignored by the influential critics, but they were seldom evaluated at their true worth.

We've already discussed most of the band's principals. Bassist Curtis Counce had played with Shorty Rogers and numerous West Coast groups, and was one of the few black musicians to have gained acceptance in the Hollywood studios; he had just returned from a European tour with the Stan Kenton orchestra when he set about forming a band in August of 1956. Tenor saxophonist Harold Land had of course been a mainstay of the Max Roach–Clifford Brown quintet. Trumpeter Jack Sheldon, who shared the front line with Land, was born 30 November 1931 in Jacksonville, Florida and moved to LA in 1947, where he studied music for two years at LA City College. Following a two-year stint in the air force, he gigged around town with Jack Montrose, Art Pepper, Wardell Gray, Dexter Gordon and Herb

Geller; he was also a charter member of the group centred around Joe Maini and Lenny Bruce. The rhythm section of the Curtis Counce Group was anchored by two exceptional musicians, pianist Carl Perkins and drummer Frank Butler. Carl Perkins (no relation to the rock-and-roll singer) had been born in Indianapolis, Indiana, 16 August 1928. A self-taught pianist, Perkins had come up through the rhythm-and-blues bands of Tiny Bradshaw and Big Jay McNeely, and had forged a blues-drenched modern style for himself. He had developed an unorthodox style and often played with his left arm parallel to the keyboard. Frank Butler was born on 18 February 1928 in Wichita, Kansas and had made jazz time with Dave Brubeck, Edgar Hayes and Duke Ellington, among others.

None of the musicians in the band was a household name, although Harold Land had gained some fame during his stay with the Clifford Brown–Max Roach band. But this was, above all, a *group*, and it was as a co-operative unit that the band excelled. Everyone is familiar with all-star bands that somehow or other don't quite make it – the chemistry between the players is somehow wrong; perhaps an ego or two gets in the way. The Curtis Counce Group was that sort of band's antithesis; a living, working example of a unit wherein the whole is much greater than the sum of its components. Although the original idea to form the group was Curtis Counce's, the band functioned as a collaborative affair. 'We were all close friends within the group,' Harold Land remembers, 'so it was a good idea for all of us, because we all liked each other personally as well as musically.'

The Curtis Counce Group was formed in August 1956, played its first gig at The Haig in September, and entered the recording studios a month later. Lester Koenig always had an ear for promising musicians, and in the latter part of the 1950s he recorded a fascinating assortment of exciting and forward-looking groups and musicians, including Ornette Coleman and Cecil Taylor, for his Contemporary label. The Curtis Counce Group was one of his happiest finds. The musicians entered the studio on 8 October for their first session, and the band's chemistry was evident from the start. The first tune recorded was Harold Land's 'Landslide', a dark yet forceful hard-bop theme. Harold leads off with some big-toned tenor work and is followed by some thoughtful Sheldon and grooving Carl Perkins. Two other originals were contributed by members of the band: 'Mia' by Carl Perkins, and Jack Sheldon's blues line 'Sarah'.

'Mia' sports a bright, bouncy tune with unexpected chord progressions and sparks swinging solos by all hands. Everybody digs deeply into the blues on 'Sarah', but Carl Perkins is especially impressive in his solo; throughout his all too short career Perkins displayed a close affinity for the blues. 'Time after Time' serves as a vehicle for Harold Land's tender yet muscular ballad style. 'A Fifth for Frank', as the title suggests, is a showcase for Frank Butler. Frank's driving support for the band throughout the session belies his relative inexperience – this was in fact his first recording. A sixth tune, Charlie Parker's 'Big Foot' (recorded by Parker as both 'Air Conditioning' and 'Drifting on a Reed' for Dial), was also recorded at this original session, but was not issued until later. To round out the initial album, a tune recorded at the group's second session – held a week later on 18 October – was used. 'Sonar' (written by Gerald Wiggins and Kenny Clarke), is taken at a bright tempo and has plenty of room for stretching out by all of the musicians.

The first album, titled simply *The Curtis Counce Group*, was released early in 1957 and immediately gained favourable attention. Nat Hentoff awarded the album four stars in an admiring review in *Down Beat* magazine. Yet somehow national stature seemed to elude the band. Undoubtedly the main reason for this was that the Curtis Counce Group was not a travelling band. Harold Land does remember that the group 'went to Denver one time, but as far as getting back east, it never did happen'. In Los Angeles the band enjoyed an in-group reputation – they were especially well-liked by fellow musicians – but they never achieved the popularity of, say, the Chico Hamilton Quintet. They did play regularly around Los Angeles. 'There was another spot down on Sunset: the Sanborn House,' Harold remembers. 'We played there quite a while, longer than we did at The Haig, and the group built up quite a following. The Haig was very small, but this was a larger club.'

In the meantime, the band continued to record prolifically for Contemporary. The group's second album contained tunes cut at various sessions held in 1956 and throughout 1957. In addition to 'Sonar', the band recorded a swinging version of 'Stranger in Paradise' at the second session of 15 October 1956; this tune and the aforementioned 'Big Foot' were on the second album, which was originally entitled *You Get More Bounce with Curtis Counce*. Two more tunes were recorded 22 April 1957 – 'Too Close for Comfort' and 'Counceltation'. The latter is an original by the leader. Curtis was studying composition with Lyle 'Spud' Murphy at the time, and 'Counceltation' is an experimental piece based on Murphy's twelve-tone system. The tune is interesting, but smacks a little too much of the classroom. As if to balance this, another tune of Counce's, a bright blues named 'Complete', was recorded at a session in May. Everybody gets to let down his hair on 'Complete', and Jack Sheldon contributes a funky Miles Davis-influenced solo in Harmon mute. A ballad version of 'How Deep is the Ocean', also recorded at the May session, and an up-tempo 'Mean to Me', recorded in September, complete the album. When the album was released late in 1957, the Curtis Counce Group was riding high, but unfortunately several unforeseen events would soon contribute to the band's early demise. Chief among these was the tragic death of pianist Carl Perkins in March of 1958; an additional strong factor was the rapid decline of jazz clubs in LA in the closing years of the decade. But before we examine the final recordings of the Curtis Counce band, let's look at a couple of other hard-swinging groups that were playing around southern California during this same period.

Perhaps the most famous neo-bop group to be formed in LA in the mid-fifties was that of Chet Baker. As you'll remember, Chet formed his own quartet following the break-up of the original Gerry Mulligan Quartet in 1953, and worked mostly in a quartet format for the next several years. He spent the autumn of 1955 and the winter and spring of 1956 in Europe, headquartered in Paris, recording in a variety of contexts with groups composed of American and European musicians. The most interesting of these recordings were made with the quartet he accompanied to France, which featured the highly original pianist Richard Twardzik. Unfortunately Twardzik died suddenly in Paris in October 1955, another young victim of drugs. When Baker finally returned to the US in the spring of 1956, he went about forming a quintet that would change his image among jazz fans, and which would temporarily slow the decline in his fortunes.

For his front-line companion Baker chose Phil Urso, a tenor saxophonist in the Zoot Sims, Al Cohn tradition. Born 2 October 1925 in Jersey City, New Jersey, Urso had played with the bands of Elliot Lawrence, Woody Herman, Terry Gibbs and Oscar Pettiford, among others. Chet's rhythm section featured three young lions. Pianist Bobby Timmons and bassist Jimmy Bond were both born in Philadelphia; Bond on 27 January 1933 and

Timmons on 19 December 1935. Both had played with name jazzmen while still in their teens, and Bond was in addition a graduate of Juilliard. Drummer Peter Littman was born in Medford, Massachusetts 8 May 1935 and had worked with Boston musicians Herb Pomeroy and Charlie Mariano before joining Chet Baker's quartet prior to the European tour. The quintet this formed, while not as powerful or exciting as the Curtis Counce Group, was a solid, swinging modern unit, and definitely more extroverted than the trumpeter's previous groups had been.

The new Chet Baker Quintet soon got a chance to record for Pacific Jazz. In a series of sessions held in late July 1956, the quintet taped sixteen numbers, and eight of these found their way on to an album entitled *Chet Baker & Crew*. (Some of the remaining tunes were eventually released on a Crown LP, and several more were issued on various Pacific Jazz anthologies.) The album's opener – and hardest-swinging number – is a piece entitled 'To Mickey's Memory', an original by Harvey Leonard based on 'I'll Remember April' changes. For this one number the quintet is augmented by percussionist Bill Loughbrough, playing an invention of his called 'chromatic timpani'. The experimental percussion set is interesting, but doesn't add anything to jazz drumming that Max Roach hadn't introduced years before. Worse, the extra drum set exacerbates Peter Littman's tendency to rush the beat. Still, it is a swinging performance, and Chet Baker's forceful new personality on trumpet comes through marvellously.

None of the album's remaining performances exceeds that of 'Mickey's Memory', but there is no serious let-down either. Bob Zieff's 'Slightly above Moderate' features some unusual progressions and elicits thoughtful solos by Baker, Urso and Timmons. Another number by Zieff, 'Medium Rock', also has unexpected changes, but in this case the solos are rather pedestrian. Phil Urso contributes two originals to the proceedings: 'Halema', a ballad, and 'Lucius Lu', a funky number in the 'Doxy' mould. 'Revelation', by Chet's former boss Gerry Mulligan, is given a driving performance, but once again the tempo picks up slightly. Al Cohn's 'Something for Lisa' is taken at a brisk but comfortable pace that sparks especially happy solos by Urso and Baker. The album's most unexpected number is Miff Mole's tender 'Worrying the Life out of Me', which features a sensitive solo by Chet. Strangely enough, a stronger performance than any of those on the album was relegated to a Pacific Jazz anthology. A version of Al Haig's 'Jumpin' Off a Clef' features hard-driving solos by Baker, Urso and Timmons, and an especially tight rhythm section. The performance was later released on an album entitled *The Hard Swing*.

Perhaps because Chet Baker's contract with Pacific Jazz was soon to be up, Dick Bock recorded his star trumpet player often in a variety of contexts during the latter part of 1956. There were no further recordings by his working quintet, but different sessions saw Chet backed by a quartet, a sextet and even a (small) big band. We'll examine the sextet recordings in a later chapter, but one of the two quartet sessions from this period deserves special attention here. On 6 November Chet was reunited with his former pianist Russ Freeman. Actually it was Freeman's session, but the band was billed as the Chet Baker–Russ Freeman Quartet on the album. The rhythm section included Freeman's fellow members of the Shelly Manne Quintet of the time – Shelly and Leroy Vinnegar. The three had been working together for well over a year and it showed. Few rhythm sections of the day were tighter, or exhibited more strength. Certainly their playing goaded Chet Baker into a superior performance. Shelly Manne remembers the date as an especially happy occasion:

> Sometimes you go into a studio, and for some strange reason – the set-up is right, everything feels right, you can hear clearly, all your creative juices are flowing, and everything is perfect – it's kinda like magic almost. And those are the times when you really make some great records ... Russ and I had found almost a new way of playing in the rhythm section together: a kind of looser, freer way, where we were an integral part of melody lines and what was happening rhythmically, without just being stuck in the background ... Leroy was such a strong walker; he gave us a foundation to lean on ... And Chet was such a loose, free player that it worked perfectly with him.

Certainly Chet Baker never played with more fire than he did on this date. The album opens with a blistering 'Love Nest'. Woody Woodward, Bock's right-hand man at Pacific Jazz, remembers that a couple of earlier attempts at the piece had produced unsatisfying takes. Woodward then suggested that the trumpeter use a Harmon mute on the next take. Baker – who was suffering from some bad teeth – was reluctant, due to the increased pressure needed to blow through the mute, but agreed to try anyway. The resulting performance proved Woodward right; Chet seems to pull out all the stops in his driving solo. The next piece, Billy Strayhorn's 'Lush Life', is given an exquisite ballad performance; neither Freeman nor Baker strays far from the written tune. The rest of the album's numbers are all Russ Freeman originals. 'Say When', based on the time-tested 'I Got Rhythm' changes, is the most conventional. 'Amblin'', a slow blues, shows off Freeman's sparse, sinewy style to great advantage. Never one to waste resources, Freeman places each note with care in exactly the right spot. 'Fan Tan' starts out in a remote key, then bounces blithely along to its tonic. Perhaps Freeman's finest composition on the album is the beautiful mood piece 'Summer Sketch', a languid ballad that evokes sultry afternoons. 'An Afternoon at Home' is taken at an engaging middle tempo, while 'Hugo Hurwhey' is pushed along at a rapid, but not breakneck, pace. In the fascinating fours on the latter piece each musician truly takes a solo, unsupported by the other instruments. All four musicians acquit themselves admirably on this album; it remains one of the high points of the Pacific Jazz catalogue.

Two other short-lived groups in the hard-bop mould had a brief moment on the LA stage around this time, and strangely enough, one of these bands had its genesis in the Stan Kenton orchestra. The first of these groups was the Red Mitchell Quartet, which was formed early in 1957. This was definitely a young and forward-looking band. Tenor saxophonist James Clay had been born in Dallas, Texas on 8 September 1935. A proponent of the big-toned tenor style favoured in the south west, Clay also played a singularly muscular flute. Lorraine Geller was the group's pianist. The youngest member of the quartet was Billy Higgins. Higgins was born in Los Angeles on 11 October 1936 and took up drums at the age of twelve, serving his apprenticeship in rhythm-and-blues bands around the area.

Once again Lester Koenig recognized the potential of the young musicians and invited them to record. A session was held the night of 26 March 1957, and enough tunes for a complete album were taped in one sitting. The direction favoured by the musicians can be charted by listing the tunes chosen for recording. These include Charlie Parker's 'Scrapple from the Apple', Miles Davis's 'Out of the Blue', Sonny Rollins's 'Paul's

153

Pal' and Clifford Brown's 'Sandu'. There are also two originals by Red Mitchell, 'Rainy Night' and 'I Thought of You', as well as a burning version of the Irving Berlin standard 'Cheek to Cheek'. The leader's mastery of the bass is exhibited throughout. On 'Scrapple from the Apple', taken at the expected rapid pace, Mitchell doubles the lead line with James Clay on the head. And on his own ballad 'I Thought of You', Red states the theme on his very melodic bass. James Clay plays flute on both 'I Thought of You' and 'Rainy Night', as well as on 'Paul's Pal'. The quixotic Sonny Rollins line on the latter tune lends itself admirably to Clay's approach on the flute. Still, the most satisfying performances are those which feature straight-ahead blowing by all hands: 'Scrapple', 'Sandu' and 'Cheek to Cheek'.

This was an auspicious debut for the quartet (it was, incidentally, the first appearance on record for Billy Higgins) but unfortunately it didn't lead to any further albums. The Red Mitchell Quartet was an early victim of the deteriorating Los Angeles club scene that took place in the waning years of the decade. A short time after recording this album, the group disbanded. For Lorraine Geller, whose sympathetic piano work contributed so much to the quartet's sound, it would be a maternity leave: she became a mother before the year's end. Tragically, she died of an apparent heart attack the following year, on 10 October 1958. James Clay, discouraged by the lack of job opportunities, returned to Dallas, although he later recorded heavily with both Ray Charles and Hank Crawford. Billy Higgins, of course, went on to become one of the most influential drummers of the 1960s. We'll return to both Higgins and Red Mitchell later in this narrative.

In the summer of 1957 LA also had a brief taste of another group with an even harder edge than the Red Mitchell Quartet. This was the Pepper Adams–Mel Lewis group. Baritone saxophonist Park Adams was born in Rochester, New York, on 8 October 1930, but spent his formative jazz years in Detroit. He began on tenor sax but switched to the larger horn when he got the chance to buy one at a discount while working in a music shop. While in Detroit from 1946 to 1951 he grew close to a group of local musicians who would loom large in the New York jazz scene of the fifties: Kenny Burrell, Paul Chambers, Tommy Flanagan, Frank Foster, Bill Evans (later Yusef Lateef), Elvin and Thad Jones, Donald Byrd and Doug Watkins. These and other Motor City jazzmen, under the tutelage of pianist Barry

Harris, forged an exciting musical environment in Detroit in the post-war years. When Adams was hired by Stan Kenton in 1956, his brusque, aggressive baritone style was a revelation for the Kentonians. Drummer Mel Lewis would later recall, 'We called him the Knife because when he'd get up to blow, his playing had almost a slashing effect on the rest of us. He'd slash, chop, and before he was through cut everybody down to size.'[1] Following a brief stint with Kenton, Pepper Adams moved on to the Maynard Ferguson big band, then to Chet Baker's quintet. (Unfortunately, this particular Baker group was never recorded.) Then, in 1957, he moved to LA to freelance, and renewed his friendship with Mel Lewis. Undaunted by the sparseness of clubs in the area, the two decided to form a band. The group worked only two paid engagements, at Zucca's Cottage in Pasadena, before they were forced to disband due to lack of jobs. Fortunately, Adams and Lewis were able to record two albums in the summer of 1957, leaving posterity at least a taste of what might have been.

The first session, for the Mode label, was held on 12 July. Lewis and Adams were joined by trumpeter Stu Williamson, pianist Carl Perkins and bassist Leroy Vinnegar for the date. The album opens with a relaxed 'Unforgettable', on which Stu Williamson's fluid trumpet balances Pepper Adams's horn nicely. A burning, searing 'Baubles, Bangles and Beads' shows how Adams gained his nickname of the Knife: he indeed cuts the others down to size. Adams also provided two original compositions for the date. 'Freddie Froo' has an up-tempo hard-bop theme, and Stu Williamson and Carl Perkins both take solos that show them to be more than comfortable in the genre. 'Muezzin'', taken at a slightly slower tempo, sports a Latin-tinged theme. 'My One and Only Love', the album's ballad, showcases Pepper Adams's tender side. Mel Lewis and Leroy Vinnegar provide propulsive support to the soloist throughout the proceedings.

The second album was recorded for Pacific Jazz (which by now had adopted the World Pacific label) a month later, on 22 August. For this date the co-leaders were joined by Lee Katzman, who had played trumpet with the two in Kenton's band, as well as pianist Jimmy Rowles and an old friend of Pepper's from Detroit, bassist Doug Watkins. The album was released under the title *Critics' Choice*, in honour of Pepper Adams having recently been chosen New Star on baritone sax in the *Down Beat* critics' poll. It is, on the whole, a more satisfying album than the previous one, exhibiting a larger range of moods. Four of the album's six tunes are originals by Adams's youthful companions from Detroit. Tommy Flanagan's 'Minor Mishap' has a rhythmically propulsive theme that spurs both Adams and Katzman into strong solos. 'High Step', by Barry Harris, has a very relaxed feel, although Mel Lewis does prod Adams into some exciting double time. Thad Jones supplied two of the album's tunes: the storming 'Zec' and the laid back '5021'. On '5021' the theme breaks in and out of 3/4 time, although the solos are all in straight four. Bassist Doug Watkins states the theme in the ballad 'Alone Together', which is mostly a vehicle for Pepper Adams's baritone. The remaining number is 'Blackout Blues', wherein each musician contributes to a searching look into the heart of the blues.

Shortly after the two albums were recorded, Pepper Adams gave up on LA and moved back to the Apple. There he was featured on a series of exciting Blue Note and Riverside recordings, usually in the company of fellow Detroiter Donald Byrd. The Los Angeles recordings, and especially *Critics' Choice*, hold up well when compared with those cut later in NYC. It's a shame the Pepper Adams–Mel Lewis group couldn't make a go of it on the Coast, but they were by no means the only musicians to face hard times in those years.

Perhaps the most poignant example of the break-up of a working band was that of the Curtis Counce Group, if only because the group had shown so much promise from its inception. They did manage to hold together through 1957, when so many bands fell by the wayside, but finally broke apart early in 1958. But before the group disbanded they managed to produce two more albums, both enduring legacies of jazz in the fifties.

The group's final recording for the Contemporary label was titled – when it was finally released in 1960 – *Carl's Blues*. The title was, unfortunately, especially apt, both because 'Carl's Blues' by pianist Carl Perkins is one of the album's highlights, and because Perkins died shortly after the tune was recorded. The album contains tunes cut at three sessions in all. Jack Sheldon's 'Pink Lady', a smoking work-out on the standard 'I Got Rhythm' changes, and a spirited version of 'Love Walked in' are from the earliest date, held on 22 April 1957. There is also a grooving version of Horace Silver's Latin-flavoured tune 'Nica's Dream', recorded 29 August. The tempo here is slower and more deliberate than Horace Silver's justly famous Blue Note recording, but the Curtis Counce performance is no less expressive.

The album's remaining tunes were recorded at Carl Perkins's final session on 6 January 1958. For this date, Gerald Wilson replaced Jack Sheldon in the group's trumpet chair, although Wilson plays on only two tunes. One track, 'The Butler Did It', is an unaccompanied drum solo by Frank Butler. 'I Can't Get Started' features Harold Land and the rhythm section, and the performance gives a strong indication of Land's growing powers as an improviser. The two tunes featuring the entire quintet are 'Larue' and the aforementioned 'Carl's Blues'. The ballad 'Larue' was written by Clifford Brown for his wife; Harold Land plays an especially tender solo on the tune. 'Carl's Blues', written by Carl Perkins expressly for the session, is a leisurely examination of the blues and a fitting epitaph for the pianist.

Carl Perkins died on 17 March 1958, just five months short of his thirtieth birthday, another victim of drug abuse. He was the heartbeat of the Curtis Counce Group, and it is not surprising that the quintet did not long outlive him. When Les Koenig finally issued his third album, several years after the selections had been recorded, he had this to say about the band.

> While it lasted, the Curtis Counce Group was one of the most exciting ever organized in Los Angeles. Counce picked four men who almost immediately achieved a togetherness only long-established bands seem to have. Today, Carl Perkins is dead, and the members of the group have gone off in different directions ... It would be difficult under the best of conditions to recapture the feeling of the 1957 quintet. Without Perkins, whose unique piano style was basic to the group's special sound, it is impossible.[2]

It is tempting to wonder how the band would have been received had it been based in New York; certainly it would have given some of the more famous groups of the fifties a run for their money.

Carl's Blues was not, however, the final recording of the band. A month after Perkins's death the restructured quintet recorded for Dootsie Williams's Dooto (Dootone) records. Counce, Land and Butler remained from the original group. The trumpeter for the date was Rolf Ericson. Ericson, born in Stockholm, Sweden, on 29 August 1927, had moved to the States in 1947 and had worked with various bands including those of Charlie Barnet, Elliot Lawrence and Woody Herman. He was a member of the Lighthouse All-Stars in 1953. The new pianist was Elmo Hope, a native New Yorker, whose brief tenure on the Coast in the late fifties sparked several outstanding recordings. Hope, born on 27 June 1923, was a childhood friend of Bud Powell and an active participant of the New York jazz scene of the forties and early fifties, although he remained little known to the public at large. Hope's piano was not as blues-oriented as that of Carl Perkins but was instead sinewy and spare, the hard-bop piano style pared to its very essence. In view of the band's restructuring, it is significant that the group was billed as the Curtis Counce Quintet rather than the Curtis Counce Group.

This set is unfortunately something of a let-down after the three previous albums. Contemporary and Pacific Jazz were the class of the West Coast independents, and however one may quibble over Les Koenig's or Dick Bock's choice of artists or material on any given record, their records were always superbly engineered and professionally produced. The Dootone album, *Exploring the Future*, is noticeably inferior to the Contemporaries in recording quality, and there seems to have been a lack of rehearsal time as well. Of course this was not the tight working band of a year earlier – Carl Perkins's death and Jack Sheldon's departure obviously disrupted the group's cohesiveness – but a couple of the numbers could have benefited from an additional take or two.

There is also the matter of the album's 'theme'. The group was definitely not *Exploring the Future*, but was diligently labouring in the well-established vineyards of hard bop. The futuristic album cover, showing Curtis Counce floating through the void in a space suit, and the choice of titles, which include 'Into the Orbit', 'Race for Space', 'Exploring the Future', and 'The Countdown', promise things the album simply can't deliver. (It is possible that some of the names were tagged on to untitled numbers after they had been recorded, a common enough practice.) All of this is not to say, however, that the album is a failure: the record does deliver a satisfying amount of modern, hard-driving jazz.

Four of the album's eight numbers were written by Elmo Hope; all are decidedly in the hard-bop vein. 'So Nice', the record's opener, has a catchy tune and driving solos by Ericson, Land and Hope. Rolf Ericson's tone is brash, and fits well in the hard-bop context, but his trumpet playing suffers in comparison with Jack Sheldon's fluid yet funky work. 'Into the Orbit' seems well named, since each soloist is launched into his solo at a doubled-up tempo. 'Race for Space' is a rapid minor-key theme which has a burning solo by Harold Land. And 'The Countdown', the album's closing number, sounds very much as if it were used by Hope as a set-closer; it features the rhythm section working as a trio. 'Exploring the Future' has a nice theme that is attributed to Dootsie Williams, but since he is also credited on the album for Denzil Best's classic 'Move', one wonders. 'Move' serves largely as a drum solo for Frank Butler. The album also has two ballads. 'Someone to Watch over Me' is a solo vehicle for Curtis Counce's bass, while Ericson, Land and Hope all contribute tender solos on 'Angel Eyes'.

Although this was the last recording of the band under Curtis Counce's leadership, two additional sessions featured largely the same personnel. The first of these was under the leadership of Elmo Hope. On 31 October 1957 the Elmo Hope Quintet – Stu Williamson, Harold Land, Hope, Leroy Vinnegar, Frank Butler – recorded three tunes for Pacific Jazz: 'Vaun Ex', 'St Elmo's Fire' and 'So Nice'. All three of course were the pianist's compositions. Whether Dick Bock had originally planned on an entire album for the group or not, these were the only tunes recorded (or at least ever released) by Pacific Jazz. Two of the numbers were released on anthologies the following year; all three eventually found their way on to an Art Blakey reissue in the early 1960s. The recording quality on these Pacific Jazz sides is noticeably superior to that of the Curtis Counce Dooto album, but it's also true that the Dooto sides exhibit a bit more uninhibited fire.

Perhaps the definitive recordings from this period came under the leadership of Harold Land for Contemporary records. *Harold in the Land of Jazz* (reissued later as *Grooveyard*) is significant both as the first album released under Harold Land's name and as Carl Perkins's last recording. The sessions were held on 13 and 14 January 1958, and the musicians were Rolf Ericson, Land, Carl Perkins, Leroy Vinnegar and Frank Butler. These Contemporary recordings combine the fire of the Dooto recordings and the recording quality of the Pacific Jazz session.

The album opens with a driving arrangement of Kurt Weill's 'Speak Low'. The interplay between Land and Frank Butler here – as always – seems nothing short of miraculous. The two had been playing together almost daily since the formation of the Curtis Counce Group, of course, but beyond that Land and Butler could communicate on a telepathic level that was sometimes almost frightening. 'We've always been close friends,' Land would later remember, 'and we were born on the same day of the month in the same year [Butler on 18 February, Land on 18 December 1928] ... and even our wives get sick and tired of our talking about how "in tune" we are with each other [laughs].' At times during one of Land's solos, the saxophonist will begin a phrase and Butler will immediately jump in, the two finishing together. 'Delirium', Harold Land's tune, is composed of descending sixteen-bar phrases following each other like an endless succession of waves. 'You Don't Know what Love is' serves as a solo vehicle for Land, who names it as one of his favourite ballads. Elmo Hope's 'Nieta' features Latin rhythms and some unconventional chord progressions. Two of the remaining tunes were written by Land. 'Smack Up' is a boppish tune which is propelled by some strong rhythmic accents, while the ballad 'Lydia's Lament' is a tender tribute to Harold's wife.

The remaining tune, and the album's high point, is the Carl Perkins composition 'Grooveyard'. It has a relaxed and timeless theme with roots in both gospel music and the blues, yet it has none of the self-conscious posturing of so many of the soul tunes of the day. Land, Rolf Ericson and especially Carl Perkins reach deep into the jazz tradition with their solos. The performance remains a fitting tribute to its composer. Bassist Leroy Vinnegar, a childhood friend of Perkins from Indianapolis, described the pianist as:

> the kind of musician who played *with* you; who played the things you heard. He not only played the chords, he played the beauty in the chords – his own way. And his time was perfect. In that respect he was what you'd call a rhythm-section pianist. A man with time like Carl's was so important to a bassist, because you're supposed to play those changes *together*.[3]

The album *Grooveyard* remains in print to this day, and like many of the Blue Note albums cut at the same time, it has survived the changing winds of fashion and still offers a moving listening experience.

Two other albums recorded around this same time also feature

Harold Land, albeit as a sideman, and round out the picture of his growing maturity on the tenor sax. The first, cut almost a year earlier (the same month as *Way Out West*) was Herb Geller's *Fire in the West*. As was the case with the *Way Out West* album, this one featured some visiting musicians. Kenny Dorham, Clifford Brown's replacement, was in town with the Max Roach Quintet and played trumpet on the date; Ray Brown, visiting with the Oscar Peterson Trio, sat in on bass. The rest of Geller's sidemen were all locals of the harder persuasion: Harold Land, pianist Lou Levy and drummer Lawrence Marable.

In a way, the album reflects its hybrid origins. Many of the arrangements – they are all by Geller – sound somewhat in the West Coast vein, but once the soloing begins there is (as the album title suggests) plenty of fire. Four of the tunes are Geller originals: 'S' Pacific View', with its minor-key theme; 'Marable Eyes' and 'An Air for the Heir', both boppish up-tempo swingers; and 'Melrose and Sam', which features a contrapuntal head. As a ballad vehicle, Herb chose the Harold Arlen tune 'Here's what I'm Here for'. All of the soloists swing hard in three on Fats Waller's 'Jitterbug Waltz'. Probably the most satisfying performance of all comes on Bud Powell's 'The Fruit', which spurs all hands into driving solos. The album was recorded for the Jubilee label, has long been out of print, and is somewhat scarce even on the second-hand market.

One year later (17 March 1958) Harold Land again recorded as a sideman, this time for Hampton Hawes. The album *For Real!* features a quartet composed of Land, Hawes, a fast-rising young bassist named Scott La Faro and drummer Frank Butler. Although this was a pick-up group, assembled only for the recording session, Butler, Land and Hawes had gigged with one another often enough to feel familiar with each other's styles. Moreover, the blowing-session format is one that held special appeal for Hawes and Land, both of whom favour straight-ahead swinging.

The album opens with 'Hip', a basic B flat blues of Hamp's that is given an interesting twist in the head, which consists of eleven-bar phrases. 'Wrap Your Troubles in Dreams', taken as a slow ballad, elicits tender yet soulful solos from both Hawes and Land. Everybody grooves on Little Benny Harris's bebop standard 'Crazeology'. Two pieces, 'Numbers Game' and 'For Real', are attributed jointly to Hawes and Land; they are based – very loosely – on 'Has Anybody Seen My Gal' and 'Swanee

River', respectively. The album is brought to a burning conclusion with a flying run-down of 'I Love You'. Throughout the album Scott La Faro exhibits the chops that would shortly thrust him into the front ranks of bassists, while Frank Butler provides his usual propulsive accompaniment on all tunes.

Unfortunately, this was Hampton Hawes's last album for quite some time. Shortly thereafter he was busted for a narcotics violation and spent several years removed from the scene. His playing was sorely missed by the Los Angeles musicians. Leonard Feather, in the liner notes for this album, recounts a conversation he had regarding Hampton Hawes with pianist André Previn. Previn told Feather, 'Hamp has never been fully acknowledged for his influence. Half the people who are said to have been influenced by Horace Silver actually owe a lot to Hamp, who's more technical than Horace; that technique, combined with the feeling, has shaped the style of a lot of people.'[4]

A similar argument might be made for Harold Land. At the time this album was recorded, Land was coming into his own as one of the finer tenor saxophonists in jazz, and certainly he was not – during this period, anyway – given his due. For the most part, this was directly related to his refusal to move from Los Angeles. New York City has long been recognized as the jazz capital of the world (dating at least from 1924, when Louis Armstrong moved east from Chicago to join Fletcher Henderson's band), and any serious musician who failed eventually to move there has been somewhat suspect in the eyes of both fellow musicians and the more influential critics. Moreover, Land just as steadfastly refused to involve himself in the Hollywood studio scene, which would have at least paid him handsomely. 'I never had any urge, despite the financial rewards, to be programmed to play anything and everything on any day at any hour,' he once told Leonard Feather.[5] Instead, Land devoted his energies totally to his music, and without fanfare slowly established himself as a major soloist. How well he succeeded will become apparent when we examine a series of albums he recorded around the turn of the decade.

9.

art pepper

When I first met Art he was the greatest saxophone player that I had heard. Far above anybody else. I couldn't believe how beautifully he played. And at that time there was the battle going on: a lot of writers were writing about East Coast jazz and West Coast jazz. Art to me was the *sound* of West Coast jazz, that melodic style he played, rather than the hard-driving New York style that a lot of players were playing. I just fell in love with him the first time I heard him. And then eventually we worked together.[1]

The speaker here is not some star-struck kid but Marty Paich, a highly respected musician in his own right, and his tribute pretty much sums up the way many musicians felt about alto saxophonist Art Pepper. Many of the white musicians mentioned in this book were (and are) primarily studio musicians, who also played jazz; Art Pepper was first and always a jazz musician, as serious about his art as the most dedicated black musicians. He had his problems: he was a heroin addict most of his adult life and spent many of what could have been his most productive years in various jails and prisons, as he makes clear in his powerful and painfully honest autobiography *Straight Life*. Nevertheless, he managed to make a series of albums that offered some of the finest jazz to be recorded in the 1950s.

Art Pepper was born 1 September 1925 in Gardena, a southern suburb of Los Angeles, and although he moved often during his childhood, it was always within the southern California area. He started on clarinet at the age of nine and took up alto sax at thirteen, playing in the school bands at Fremont and San Pedro high schools. His first professional job was with the Gus Arnheim band, and while still in his teens he was hired by Lee Young for the house band at the Club Alabam on Central Avenue. A short time later he joined Benny Carter's big band.

When I went with Benny Carter I played all my jazz by ear. I was good at reading, but I didn't know about chord structure, harmony, composition. Also, I had never played much lead alto, so with Benny I played second alto ... and sometimes, if there wasn't a large audience, Benny would just get off the stand and let me play his parts. I'd get all his solos. I learned that way how to play lead in a four-man saxophone section. And I learned a lot following Benny, listening to his solos, what he played against the background. The guys in the band were all great musicians – Gerald Wilson, Freddie Webster, a legendary trumpet player, and J.J. Johnson, a jazz superstar. We played all over LA. We did well. I was making fifty dollars a week, which was big money in those days.[2]

This was during the war years, and the personnel in all of the big bands turned over rapidly as musicians were drafted. When Art heard about an opening in the Stan Kenton band, he auditioned and landed the job. The year was 1943 and he was seventeen years old.

Shortly thereafter Pepper was himself drafted and spent several years in the army, mostly in England. When he was discharged in 1946, Art moved back to LA and began freelancing, but soon he was called again by Stan Kenton. From 1946 to 1951 Art was a mainstay of the Kenton band. During this period he began friendships with Shorty Rogers, Shelly Manne and others who would form the nucleus of the West Coast school of the 1950s; he also acquired the narcotics habit that would plague him the rest of his life. The seminal recordings that Art made in the opening years of the decade – 'Art Pepper' with the Kenton orchestra and 'Over the Rainbow' with Shorty Rogers – have already been mentioned. When Art Pepper left Kenton at the end of 1951 he had already established his credentials as a major jazzman.

For the next year or so Art freelanced around LA. He formed a quartet composed of himself, Hampton Hawes, bassist Joe Mondragon and drummer Larry Bunker. The band landed a steady gig at the Surf Club, a bar in downtown LA, and began to attract a following. On 4 March 1952, the quartet recorded four numbers for the Discovery label; these were the first records to be issued under Art's name. All four of the tunes are simple launching-pads for the soloists. 'Brown Gold' is based on 'I Got Rhythm' changes; both the up-tempo 'Surf Ride' and the medium 'Holiday Flight' are B flat blues. 'These Foolish Things' is Art's ballad vehicle. In October Art recorded four more tunes for Discovery using a different rhythm section: pianist Russ Freeman, bassist Bob Whitlock and drummer Bobby White. The mix of tunes remained much the same, however. 'Chili Pepper' and 'Suzy the Poodle' are Art's originals, Lester Young's 'Tickle Toe' gets an exciting up-tempo run-down, and 'Everything Happens to Me' serves as the requisite ballad.

During this same period Art often joined the Lighthouse All-Stars for the marathon Sunday sessions; he also appeared as a sideman on the Shorty Rogers *Giants* and *Cool and Crazy* recordings, as well as the first Shelly Manne Contemporary recordings. But in 1953 he was busted for the first time and thereafter spent an increasing amount of time in various lock-ups. In August, 1954 – temporarily at liberty – he recorded a final time for Discovery, this time with a quintet. Tenor saxophonist Jack Montrose was the other horn, and the rhythm section was composed of pianist Claude Williamson, bassist Monty Budwig and drummer Larry Bunker. Eight tunes were recorded, enough for a ten-inch LP. Several of the tunes were named after various spices: 'Nutmeg', 'Cinnamon', 'Thyme Time', 'Art's Oregano'. This adds a nice homey touch to the album, unless you are aware that nutmeg can be used to achieve a cheap 'high' in the absence of any more potent, but illegal, drugs. The high point of the album is the performance of 'Straight Life' (ironic title!), an extremely rapid flag-waver of Art's based on 'After You've Gone'. A few months after this session, however, Art once again fell foul of the law, and was off the scene until 1956.

The years 1956 to 1960 saw Art Pepper both at the apex of his profession and at the nadir of his personal life. His description of these years in the autobiography *Straight Life* makes painful reading. Most of his recording sessions from these years – the ones which produced such beautiful and lasting performances – are mentioned only in passing, as backdrops to his constant obsession with drugs. Nevertheless he did manage somehow to record prolifically during this period, so much so that we'll be able to examine only the highlights of his recording activity.

Pepper's first session following his release, as sideman on the Shorty Rogers big-band date that produced 'Blues Express', has already been mentioned. Later the same month, on 26 July 1956, he recorded for the first time for the Pacific Jazz label. The group was a collaborative affair – the Chet Baker–Art Pepper Sextet – with tenor saxophonist Richie Kamuca and a driving rhythm section composed of Pete Jolly, Leroy Vinnegar and Stan Levey. Johnny Mandel shared arranging credits with Art. Unfortunately, given all the talent that appeared on the session, the results are something of a let-down. The basic problem is that the arrangements tend to overshadow the soloists. Art Pepper's arrangements of his own tunes 'Tynan Time' (for John Tynan, West Coast editor for *Down Beat*) and 'Minor Yours' both feature contrapuntal arrangements, and Johnny Mandel's scoring on 'Sonny Boy' and 'Little Girl' hews very closely to the 'West Coast sound'. By far the best sextet performance comes on a basic blues, 'The Route', which is obviously a head arrangement. 'The Route' opens with a walking chorus by Leroy and Stan, adds Pete Jolly's piano for another couple of choruses, and then the horns solo in turn, with Jolly laying out for the first chorus or two in each case. Freed from the constraints of written scores, all of the soloists dig deeply into the blues. It is the date's one fully satisfying performance.

Three additional tunes were cut by Art Pepper with rhythm accompaniment. 'Old Croix' (marvellous pun) is a ride through the 'Cherokee' changes by the quartet at an easy lope. On the two remaining numbers, Art dispenses with the piano as well. His performances on 'I Can't Give You Anything but Love' and 'The Great Lie', backed solely by bass and drums, are fascinating. Art Pepper had always been a strongly rhythmic player, but here – with only the most basic support – he probes deeply into the subtleties of jazz rhythms. At times he overreaches and finds himself cornered, but he simply backs away and tries a new approach. In his own way, Art was exploring the area that Sonny Rollins would be working on the following year in *Way Out West*. The unorthodox use of space and subdivided rhythms that Art was tentatively exploring here would add greatly to the strength of his playing in the years to follow.

The results of the session must have been disappointing to Dick Bock; only a few of the titles were issued, and those – often sharply edited – on various anthologies. This couldn't have bothered Pepper, however, for he was much in demand and spent the next half year in a hectic round of recording activity. On 6 August he recorded under his own name for the Jazz West label. This session was a much looser affair and Art seems much more comfortable. His sidemen for the date were Jack Sheldon on trumpet and the rhythm section of Russ Freeman, Leroy Vinnegar and Shelly Manne. Since this was Shelly's working rhythm section, the three were very tight. This was Jack Sheldon's first recording with Pepper and the two proved very compatible; they would collaborate often in the years ahead.

The Jazz West date was a blowing session, pure and simple, and everybody was cooking. Several of the tunes were Art's originals, but his method of composition fell right in with the jam-session atmosphere of this and similar recordings of the time:

> I'd just wait until the night before the date, and then sit down and write however many tunes were needed. I didn't have a piano, and I wasn't writing on the alto, so I'd just compose them in my head and write them down. They were very loose, just arrangements to play from ... but some of them were pretty good, I think. I liked 'Straight Life', of course. And 'Pepper Returns' and 'Angel Wings' both have two-part counterpoint lines for Jack Sheldon and me that came off very well. And 'Patricia', which I wrote for my daughter, is a good tune. And 'Mambo de la Pinta', which I wrote for guys in different jails I'd been in – 'la pinta' is 'the joint'.[3]

With the exception of 'Straight Life', all of the tunes mentioned above are on the Jazz West album. 'Pepper Returns' is a very rapid trip through 'Lover Come Back to Me' changes, and the counterpoint between Pepper and Sheldon sounds more like that of Bird and Miles Davis on records like 'Chasin' the Bird' and 'Ah-Leu-Cha' than the studied contrapuntal lines of the West Coast school. Much the same goes for 'Angel Wings', an 'I Got Rhythm' clone. Three of the album's tunes are blues: 'Five More', 'Funny Blues' and 'Walkin' Out Blues'. 'Funny Blues' does indeed prod Pepper, Sheldon and Freeman into quirky solos (Sheldon gets off a double-time cavalry charge), while 'Walkin' Out', as the name implies, begins and ends with Pepper supported solely by Leroy Vinnegar's muscular bass. On the album's two ballads, 'Patricia' and 'You Go to My Head', Sheldon lays out to provide Art more solo room. Art's work here proves once again that he is one of the premier ballad interpreters in jazz.

We can skip lightly over Art Pepper's next few recording sessions. In August 1956 there were two quartet dates for the Tampa label, the first with Russ Freeman, Ben Tucker and Gary Frommer, the second with Marty Paich, Buddy Clark and Frank Capp. Both have their moments; neither adds significantly to Art's accomplishments. In September he played lead alto (and had a couple of solos) in a big band backing Hoagy Carmichael for a Pacific Jazz date. The following month he took part in a Chet Baker big-band date for the same label. And on 31 October there was another sextet session with Chet Baker, also for Pacific Jazz.

The sextet this time consisted of Chet, Art, Phil Urso, Carl Perkins, Curtis Counce and Lawrence Marable, and the guest arranger for this date was Jimmy Heath. Jimmy contributed charts on five of his own tunes, 'Picture of Heath', 'For Miles and Miles', 'CTA', 'For Minors Only', and 'Resonant Emotions'. Art brought back his arrangement of 'Tynan Time' and 'Minor Yours'. The Heath arrangements are spare and straightforward, excellent launching-pads for soloists, and the musicians play with a fire that seems missing in the earlier sextet date. Chet Baker in particular seems liberated by the circumstances and responds with some driving, extroverted solos. (Less than a week later he would play with similar heat on the Russ Freeman–Chet Baker Quartet session.) Phil Urso, like Richie Kamuca, favours the Four Brothers tenor sound, but he is closer to the extrovert Al Cohn–Zoot Sims end of the spectrum. It is instructive to compare the performances on the two Art Pepper charts; 'Tynan Time' is taken at a slightly faster tempo the second time around, but both it and 'Minor Yours' are played with more verve at the second session. The rhythm section had much to do with the flavour of the October date, of course. Lawrence Marable is especially impressive in trading eights with the horns on both 'Picture of Heath' and 'CTA', and Carl Perkins plays with his usual joy and swing. In any case, there was no doubt in Richard Bock's mind; the seven tunes were almost immediately released on a Pacific Jazz LP.

Interestingly enough, Art Pepper's next Pacific Jazz session returned to a conservative West Coast format. This date was under the leadership of Bill Perkins and only four tunes were recorded – half an LP's worth. The album's remaining performances came from a session featuring Bill Perkins and Richie Kamuca. Perkins and Kamuca were both in the direct lineage of the Lester Young–Four Brothers tenor-sax style (both were in fact alumni of the Woody Herman band), and their work on this album *(Just Friends)* is intriguingly similar, with just enough subtle differences to keep interest from flagging. Backed by the swinging and tight-knit rhythm section of Hampton Hawes, Red Mitchell and Mel Lewis, Perkins and Kamuca breeze through performances of 'Just Friends', 'All of Me' and 'Limehouse Blues'. On two numbers, 'Sweet and Lovely' and 'Solid DeSylva', Perkins switches to bass clarinet, which he plays with a lovely dark-burnished sound. The bass clarinet is particularly effective on 'Solid DeSylva', a blues line honouring disc jockey Walt DeSylva of radio station KBIG. All of the arrangements, as well as the original blues, were written by Bill Perkins.

The Perkins–Art Pepper session, with a completely new rhythm section of Jimmy Rowles, Ben Tucker and Mel Lewis, was recorded 11 December 1956. As is so often true of Pacific Jazz recordings of the time, the arrangements are given at least as much weight as the blowing. The Bill Perkins arrangement of 'A Foggy Day' features some complex rhythmic suspensions, but the solos which follow are unexceptional. Art Pepper's arranging is much more conservative than his playing, and his charts on two originals – 'Diane-A-Flow' and 'Zenobia' – as well as an arrangement of 'What is this Thing Called Love', are all pretty much in the West Coast bag. The high point of the date comes with his solo on 'What is this Thing Called Love', which pumps some needed emotion into an otherwise staid session.

Shortly after the Bill Perkins session Art Pepper recorded for the Intro label, both with a quartet (Pepper, Russ Freeman, Ben Tucker, Chuck Flores) and a quintet (Pepper, Red Norvo, pianist Gerald Wiggins, Ben Tucker and drummer Joe Morello). As had been the case with the earlier Tampa recordings, the blowing was – for the most part – competent but unexceptional. Russ Freeman contributes some typically hard-driving piano work to the quartet sessions, but the most interesting tracks from the quartet dates are two duets featuring Art and bassist Ben Tucker, 'Blues In' and 'Blues Out'. Similarly, the most fascinating track on the quintet session comes when Art switches to tenor sax on a cut entitled 'Tenor Blooz'. Red Norvo's vibes add much to the proceedings on this date, although he does lay out during a searing run-down of 'Straight Life'.

Less than a week after the final Intro session, Art recorded for Contemporary, in what was to be the first of many great albums for that label. These Contemporary albums mark the apogee of Art's playing in the fifties, and it is all the greater wonder that they were recorded during a time when Art's personal life was floundering ever deeper into a self-imposed abyss. As a matter of fact, Art's first recording for Contemporary came as a complete surprise to the altoist himself, according to a possibly romanticized account in his autobiography. By January 1957 Art Pepper was once more deeply ensnared by narcotics and was letting his musical life slide. Art's second wife, Diane, got together with Les Koenig to arrange for a recording session, the two figuring that Art's pride as a musician would force him to make the date. The Miles Davis Quintet was in town and Koenig made arrangements to borrow the trumpeter's rhythm section, one of the most powerful and respected in jazz: Red Garland, piano; Paul Chambers, bass; and Philly Joe Jones, drums. Art says that Diane sprung the news on him the morning of the session; he was completely unprepared, his horn was messed up, and he was in awe of the musicians he would be playing with. After struggling to get his horn in shape (the cork which held the mouthpiece had come loose) he drove to the recording studios, where he met a sheepish Les Koenig.

So here he is at the door, and I walk in, and I'm afraid to meet these guys because they've been playing with Miles and they're at the pinnacle of success in the jazz world. They're masters, practising masters. But here I am and here they are, and I have to act like everything's cool – 'Hi' and 'What's doin'?' 'Hi, Red, what's going on?'

When the amenities are over and Les gets everything set up, the balance on the horn and all the microphones, then it's time to start making the album. Red Garland is looking at me, and my mind is a total blank. That's always been one of my faults – memory. I have a poor memory, and I can't think of anything to play. Red says, 'Well, I know a nice tune. Do you know this?' He starts playing a tune I've heard before. I say, 'What's the name of it?' He says, '"You'd be So Nice to Come Home to".' 'What key?' 'D Minor.'

It came out beautiful. My sound was great. The rhythm was

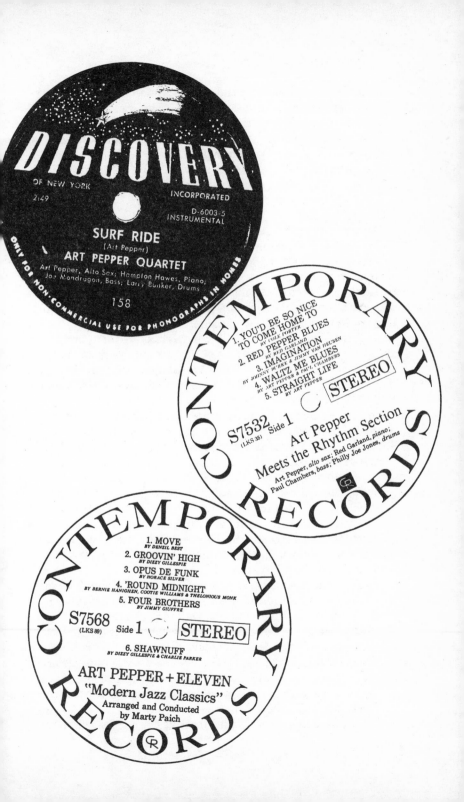

great. And I remember in the reviews, by people like Leonard Feather, Martin Williams, they said, 'The way Art plays the melody is wonderful. He's so creative. He makes it sound even better than the actual tune.' Well, what I'm doing, I don't *know* the melody so I'm playing as close to it as I can get, and that's the creativity part. It does sound good because I play it with a jazz feeling, and it's like a jazz solo, but I'm really trying to play what I recollect of the song.[4]

Whatever the difficulties surrounding the session, the resulting album, *Art Pepper Meets the Rhythm Section*, sounds warm and relaxed. 'You'd be So Nice to Come Home to', taken at a relaxed pace, is indeed a classic performance, as is that on the ballad 'Imagination'. 'Star Eyes' had been a favourite vehicle for jazz musicians since Charlie Parker had cut a classic version of the number earlier in the decade. There are also three jazz standards, 'Tin Tin Deo', 'Birk's Works' and a somewhat surprising pick, 'Jazz Me Blues'. Two tunes were obviously improvised on the spot, 'Waltz Me Blues' (attributed to Art Pepper and Paul Chambers) and Red Garland's 'Red Pepper Blues'. Art, always at home in the blues, is especially impressive in the latter number. Finally there is a smoking rendition of 'Straight Life', where an explosively propulsive Philly Joe Jones boots Art into a superlative performance.

Art Pepper Meets the Rhythm Section is a completely satisfying album, the first where Art lived fully up to his artistic promise. Certainly the support of this rhythm section, 'practising masters' as Art calls them, is central to this achievement. John Koenig, the present head of Contemporary records, remembers the part Les Koenig played in the gestation of the album and in trying to steady Art Pepper's career during this period.

My father always told me Art was the best alto player in town. He responded to Art early ... He thought Art wasn't getting a chance to play with people that were up to him, which was why he wanted to make those records like *Meets the Rhythm Section* and *Gettin' Together*. But, unfortunately, Art started getting into trouble, and that effectively took him off the scene. He would come back for a brief stay and try to get something together. Les was genuinely disturbed but he couldn't prevail upon Art to stop.

I'd say the first thing Les liked about Art was that he didn't play like anybody else. He wasn't anybody's man but his own. Art was the best player around then ... There were a couple other good alto players in the country at the time: there was Cannonball, and there was Jackie McLean, Phil Woods. It's hard to think of anybody else that you could identify as a powerful individual force. And Art was *here*. Les responded to Art basically because Art was something special.[5]

With the release of *Meets the Rhythm Section*, Art Pepper won critical acclaim and should have gained the rewards that were his due as one at the forefront of his profession, but unfortunately his life was becoming increasingly schizophrenic due to his personal problems. In the recording studios he was recognized as a master, and was a welcome addition to any session. In the shrinking LA jazz-club scene, he played some of the smaller and sleazier clubs, working with available pick-up groups – usually just a rhythm section. And as the decade drew to a close, even these few jobs fell through; for a time he was reduced to selling accordions door to door to keep his head above water!

Although he was much in demand as a sideman for recording dates at the time, the only other session which featured Art as leader in 1957 came in August for Pacific Jazz. It was a reunion of sorts between Art and Shorty Rogers, with Art and a nine-piece band reworking some of the Rogers charts that had been so important to their careers earlier in the decade: 'Popo', 'Bunny', 'Powder Puff', 'Didi' and 'Diablo's Dance'. The instrumentation was that of the RCA *Giants* album, except that the French horn had been replaced by a baritone sax. The musicians were Don Fagerquist, trumpet; Stu Williamson, valve trombone; Red Callender, tuba; Pepper, Bill Holman and Bud Shank on alto, tenor and baritone saxes; and the rhythm section of Russ Freeman, Monty Budwig and Shelly Manne.

If the premise underlying this session – that is, rehashing past success – sounds less than promising, the results are more than satisfactory. The Shorty Rogers charts are still full of verve and energy, and the musicians blow with an invigorating gusto. Art's tone is fuller and he exhibits much more emotion than he had on the original recordings. The growing tendency towards asymmetrical lines in his solos is perhaps exaggerated here because the charts are so familiar, but his blowing seems much more interesting than on the earlier sides. This is especially true of his solo on 'Diablo's Dance', though it is true to some degree on each tune.

With the exception of 'Popo', the other musicians don't have much solo space; this is Art's session start to finish. This seems a shame, for some of the other musicians had been growing also. Bud Shank, whose alto work had originally been highly influenced by Art, shows signs here of what would become an increasingly original voice on baritone sax. Unfortunately, his only extended solo is on an alternate take of 'Popo', which has been unearthed only recently. This is also true of Don Fagerquist, a much underrated soloist. No doubt Fagerquist was largely ignored at the time because he laboured so often in the commercial vinyards of the Dave Pell Octet. His solo on the alternate take of 'Popo' and his fours on the version that was released showcase his fluid and imaginative trumpet work. Bill Holman and Stu Williamson solo on both versions of the tune. Russ Freeman contributes some typically swinging and thoughtful solos on 'Popo' and 'Didi', as well as some rock-solid support in the rhythm section throughout. In fact the rhythm section is especially tight, since the three men worked together nightly in Shelly Manne's regular quintet – Monty Budwig having replaced Leroy Vinnegar earlier in the year.

Unfortunately, as was so often the case in those years, the tunes recorded on the date were issued only piecemeal by Pacific Jazz, so the full impact of the session was not felt at the time. In any case, the performances failed to help Art Pepper's deteriorating situation. He appeared as a sideman on a couple of other sessions in 1957, but in 1958 he recorded only twice. The first was a quartet date of his own in January for the Aladdin label. Even here Art's bad luck held, for Aladdin folded before the records could be released. (The performances were later issued on two Omegatape albums, but the reel-to-reel tape format worked against extended sales.) This quartet date featured pianist Carl Perkins (in one of his last performances), bassist Ben Tucker and drummer Chuck Flores, and a couple of the tunes – 'Holiday Flight' and 'Surf Ride' – are reworkings of numbers he had done on his first Discovery date. Carl Perkins and Art work well together, but the session as a whole suffers from the obviously impromptu nature of the date. On his one other recording session of 1958, Art was buried in a big band led by John Graas.

Things began to pick up once more in 1959. In February Art

played on a Marty Paich session with a mid-sized group. This seems to have led directly to one of his most memorable albums, *Art Pepper Plus Eleven*. Once again, the album was Les Koenig's idea – to back Art with a big band composed of the best musicians available. Marty Paich, who had been growing continuously as an arranger, got the call to write the charts. Marty still has good feelings about the album.

> I was with Shorty Rogers at the time, and Art used to come and sit in an awful lot, and I was starting to write a lot of arrangements ... Art liked certain things I did, and that's when he asked me to [do] the *Art Pepper Plus Eleven*. We collaborated on that album ... When the word got around that we were going to do *Art Pepper Plus Eleven*, I had innumerable calls from practically everybody in town, top players, wanting to be on the session because they had the feeling that ... it was just electrifying all the time Art was around.[6]

The album is subtitled *Modern Jazz Classics*, and all of the tunes are indeed jazz standards of the forties and fifties. And, as advertised, the sidemen are all heavyweights.

The album's twelve tunes were cut at three different sessions. On the first date, 14 March 1959, the musicians were Pete Candoli and Jack Sheldon, trumpets; Dick Nash and Bob Enevoldson, trombone and valve trombone; Vince DeRosa, horn; Art Pepper and Herb Geller, altos; Bill Perkins, tenor; Med Flory, baritone sax; and Russ Freeman, Joe Mondragon and Mel Lewis, rhythm. The tunes recorded were 'Opus de Funk', 'Round Midnight', 'Walkin' Shoes' and 'Airegin'. As is so often the case, Pepper's stongest performance comes on the ballad, in this instance Thelonious Monk's haunting master-piece. Art expresses some deeply felt emotion on the tune. Horace Silver's 'Opus de Funk' and Gerry Mulligan's 'Walkin' Shoes' are both taken at loping middle tempos, although 'Opus' is slightly faster. Marty Paich's arrangements are gems of control and restraint; they boot the musicians along without unduly distracting attention from the soloists. Sonny Rollins's 'Airegin' really moves out; Art's lead alto work here shares equal honours with his solo. Jack Sheldon contributes some typically wry solos on 'Walkin' Shoes' and 'Airegin'.

The second session, held 28 March, featured four numbers

from the bebop era, 'Groovin' High', 'Shaw Nuff', 'Donna Lee' and 'Anthropology'. On this date, Al Porcino took over lead trumpet from Pete Candoli and Bud Shank replaced Herb Geller on alto. Jack Sheldon's and Art Pepper's flying unison lines on the heads of 'Shaw Nuff' and 'Donna Lee' recall the original impressive work-outs of Diz and Bird and Miles Davis and Parker, respectively. 'Groovin' High', on the other hand, is taken at a more relaxed pace than the original. The outstanding performance from this second session, though, is 'Anthropology', which features Art's grooving clarinet. Art has never been given his due as one of the finest modern jazz clarinettists, possibly because he recorded on the instrument so infrequently, but he shows here in three skilfully constructed and swinging choruses that he is a master of the often neglected horn.

The final session, held on 12 May, featured Art's tenor sax. The tunes were 'Bernie's Tune', 'Four Brothers', 'Move' and 'Walkin''. Art does play alto on 'Bernie's Tune', but switches to the bigger horn for the other numbers. For this Charlie Kennedy replaced Bud Shank and Richie Kamuca replaced Bill Perkins. 'Four Brothers' hews closely to the traditional Jimmy Giuffre arrangement, with Art on lead tenor. (Bob Enevoldson and Charlie Kennedy switch to tenor to achieve the requisite sound.) The Denzil Best classic 'Move' does indeed move out, with solos by Pepper, Sheldon and Bob Enevoldson (back on valve-trombone). Richard Carpenter's 'Walkin'', taken at a very relaxed pace, has a fine big-toned solo by Pepper. As Nat Hentoff remarks in the album's liner notes, 'this would make an interesting *Blindfold Test* for a musician who claimed to be able to identify an "East Coast" from a "West Coast" player'.[7]

With the release of *Art Pepper Plus Eleven*, Art's fortunes improved. He was once again much in demand for record dates and landed a steady gig with the Lighthouse All-Stars. For a while, he even managed to stay clear of narcotics. He recorded with Marty Paich, backing singers as disparate as Joanie Sommers and Jesse Belvin. In November he recorded at MGM for the soundtrack of the movie *The Subterraneans,* both in a jazz combo (with Art Farmer, Gerry Mulligan and others) and as soloist backed by a large string orchestra. And in February 1960 he cut his second album for Contemporary with a Miles Davis rhythm section.

By this time the personnel in the Miles Davis band had changed: Wynton Kelly had replaced Red Garland as pianist and

Jimmy Cobb had taken over the drum chair. Bassist Paul Chambers still anchored the section, however. Art's co-worker in the Lighthouse band, Conte Candoli, was brought along as an added starter, although he plays on only three tunes. Two of these were arrangements Art and Conte had been playing nightly at the Lighthouse, Thelonious Monk's 'Rhythm-a-ning' and Art's 'Bijou the Poodle'. 'Rhythm-a-ning' blasts out of the starting-gate and never lets up. Art had by now perfected his own version of thematic improvisation; he states a motif, then explores its various permutations, siblings and offspring. It's a technique that Thelonious himself favoured (although Monk was reportedly not pleased by the pick-up note that had been added to his melody). For that matter, 'Bijou the Poodle' has a very Monkish-sounding line and contains some unconventional chord changes. On 'Bijou', Art switches to tenor sax. The third tune on which Conte Candoli plays is 'Whims of Chambers', a blues written by the bassist.

The remaining tunes from the session were all done as a quartet. 'Softly, as in a Morning Sunrise' is a happy choice; Art's interpretation seems especially congenial to this rhythm section. Wynton Kelly's solo is fluid and swinging, as always, and Paul Chambers gets off one of his patented arco solos. There are two ballad performances. 'Why are We Afraid' is an André Previn tune from the score of *The Subterraneans,* and Wynton Kelly provides an especially sensitive accompaniment to Art's plaintive solo. 'Diane' is Art's own tune, and he demonstrates an ability to project emotion without sentimentality in both his writing and his playing on this number. The album's final tune, 'Gettin' Together', has Art once again switching to tenor sax for an extended examination of the blues.

Gettin' Together was as well received as the earlier *Meets the Rhythm Section,* and Art Pepper was once again at the very door of success. And once again, some perverse demon in Art's personality turned him deliberately away. He returned to drugs, missed a couple of recording sessions, lost his job at the Lighthouse, and was back on the streets. His frank descriptions of this period in his autobiography are at first fascinating, then terrifying, and finally sickening. With little money coming in from recording (Les Koenig or Marty Paich would call him as a sideman when they could) and none at all from club dates, he was reduced to burglarizing to support his habit. He was simply awaiting the inevitable bust, and as a three-time loser, he knew that meant many years in prison. And yet somehow, right in the middle of this nightmare, he was able to record what is probably his best album of the entire decade.

The album is *Smack Up!*, and it was recorded 24 and 25 October 1960. Once again Les Koenig had come through and set up a date with musicians who matched Art's standards. The rhythm section was one of the strongest available in LA at the time: pianist Pete Jolly, bassist Jimmy Bond and drummer Frank Butler. Joining Art in the front line was Jack Sheldon, whose trumpet work was so compatible with the altoist's. The album's six tunes were all compositions by saxophonists, and all (with the exception of an original Art introduced at the session) had been recorded for Contemporary by the composers. The title tune was perhaps a bit too apt – 'smack up' being a slang expression for shooting heroin. The tune had originally been recorded by Harold Land on his *Grooveyard* album; Art's version is faster and hence more boppish in feeling. Art's own tune, 'Las Cuevas de Mario', is next. The title refers to the family of Mario Cuevas, friends of Art's from East LA. The tune is a 5/4 blues with a recurring vamp. (It must be remembered that in 1960 even a piece in 3/4 time was a rare addition to a jazz musician's repertoire.) The players are totally comfortable in the unaccustomed setting and swing as if it were the most natural thing in the world. (Which of course it should be.) Buddy Collette's 'A Bit of Basie', a more conventional blues, is taken at a bright tempo, sparked by the propulsive drumming of Frank Butler. A tune written by Art's old boss is next: Benny Carter's 'How Can You Lose'. The minor-to-major theme elicits some funky blowing by all hands. 'Maybe Next Year', a strikingly original composition by Duane Tatro, serves as the album's ballad. The chord sequence is quite unorthodox, and Art later admitted having some difficulties with it to Leonard Feather. 'It's really a strange tune. It wasn't easy to play. But the more you hear it, the more logical and inevitable the chord structure sounds.'[8] Despite the initial reservations, Art turns out a beautiful and very natural-sounding solo; it seems strange this tune hasn't found its way into more musicians' repertoires.

The final tune on the album is another blues, but this one is also quite unorthodox. The tune is 'Tears Inside', and the composer is Ornette Coleman, whom Les Koenig had recorded earlier. Art Pepper was always a superior blues player, and Ornette's tune somehow sparks Art into one of his finest recorded performances. Pete Jolly quite suitably lays out on the head, and his entrance – halfway through Jack Sheldon's solo – is all the more welcome because it releases tension built by the delay. Jolly's solo, which comes next, has an infectious swing (backed by Frank Butler's potent brush work) and serves as an admirable launching-pad for Art. Art begins casually enough (wryly including a quote from 'Silver Threads among the Gold') but then turns serious. He begins working on seemingly random phrases, probing and then discarding them one by one. It's as if the solo mirrors his tortured search for a meaning in life. The solo builds in intensity to an almost unbearable level; even the most casual listener must finally be moved by the stark emotions revealed in Art Pepper's solo on 'Tears Inside'.

Given Art's intuitive feel for the dramatic, it must have seemed almost fitting that the denouement he had building towards throughout the decade came hard on the heels of one of his finest recording efforts. The very next day he was arrested for narcotics possession for the third and final time. He was held in the LA County jail while awaiting trial and Les Koenig and a few of his friends made his bail. Les also hastily arranged for a final album so Art could cover some court costs. It was a simple affair: Art and a rhythm section playing a set of standards. Jimmy Bond and Frank Butler, who contributed so heavily to the success of the *Smack Up!* album returned for this one also. The only newcomer was pianist Dolo Coker. Coker was born in Philadelphia, 16 November 1927. He had originally wanted to be a doctor, but later found the piano to be his true calling. Dolo had been playing professionally since the late forties, and had made jazz time (and paid some R & B dues) with musicians as diverse as Ben Webster, Erskine Hawkins, Clyde McPhatter, Ruth Brown, Sonny Rollins and Kenny Dorham. He had also worked with Dexter Gordon in the LA stage production of Jack Gelber's *The Connection*.

The setting for the recording – Art backed only by a rhythm section, playing seven well-known standards – whether by design or no, placed Art's powers as an improviser in stark relief. There was no place to hide. And, as he usually did in such instances, Art more than met the challenge. The first side of the album especially shows the range of emotions that can be wrung from four basically similar tunes. Art charges out on 'I Can't Believe that You're in Love with Me' accompanied only by Jimmy Bond's powerful bass, then the rest of the rhythm section joins in

and backs the altoist on a deeply felt yet swinging flight. Cole
Porter's 'I Love You' starts out in a relaxed two, then breaks into
four for thoughtful solos by Art and Dolo Coker. 'Come Rain or
Come Shine' is the only tune played strictly as a ballad. 'Long
Ago and Far Away', on the other hand, is taken at a blistering
pace that finds Art completely at ease yet furiously swinging.

There is less variety on the album's second side. The three
tunes, 'Gone with the Wind', 'I Wished on the Moon' and 'Too
Close for Comfort', are all taken at a relaxed middle tempo, and
although Art's inspiration never fails, the similarity of the
approach causes the listener's interest to flag. Nevertheless, the
album's title, *Intensity*, is quite apt; Art Pepper plays throughout with an intensity of emotions that can be palpably felt. If
Intensity feels somewhat anti-climatic after *Smack Up!*, it is none
the less a major statement by a major artist.

Unfortunately, by the time the two albums were released –
Smack Up! in 1961 and *Intensity* in 1963 – Art was serving time
in San Quentin. When he was finally released in 1966, his career
and life were in a shambles and a new revolution in jazz had
passed him by. But his was, finally, a happy ending. With the
help of the Synanon programme and, more importantly, his
fourth wife Laurie, Art was eventually able to straighten out his
life. Beginning in 1975 he recorded a series of critically acclaimed
albums that returned him to the front ranks of jazz soloists. (The
first of these albums was, naturally enough, a recording for Les
Koenig entitled *Living Legend*.) In Art's final years – he died in
1982 – he was secure in the knowledge that his stature as a major
jazz voice was recognized throughout the world.

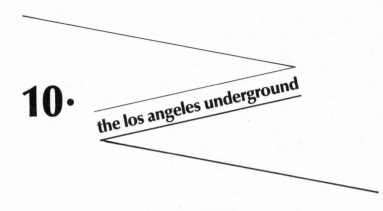

10·
the los angeles underground

In the autumn of 1959, the jazz world was set on its ear by a new group which appeared in New York's famed Five Spot bar. The Ornette Coleman Quartet – Don Cherry, trumpet; Coleman, alto sax; Charlie Haden, bass; Billy Higgins, drums – had launched a revolution as sweeping as that of Dizzy Gillespie, Charlie Parker and the beboppers a decade earlier. But whereas bop had been incubated in New York's Harlem itself, in clubs like Minton's Playhouse, the new jazz of Ornette and company had first been formulated in Los Angeles.

It would hardly be fair, of course, to credit Los Angeles as the birthplace of free jazz. In the first place, pianist Cecil Taylor and other New Yorkers had been stretching the boundaries of modern jazz to the breaking-point since the mid-fifties. More importantly, the Los Angeles musicians and jazz audience gave Ornette and his fellows little nurture during their stay in the west; Ornette's small circle formed, in effect, an underground within an underground. Nevertheless, many important steps leading to the jazz revolution of the 1960s took place on the Coast during the fifties. In fact some of the roots of that revolution may be traced back to the years before Ornette's arrival on the Los Angeles scene.

Some time in 1946, on one of many similar casual gigs, Charles Mingus played for a dance. The alto saxophonist that evening was a youngster from Dorsey High School on his first paying job, Eric Dolphy. In later years, of course, Eric would figure prominently in some of Mingus's finest groups, but this early meeting apparently left little impression on either musician.

Nevertheless, the two had much in common. Both were extremely dedicated musicians with insatiable appetites for practising, and both remained steadfastly opposed to the status quo in music throughout their careers.

Eric Dolphy was born in Los Angeles on 20 June 1928. He was an only child and was brought up in a loving, middle-class home. Eric demonstrated a love for music at an early age and began playing clarinet in grammar school; by the time he was a student at Foshay Junior High he was playing in the Los Angeles City School Orchestra. His parents, recognizing Eric's dedication, had a studio built in the back yard so that he could practise undisturbed; the room would later serve as a favourite jamming spot for like-minded musicians. He was also one of the many distinguished musicians who studied with Lloyd Reese.

After graduating from Dorsey High, Eric attended Los Angeles City College as a music major. One of his section-mates in the LACC band was altoist Vi Redd, who had also played alongside Eric throughout grammar and high school. Vi would later remember Eric not only as an extremely dedicated and hard-working musician, but also as a thoughtful and considerate friend. As an example, she recalls the time she ran into trouble during a gig. ' ... I was playing a job in El Monte [a suburb of LA] and I broke my own mouthpiece while taking my horn out of the case. I hurriedly called Eric and he came all the way out from town to bring me one I could use.'[1] Everyone agrees that the incident was typical of the man.

During this same period Eric joined the Roy Porter big band, a legendary proving-ground for budding jazz musicians. Among the youthful musicians who spent time in the band during its short life (1948 to 1950) were Art and Addison Farmer, Chet Baker, Jimmy Knepper, Joe Maini, Herb Geller, Teddy Edwards, Hadley Caliman, Bob Gordon and Russ Freeman. Eric, who played lead alto during his tenure, cut his first records with the band. Although most of the sides were not issued at the time, eight numbers recorded by Savoy in 1949 have been unearthed and issued on the anthology *Black California*.

The tunes were recorded at two sessions early in 1949, just after the recording ban was lifted. (It's possible the earlier session – listed in Savoy's archives as being held in January – actually took place in late 1948, when the ban was still in effect.) The cuts are fascinating for the glimpse they afford into the early work of future jazz stars. Art Farmer takes all of the trumpet solos (his twin brother Addison is the bassist on the second session) and Jimmy Knepper handles the trombone solos. Most interesting of all, of course, are Eric Dolphy's alto solos.

There has been some disagreement over which solos may be attributed to Dolphy. Everyone connected with the band remembers that the bulk of the jazz alto solos were assigned to the second altoist, Leroy 'Sweetpea' Robinson. Roy Porter himself, according to Dolphy's biographer Vladimir Simosko, has stated that Eric was featured on only one piece (not recorded by Savoy), 'Moods at Dusk'. However, the eight Savoy titles – issued since the publication of the biography – belie that claim. To begin with, there is a chase sequence featuring both altoists on the tune 'Sippin' with Cisco'. The chase reveals two good but not quite mature soloists; both are heavily influenced by Charlie Parker (naturally), but one is a bit more adventurous. Moreover, the adventurous youngster exhibits certain stylistic traits that were typical of the mature Eric Dolphy's work. It is of course possible that Dolphy was the more conservative soloist on the Savoys, and that he would later incorporate portions of Leroy Robinson's style into his own work, but it's certainly much easier to assume that the altoist who sounds like Eric Dolphy *was* Eric.

Only two of the titles recorded by Savoy were released at the time, and it is easy to understand why when one listens to the entire set. The youthful crew is brash and exuberant, full of fire and spirit, but the ensembles are frequently sloppy and the intonation terrible. The trombones are painfully out of tune on 'Pete's Beat', and every performance has moments when the listener winces at the pitch. The vocals by Paul Sparks on 'This is You' and 'Love is Laughing at Me' are undistinguished and the lyrics trite. Still, the band is exciting and some of the solos are well worth hearing. Art Farmer shows promise of things to come in his solos on 'Pete's Beat', 'Sippin' with Cisco' and 'Howard's Idea', and Jimmy Knepper has a very exciting half chorus on 'Little Wig'. Clifford Solomon and Joe Howard engage in a tenor-sax chase on 'Sippin'', and one of the men – probably Solomon – contributes journeyman solos on 'Pete's Beat', 'Howard's Idea' and 'Little Wig'. The best solo by far is that of Eric Dolphy on 'Gassin' the Wig', one of the two tunes originally issued. The restless lines and wide-interval leaps that would become hallmarks of Dolphy's mature style are already very evident. The alto solo on 'Little Wig', the other original release, is briefer and more conservative; the liner notes to *Black*

California credit this one to Eric also, but it may well have been Leroy Robinson's. Robinson's solos on 'Pete's Beat', 'Phantom Moon' and 'Love is Laughing at Me' are very Parkeresque, and it is easy to understand that he would have been the favoured alto soloist in 1949.

At the time, most listeners probably would have agreed with the assessment of Dolphy's playing given many years after by the band's leader and drummer, Roy Porter. Porter was asked by an interviewer if he had any idea of Eric's future potential. His answer:

> Well, frankly speaking, no. But don't get me wrong. Everybody were youngsters – a lot of them had just come out of high school. Eric was studying music at LA City College. He was very young. Because he could read so well, Eric was playing first alto, and was good, but he was really a section man at the time. The heavy solos would fall on Leroy 'Sweetpea' Robinson. Eric soloed too, but he wasn't the heavy in the band. So I had no idea he would go to New York and become a legend. I'm glad he did.[2]

But even if he wasn't considered a major soloist at the time, Eric's musical and extra-musical influence on the band was considerable. One friend has written that:

> Clifford Solomon ... probably one of the few survivors of that band, relates how giving Eric was with the other musicians. Eric was no doubt the best reader in the band and the one with the best technique, but he was never too busy to help anyone. If any musician needed help, it was Eric who patiently played the passage and explained. The band was riddled with young junkies, and wine was consumed in large quantities but Eric never participated in any of this. Yet he was respected – not considered an oddball. Usually, if you don't partake with the cats, then you're almost an outcast. But somehow Eric gained respect even though he had no habit of any kind.[3]

A second recording session for Knockout records is known to have been held shortly following the Savoy sessions, but the records were distributed only locally and none is available today. The personnel given for the Knockout recordings is certainly intriguing, including – besides Dolphy – Joe Maini, Bob Gordon,

Jimmy Knepper and Russ Freeman. Despite all this talent, Roy Porter found it difficult to keep the band going. 'The only places we could play would be once a week gigs at the Elks, or the Avalon Ballroom downtown or maybe some club dance. The reason the band stayed together so long was pure love. On a lot of nights we wouldn't make more than $3.00 each.'[4]

From 1950 to 1953 Eric served in the army, in the company of tenor saxophonist Walter Benton, who had enlisted at the same time. He was stationed for a while at Fort Lewis, Washington (where he played with the Tacoma Symphony Orchestra) and later at the US Naval School of Music in Washington, DC. His tour completed, he returned to Los Angeles and once again launched on an intense round of practising and musical studies. Buddy Collette introduced him to Marle Young, a clarinet and woodwinds instructor, and Marle in turn introduced Eric to the bass clarinet. He also played around town with various groups led by Buddy Collette, Gerald Wilson, George Brown and Eddie Beal. And of course there were always the daily woodshedding sessions in his practice room that Harold Land has mentioned. Clifford Brown, Max Roach and Richie Powell would become frequent guests at the sessions. In 1954 Eric also met two musicians who would play important parts in his subsequent career: John Coltrane (in town with the Johnny Hodges band) and Ornette Coleman.

By 1956 Eric was leading his own quintet at the Club Oasis. The personnel included Norman Faye, trumpet; Wilfred Middlebrooks, bass; Earl Palmer, drums and Ernest Crawford or Fran Gaddison on piano. He also formed a ten-piece rehearsal band to serve as a vehicle for his arranging abilities. One of the musicians in this band was his close friend trombonist Lester Robinson. All of this preparation finally paid off in 1958 when Chico Hamilton needed a replacement for reedman Paul Horn, who had just left the quintet. Buddy Collette recommended Eric, and Eric thus achieved his first national recognition.

Eric's first recording with the quintet came in April 1958, shortly after he had joined the group. Two numbers were cut for Pacific Jazz, 'In a Sentimental Mood' and 'I'm Beginning to See the Light', but they were not to be issued until years later. Eric does have a brief (and apparently edited) alto solo on 'Beginning to See the Light', but there is little hint of his strongly individual style. In the summer of 1958 the Chico Hamilton Quintet was one of the groups filmed at the Newport Jazz Festival for the documentary *Jazz on a Summer's Day*. Eric can be seen and heard playing flute on a performance of 'Blue Sands'.

Late in the year the group – now made up of Eric, guitarist Dennis Budimir, cellist Nat Gershman, bassist Wyatt Ruther, and Chico – recorded for Warner Brothers records. There were two sessions in October, one of which found the quintet burdened with a string section, but Eric does get in a couple of nice alto solos on the quintet date on Fred Katz's 'Modes' and 'Under Paris Skies'. A third session in December produced several superior cuts and a fine representative album. The album, *Gongs East*, is by far the best recording by the Chico Hamilton Quintet from this period and the first recording adequately to display Eric's developing style.

There are, to be sure, some rather ornate arrangements in a typically Hamiltonian style. 'I Gave My Love a Cherry' and 'Long Ago and Far Away', both arranged by Hale Smith, allow no room for blowing whatever; Eric plays rather legit flute and clarinet on the two tunes. By contrast, two arrangements by Fred Katz – the quintet's former cellist – allow plenty of blowing room. Eric's flute solo on 'Beyond the Blue Horizon' is far from conservative, and his alto work on the ballad 'Nature, by Emerson' is impressive. Two of the album's numbers are originals by Eric's friend and former employer, Gerald Wilson: 'Where I Live' is a mood piece with a somewhat melancholy air, while 'Tuesday at Two' is a straight-ahead swinger. And although the title of Nat Pierce's 'Far East' suggests another mood piece, it is really a Latin number, while 'Gongs East' – although introduced by a gong – turns out to be an excursion through the blues. Of the two remaining tunes, 'Good Grief, Dennis' is an up-tempo feature for Dennis Budimir's fleet guitar, and Billy Strayhorn's 'Passion Flower' spotlights Eric's alto.

When Eric later emerged as one of the leaders of the new jazz of the 1960s, it was customary to suggest that the saxophonist's individualism was somehow stifled during his tenure with Chico Hamilton. To the contrary, Eric fitted in well with the quintet's disciplined approach. His solos, while conservative compared to his later recordings, suggest more that his style was not yet fully formed than that he was being held back in any way. Eric's alto solos on 'Tuesday at Two' and the ballad 'Nature, by Emerson', and particularly his bass clarinet work on 'Gongs East' are completely untrammelled. All feature imaginative lines and the sort of vocal 'cry' that Eric would employ so successfully later on.

At the same time, Eric could also effectively show his awareness of the jazz tradition in his tribute to Johnny Hodges on 'Passion Flower'.

There was one more album for Warner Brothers, but unfortunately only three of the cuts were by the quintet. One of these, 'Miss Movement', was the first composition of Dolphy's to be recorded, and Eric responded with a smoking alto solo. On the ballad 'More than You Know' Eric once again acknowledges his debt to Johnny Hodges on the head, but the solo is pure Dolphy. Eric also has a fine alto solo on Kenny Dorham's 'Newport News'. The remaining tracks on the album feature either unaccompanied drum solos by Chico or vocals by the drummer. On the vocals Chico is backed by an expanded group which includes his former reedmen Paul Horn and Buddy Collette. None of the vocals or drum solos is particularly memorable.

The quintet spent most of the following year on the road, travelling as far as New York. There were some recordings for the Sesac label, but most of these seem to be extensively edited; none of the soloists is given much room to stretch out. While playing Birdland in New York the group alternated sets with the Miles Davis Sextet, and Eric was able to renew his acquaintance with John Coltrane, by now one of the leading tenor saxophonists in jazz. When the quintet did play Los Angeles, its popularity assured there would be standing-room-only crowds. By the end of the year, however, Eric felt he had gained enough experience with Chico and was ready to strike out on his own. He moved to New York where, in December of 1959, he joined the group of another former Angeleno, Charles Mingus, at the Showplace in Greenwich Village. From then until his tragically early death in 1964 while on a European tour, Eric would play and record often with Mingus. He also would appear on seminal recordings with Ornette Coleman and John Coltrane. At the time of his death, Eric would be recognized as one of the leading voices in jazz.

In the early 1960s, as jazz turned a new corner, four men – Ornette Coleman, Cecil Taylor, John Coltrane and Eric Dolphy – were acknowledged as leaders of the New Jazz. Of the four, Ornette Coleman gained the most notoriety. In part, this was a result of his sudden dramatic appearance on the national jazz scene late in 1959. The others were well-known quantities to the jazz audiences by 1959. John Coltrane was the best-known; he had played with Dizzy Gillespie's big band in the late 1940s, and had been a sideman with two of the biggest names in jazz in the 1950s – Miles Davis and Thelonious Monk. Eric Dolphy, as we have seen, was well-known through his tenure in the Chico Hamilton Quintet. And Cecil Taylor, a native New Yorker, had made a name for himself as a leader of consistently avant-garde groups from the mid-fifties on.

Moreover, as these three began to push beyond the boundaries of 'accepted' jazz practices, they did so through a firm understanding of musical theory. Cecil Taylor had studied at the New York College of Music and had spent an additional four years at the New England Conservatory; John Coltrane and Eric Dolphy both had extensive formal training, and both had served apprenticeships with established jazz stars. Ornette Coleman, on the other hand, was almost exclusively self-taught. Where the other three eventually progressed beyond the strictures that they felt too binding, Ornette simply ignored any 'rules' that got in the way of his intuitive soloing. Certainly all four musicians paid a heavy price for their stubborn insistence on going their own way, but three of the four had at least been accepted initially by the jazz community during the early years of their careers. Ornette Coleman was an outcast from the start.

Ornette Coleman was born in Fort Worth, Texas, on 19 March 1930. As a child he was, he would later tell an interviewer, 'poorer than poor'; his father died when he was seven and his mother, a seamstress, raised Ornette and a sister with no outside help. When at the age of fourteen Ornette asked his mother for a saxophone, she replied they couldn't afford it unless he got a job. He immediately found some part-time work and soon after was given his first alto. There was of course no money for professional lessons; Ornette got some help from a cousin who played sax but mainly taught himself by listening to the radio and the occasional record that came his way. His house soon became known as a good spot for jamming by the local aspiring musicians, who included such future stars as drummer Charles Moffett, trumpeter Bobby Bradford, and reedmen Prince Lasha, Dewey Redman and John Carter.

The music Ornette listened to in those years was an eclectic hodge-podge of rhythm and blues, swing, bebop and popular songs, and he would later stress that stylistic categories meant little to him. He was heavily impressed – as were most of his contemporaries – by saxophonist Red Connors, a local and reportedly advanced musician who never recorded. Most of

Ornette's early jobs were of the rhythm-and-blues variety at dances and local bars. Soon after he graduated from high school, Ornette hit the road with a minstrel-show band that played the backwaters of the Deep South. He was fired from that job while in Natchez, Mississippi, joined a travelling rhythm-and-blues band, was beaten up outside a dancehall in Baton Rouge by some disgruntled customers, and left that band at New Orleans.

In New Orleans Ornette played with some of the underground modern jazz musicians – definitely a minority in that city – and found that his unorthodox solos were too far-out even for those jazzmen. After being stranded six months in New Orleans, he left town with the Pee Wee Crayton band, which was headed for the Coast. By the time the band reached LA, Crayton was paying Ornette *not* to play, and once again the saxophonist found himself stranded in a strange city. The year was 1949.

Ornette's first stay in LA was brief; he moved into a downtown hotel on the fringes of skid row and – supported at least in part by money sent from home – played when and where he could. Unable to land a steady job, he soon had his mother wire him some money and returned to Fort Worth. But the situation there had not improved either, and most of his friends had left town. After a few desultory years he returned in 1952 to Los Angeles, which would be his home for the remainder of the decade.

Ornette moved to Watts, where he stayed with a friend and 'ate and slept whenever I could'. Musical jobs were few and far between, so he took whatever menial day jobs were available; for a time he ran an elevator, studying books on theory and harmony between rides. At nights he would walk into LA and try to sit in with any bands that would let him. There were few takers. During his first stay in LA, when he was playing what writer A. B. Spellman would term 'a cross between his own brand of rhythm and blues and bebop', he had sat in with musicians like Teddy Edwards, Hampton Hawes and Sonny Criss. He had been at least half-heartedly accepted then, but by now his playing was simply too far removed from the accepted norm. One of the few sympathetic musicians was drummer Ed Blackwell, whom Coleman had met earlier in New Orleans. Blackwell remembered:

Ornette sounded a lot like Charlie Parker back then, and he was still hung up with one-two-three-four time. I had been

191

experimenting with different kinds of time and cadences, and since Ornette and I used to share together, we had reached some new grooves. Ornette's sound was changing too, and a lot of the musicians used to think he played out of tune. He never used to play the same thing twice, which made a lot of the guys think that he didn't know how to play.[5]

The mounting rejections would surely have discouraged a man with less indomitable will. A. B. Spellman cites a typical experience of the period:

He went down to sit in with tenor saxophonist Dexter Gordon one night and found that Dexter had, characteristically, not shown up in time for the first set. Ornette went up to play with Dexter's rhythm section only to have Gordon come in and order him off the bandstand. 'He said, "Immediately, right now. Take the tune out and get off the bandstand." ' And Ornette made the long walk back to Watts in the rain.[6]

Ornette also tried to sit in with Max Roach and Clifford Brown when they were in town. He wasn't let on the stand until after Max and Brownie had already left, and when Ornette did get on the stand the rhythm section packed up their instruments and walked off. He would later tell trumpete: Don Cherry, 'no matter how much you get rejected, you put that much more study and work into it so that you can produce more'.[7]

Nevertheless, he did manage to find a group of musicians willing to accept new ideas, and they began to practise together. Three of the musicians initially in the group were Ed Blackwell, trumpeter Bobby Bradford and tenor saxophonist James Clay. When Clay was drafted, followed soon thereafter by Bradford, their replacements were George Newman and Don Cherry. Cherry, who would become Ornette's musical partner, was originally from Oklahoma City, but had been raised in Los Angeles. When he met Ornette he played very much in a Clifford Brown bag, and unlike Ornette he was accepted by the LA jazz establishment, having gigged with musicians like Red Mitchell, Dexter Gordon, Wardell Gray and Herb Geller. Cherry also introduced a teenaged drummer named Billy Higgins to the group. Finally two additional musicians, bassist Don Payne and pianist Walter Norris, were welcomed into the fold. There were now enough instruments for a self-contained unit; Ornette would not have to depend on hostile sidemen when looking for a job.

Everyone concerned stresses that the practice sessions were a co-operative affair, and that ideas were freely exchanged by all the participants, although Ornette was obviously the keystone of the group. Despite the excitement of these sessions, however, Ornette still found it next to impossible to land a club date. Finally he decided his only hope was to get a recording session. George Newman had worked with Red Mitchell and introduced Ornette to the bassist, hoping that Mitchell in turn would introduce Coleman to Les Koenig. A meeting was set up at Don Payne's house so that Mitchell could hear Ornette and offer a professional opinion on Coleman's work. The upshot was the Mitchell liked Ornette's compositions but not his playing, and would only let his name be used in that context.

Ornette, accompanied by Don Cherry, dropped by the Contemporary studios and introduced himself to Keonig using Mitchell's name. Koenig, always ready to buy new tunes that might be recorded by his artists, agreed to listen, but things didn't go too well at first. Ornette tried to pick out some of his tunes on the piano, but he wasn't a pianist and was doing a poor job of it. Finally, in desperation, he and Cherry got out their horns and ran down some of the tunes. Koenig was impressed enough to offer Coleman a recording on the strength of their playing.

The resulting album, *Something Else!*, was recorded in three sessions held 10 and 22 February and 24 March 1958. The band consisted of Don Cherry, Ornette, Walter Norris, Don Payne and Billy Higgins. The record was far from a popular success, but it did introduce Ornette and his music to the jazz world at large, albeit in a slightly watered-down version. The use of the piano dictated that chord changes had to be adhered to (Ornette would never again use a piano on any of his own recordings) and the drumming of Billy Higgins was quite conservative compared to his later work. Nevertheless, the essence of Ornette's music does manage to come through.

It's not surprising, however, that the album failed to attract a very large audience. Much of the music undoubtedly sounded like a slightly quirky brand of bebop to the listeners of the day. All of the album's numbers were Coleman originals, and all had been written some years before in Fort Worth; most were – by Ornette's later standards – rather conservative. There are two blues, 'Alpha' and 'When Will the Blues Leave?', and two variations on the 'I Got Rhythm' format, 'Chippie' and 'Angel Voice'. Don Cherry actually quotes from a well-known Horace Silver solo from the 'Rhythm' clone 'Oleo' during his solo on 'Chippie', and the boppish theme on that tune carries strong hints of 'Anthropology'. 'Jayne', named for Ornette's wife, is based on 'Out of Nowhere'. On the other hand, 'Invisible' has a deliberately vague tonal centre (it's in D flat, one of Ornette's favourite keys); 'The Disguise', in D, has a thirteen-bar theme; and 'The Sphinx' has the sort of restless melody line and abrupt tempo changes that would soon become closely identified with Coleman. 'The Blessing', a slightly up-tempo mood piece, stands somewhere between these two extremes. On this tune, by the way, Don Cherry takes a very hard-boppish solo in Harmon mute. Nat Hentoff, in the liner notes to the album, selected some pertinent quotes by Ornette and Don Cherry that serve as a good introduction to the goals of the musicians. The most prophetic is by Ornette himself:

> I think one day music will be a lot freer. Then the pattern for a tune, for instance, will be forgotten and the tune itself will be the pattern, and won't have to be forced into conventional patterns. The creation of music is just as natural as the air we breathe. I believe music is really a free thing, and any way you can enjoy it, you should.[8]

If sales of the first album were disappointing, they failed to discourage Les Koenig, who arranged for a second recording a year later. The instrumentation for this second album would be that of most Coleman groups of the next several years: a pianoless quartet. Don Cherry was the other horn, of course, but the bass and drums were – no doubt at Koenig's insistence – Red Mitchell and Shelly Manne. Shelly remembers:

> Les knew I was adaptable; he'd done so many albums with me in so many contexts, and he felt that I would be the right choice. And so did Ornette. Ornette came out to my house and we went over some of his melody lines, and I found them very intriguing, very interesting. And Red was there, Red Mitchell. Then we did the date, and Red and Ornette got into a little scuffle...'cause Red had some changes dictated to play and Ornette wasn't following the changes. And Red said, 'I have to play the changes,' and Ornette says 'No you DON'T have to

play the changes,' and it went back and forth like that, and it got so that Percy Heath finished up the album. I remember playing the date, and it was a very free feeling, but I was almost trying to *force* the free feeling...to not play in the tradition, the way things had always been done. I think today I would do a better job of it; I understand a lot more about it.

This album also was done in three sessions. The first two, 16 January and 23 February, were done with Red Mitchell and produced three tunes: 'Lorraine', 'Turnaround' and 'Endless'. 'Lorraine', written for Lorraine Geller, is the first in a line of particularly moving dirges that Ornette would record. ('Lonely Woman' is the most famous.) The tune is infinitely sad yet never maudlin; at one point the alto races free for a short joyous passage, only to be brought up short by the return of the despairing theme. 'Turnaround' is a basic blues and best exemplifies the clashing musical philosophies of Coleman and Red Mitchell. Mitchell leads off with an extended bass solo that shows his mastery of modern jazz...to that point. But soon after Ornette begins his solo, it becomes evident that he is chaffing at the confinement of the unyielding chord changes. He almost breaks free once or twice, but is held in check by Mitchell's bass. The remaining tune, 'Endless', is an up-tempo AABA number that never quite resolves to a tonic.

These three tunes were the only ones recorded at the January and February sessions, and it became evident that Red Mitchell just wasn't fitting in with Ornette's concepts. With the money from the first dates, Ornette and Don Cherry flew to San Francisco, where the Modern Jazz Quartet was appearing. They sat in with the MJQ, strongly impressing the group's musical director John Lewis, and were able to talk Percy Heath, the unit's bassist, into flying to LA for the third Contemporary session. This was held the night of 9-10 March 1959 and produced six additional tunes.

'Tomorrow is the Question', a bright 'rejoicing-type tune', supplied the album with a title. 'Tears Inside', the tune Art Pepper would record the following year, is a much more earthy blues in Ornette's version. It's in D flat and is a precursor to 'Ramblin'', another D flat blues that would elicit one of Ornette's finest performances on a later recording; like 'Ramblin'', 'Tears Inside' is rooted firmly in the south-western blues tradition. The remaining four tunes – 'Mind and Time', 'Compassion', 'Giggin'' and 'Rejoicing' – have in common an elastic quality that allows each performer a great amount of latitude in shaping his own lines.

1. TOMORROW IS THE QUESTION!
2. TEARS INSIDE
3. MIND AND TIME
4. COMPASSION
5. GIGGIN'
6. REJOICING
All selections composed by Ornette Coleman

S7569 Side 1 ◯ STEREO
(LKS 75)

Tomorrow Is The Question!
The New Music of
ORNETTE COLEMAN
Ornette Coleman, *alto sax*; Don Cherry, *trumpet*;
Percy Heath, *bass*; Shelly Manne, *drums*

Tomorrow is the Question certainly gives a truer idea of Ornette's music than does the earlier *Something Else!*, but the lack of an empathetic bass player was still hurting the group. Actually, Ornette had already played with his future bassist before the second album was cut, but Les Koenig had wanted 'name' musicians on the album to help boost sales. The one job Ornette had landed in the year between the Contemporary recordings was as a sideman for pianist Paul Bley at the Hilcrest club in west LA. The musicians for the date were Cherry, Coleman, Bley, Billy Higgins and bassist Charlie Haden. Haden, born 6 August 1937 in Shenandoah, Iowa, came from a family steeped in folk and country music. He had played around Los Angeles with Art Pepper and Paul Bley; more importantly, he had a tremendous ear and was quite willing to adopt the methods that would fit him for working with Ornette. Coleman told the bassist:

'Forget about the changes in key and just play within the range of the idea. If I'm in the high register just play within that range that fits that register and just play the bass, that's all, all you've got to do is play the bass.' So he tried and he would have a difficult problem of knowing which range I was playing in and just what I meant by the whole range of playing anyway. I told him, 'Well, just learn.' So after a while of playing with me it just became the natural thing for him to do. All that matters in the function of the bass is either the top or the bottom or the middle, that's all the bass player has to play for me. It doesn't mean because you put an F7 down for the bass player he's boing to choose the best notes in the F7 to express what you're doing. But if he's allowed to use any note that he hears to express that F7, then that note's going to be right because he hears it, not because he read it off the page.[9]

A recording issued many years after the fact captured the Paul Bley group at the Hilcrest and gives a better picture than either of the Contemporary albums of Ornette's development to that point. The addition of the piano, which does hold Ornette back a little, is more than made up for by the supremely empathetic bass work of young Charlie Haden. Moreover, Paul Bley's playing is quite advanced in its own right; he does not constantly feed the established chord changes as would a bebop pianist. The recording was obviously done on somebody's home equipment – both the piano and bass are drastically under-recorded – although in this case it may have been a blessing in disguise, since potential clashes between the notes played by Bley and Haden are softened.

There are only four performances on the album (*Live at the Hilcrest Club, 1958*): two jazz standards – Charlie Parker's 'Klactoveesedstene' and Roy Eldridge's 'I Remember Harlem' – and two originals by Ornette – 'The Blessing' and 'Free'. Both 'Klactoveesedstene' and 'The Blessing' run well over ten minutes, so there is plenty of room for stretching out. The addition of 'Klactoveesedstene' may well have been an attempt to answer those who complained that Ornette and company couldn't play an orthodox brand of jazz. Ornette's solo begins in a very Parkerish vein and moves only slowly to the outside. The first several minutes of the performance could have been spliced into one of the many amateur recordings of Parker's club dates of the early fifties without raising most listeners' suspicions. Paul Bley's solo on this number is actually freer than Ornette's, especially when the bass and drums lay out for an extended period. 'I Remember Harlem' is a vehicle for Paul Bley, with Coleman and Cherry limited to background figures.

On his own two numbers Ornette evidently feels less strictured; his solo on 'The Blessing' achieves a freedom only hinted at on the Contemporary recording of the tune. 'Free' is exactly what the name implies – tempo, metres and tonal centres shift rapidly throughout the piece. On both these numbers Bley wisely lays out during much of Ornette's and Don Cherry's solos. Cherry's playing, by the way, is the real revelation on this album; he completely sheds the hard-bop elements of his style and shows why his trumpet is the perfect complement for Ornette's sax.

Finally, in May 1959, the recording towards which all of the previous sessions had been pointing came about. Largely through the promptings of John Lewis (the MJQ recorded for the label) Ornette landed a contract with Atlantic records. The first Atlantic recording session was held in Los Angeles, although the album would not be released until the autumn, after Ornette and the group had moved to New York. The Ornette Coleman Quartet was now set: Don Cherry, Ornette, Charlie Haden and Billy Higgins. Eight tunes were recorded at the initial session, but only six were issued on the first Atlantic album, *The Shape of Jazz to Come*.

'Lonely Woman' serves as an admirable introduction to Ornette's music. The drone bass and slashing drums set up a fast tempo that almost mocks the stately dirge played by the horns. The effect is to keep any trace of sentimentality from what could have been a maudlin piece. 'Eventually' is Ornette's homage to bop, complete with a unison theme and extremely rapid tempo. 'Peace', almost the antithesis of the previous number, once again shows the genius Coleman has for composing tunes that both state a mood and inspire the soloists to original improvisations within that mood. 'Focus on Sanity' allows each soloist to choose his own tempo and metre; the others follow the soloist's lead. Both 'Congeniality' and 'Chronology' are taken at a medium-up tempo, and both inspire burning performances by all the musicians. Listening to these latter numbers from the perspective of the 1980s, it is difficult to imagine the fuss originally made over Ornette's music. They sound so close to the mainstream of jazz, especially when compared to the performances of the second- and third-generation free-jazz musicians of the later 1960s. Nevertheless the initial breakthrough had been accomplished by Ornette and company.

Things moved rapidly from this point on. Neshui Ertegun, president of Atlantic records, paid for a trip by Coleman and Cherry to the Lenox School of Jazz in Lenox, Massachusetts that summer. There they edited the tapes from the session in May and, more importantly, were heard by critic Martin Williams. Williams liked what he heard and paved the way for an engagement at the Five Spot in New York City that autumn. With the advances from the Atlantic recordings, the group flew to New York where they cut some additional sides for Atlantic in October (most would be released on the album *Change of the Century*) and opened at the Five Spot in November. The two-week gig eventually stretched into several months as crowds packed the club, attracted by the controversy that surrounded the group. Musicians as well as jazz fans chose sides, and if Ornette had more supporters in New York than he had gained in LA, he still had a large number of vehement detractors in the Apple. Ultimately, of course, Ornette was vindicated; even those who prefer a more conservative brand of jazz are forced to recognize Ornette's position as one of the major innovators in the history of jazz. And if it is true that he had to move to New York to receive his due, it is just as true that the foundations for his revolutionary work had been laid during his tenure in Los Angeles.

11·

into the sixties

As the turn of the decade approached, the differences between jazz produced on the West Coast and that produced in New York became increasingly less discernible. On the other hand, the reaction against the excessive publicity given West Coast jazz earlier in the decade practically guaranteed that any music coming out of LA in the late fifties or early sixties would be undervalued. Many worthwhile albums were thus given short shrift at the time and have only recently been given their due – and some still languish in obscurity. This final chapter will examine some of those records and the musicians that produced them.

Two such records were produced by Dave Axelrod for the short-lived Hifijazz label. The first of these was *The Fox*, which was issued under Harold Land's name but which Harold says was more a collaboration with pianist Elmo Hope. The recording took place in August 1959, with a quintet composed of trumpeter Dupree Bolton, Land, Hope, bassist Herbie Lewis and Frank Butler. Of Dupree Bolton little is known. Harold Land discovered him playing in a club on LA's southside; *The Fox* marked his recording debut. He would appear on record only one other time, on the Curtis Amy album *Katanga*. When *Down Beat* magazine's West Coast editor John Tynan tried to interview Bolton in 1960, the only information the trumpeter would offer was, 'When I was fourteen, I ran away from home.'[1] This was also the first recording for bassist Herbie Lewis, who was born in Pasadena in 1941. He had played previously with Teddy Edwards, Bill Perkins and Les McCann.

Elmo Hope and Frank Butler have already been introduced.

Of the six tunes recorded for *The Fox*, four were written by Elmo Hope, two by Harold Land. The music is quite 'advanced', at least as advanced as the majority of the jazz then being produced in New York City. 'The major reason for that was the writing of Elmo Hope,' Land would later comment, 'because his writing, to me, was quite advanced. In listening to his writing today [1983] it *still* sounds advanced. That's the kind of talent he possessed.' Land would also tell Leonard Feather,

> Elmo was equally talented as a soloist and composer, but with a difference. He expresses things in his writing you don't hear in his playing. In his solos he's loose and free, while in his writing there's a sense of form. His lines are involved, yet never lose continuity. Elmo truly had a touch of genius. I was in awe of him.[2]

The album blasts out the starting-gate with Harold Land's 'The Fox', an extremely up-tempo blues that goads all the participants into playing at the top of their form. Harold Land had shown promise of becoming a major voice in jazz from his days with the Max Roach–Clifford Brown quintet; his work on this album announced that he had indeed arrived. The other original, 'Little Chris', refers to his son, then aged nine. (Chris Land is now a pianist in his own right, and often works with his father.) The tune has a rhythmic punch typical of Land's originals. The remaining four numbers all bear Elmo Hope's individualistic stamp. 'Mirror-Mind Rose' is the album's only ballad; Hope shares with Thelonious Monk the ability to write a moving ballad without introducing any hint of sentimentality. 'One Second, Please' comes the closest of any tune on the album to being an orthodox hard-bop number. 'Sims A-Plenty', on the other hand, has a very original theme, as well as some far from commonplace chord progressions. 'One Down' uses a mix of rhythms and accents to push the soloists along.

This is a tight unit; the musicians respond to one another as if they had been working together for years. Harold Land's tenor is very self-assured, and Hope sounds utterly relaxed at any tempo. The surprise of the album is newcomer Dupree Bolton. (A photo on the album sleeve shows Harold looking on almost incredulously as the trumpeter works out; those listening to the album are likely to have much the same reaction.) Bolton seemed poised

on the first step of an outstanding career, but once again a promising musician eventually got sidetracked by drug problems.

Not long after it was issued, *The Fox* fell victim to the vagaries of the recording business when Hifijazz records went out of business. Fortunately, the masters were bought and the album reissued in 1969 by Contemporary records. Another important album cut around the same time was not so fortunate. In March 1960 Hifijazz recorded the Paul Horn Quintet, one of the most original groups to be formed in Los Angeles. Multi-reed man Paul Horn had been Buddy Collette's replacement in the Chico Hamilton Quintet. Born 17 March 1930 in New York City, Horn received a Bachelor of Music from Oberlin Conservatory and a Master of Music from the Manhattan School of Music. He had played with the Sauter–Finnegan Orchestra and gained national prominence with Chico Hamilton. In 1959 he left Hamilton to form his own group, composed of vibraphonist Emil Richards, pianist Paul Moer, bassist Jimmy Bond and drummer Billy Higgins. Emil Richards – born Emilio Radocchia, 2 September 1932 in Hartford, Connecticut – had played with the Hartford and New Britain symphony orchestras and had made jazz time with Toshiko Akiyoshi (while in the army stationed in Japan), Flip Phillips, Charles Mingus and George Shearing. We've already met the others in the rhythm section.

Given the instrumentation of the group and Paul Horn's experience in the Chico Hamilton Quintet, it would be easy to assume that this would be another chamber-jazz group. Nothing could be further from the truth. The Paul Horn group was a hard-driving unit with plenty of fire. Billy Higgins, who was of course playing with Ornette Coleman during this period, was fast becoming one of the strongest percussionists around, and Jimmy Bond was equally muscular. When Higgins went east with Ornette, the team of Red Mitchell and Larry Bunker took over the bass and drum slots for a time, but when Higgins returned to the Coast (Ed Blackwell having joined Coleman in New York) the original personnel were reunited. Just about this time the group recorded for Hifijazz.

Aside from Ornette's debut at the Five Spot, perhaps the most important event in jazz to take place in 1959 was the recording of the album *Kind of Blue* by the Miles Davis Sextet. The album focused on performances wherein the soloists based their improvisations on modes, or scales, rather than chords. Moreover, since only a few such modes were used in each tune, each soloist was given more time to craft a melody, unhurried by ever-advancing chord progressions. The Paul Horn album, entitled *Something Blue*, was obviously influenced by the Miles Davis album, and indeed the Paul Horn group was one of the first fully to explore the new territory opened by Miles. Paul Horn's 'Dun-Dunnee', for instance, is a forty-bar AABA tune with but one chord or scale for the eight-bar A sections. (It can be thought of as either one long G7 chord or a mixolydian scale; that is, a scale starting on G using the white keys of the piano.)

On both 'Dun-Dunnee', an up-tempo scorcher, and Paul Moer's 'Tall Polynesian', a mood piece in 3/4 time, Horn plays flute. His technical mastery and control of the instrument are obvious. Emil Richards nearly burns the keys off the vibes with his smoking solo on 'Dun-Dunnee'. The solos on 'Tall Polynesian' are in double time (or 3/2). Paul Horn switches to alto for 'Mr Bond', another of his compositions. It is based on four ascending eight-bar phrases, each a minor-third above its predecessor; G7 to B flat 7 to D flat 7 to E7 and back to G7. The result is the musical equivalent of a perpetual motion machine. Emil Richards's 'Fremptz' is something of a musical in-joke; one of its phrases is derived from a cliché often played by Miles Davis. The two remaining tunes are both Paul Horn's. 'Something Blue' is a blues built on minor 7ths. Horn plays clarinet on this one and achieves a dark tone that fits well with the tune's mood. He returns to alto for the final number, 'Half and Half'. As the name suggests, the metre in this one switches back and forth from 4/4 to 6/8.

The Paul Horn Quintet managed to stay together for several years, but as was the case with several other such units, the deteriorating Los Angeles jazz-club scene ultimately forced its demise. It was, during its existence, a truly first-rate unit and seems never to have got the recognition it deserved.

As the autumn of 1959 approached, one of the longest-lived working bands in LA was booked into a San Francisco club for a short engagement. Shelly Manne had, since leaving the Shorty Rogers Giants in 1955, led a quintet that consistently produced a hard-driving brand of jazz; this in addition to a steady stream of studio calls that kept him among the busiest musicians in Hollywood. There had been changes in personnel in Shelly's group over the years, but each edition employed top-notch players. His trumpet players had been Stu Williamson (who doubled on valve-trombone) and Conte Candoli, while Bill Holman, Charlie Mariano and Herb Geller had held down the sax chair. The rhythm section was originally composed of Russ Freeman, Leroy Vinnegar and Shelly, although Monty Budwig eventually replaced Leroy Vinnegar.

In September of 1959 the front line of Shelly's quintet featured trumpeter Joe Gordon and tenor saxophonist Richie Kamuca. Gordon hailed from Boston, Massachusetts, where he was born on 15 May 1928. He had played with Boston musicians Charlie Mariano and Herb Pomeroy, as well as Charlie Parker, Art Blakey, and in Dizzy Gillespie's big band. Kamuca, whom we've already met, was best known for his work with Stan Kenton and Woody Herman. Bassist Monty Budwig was born on 26 December 1929 in Pender, Nebraska, and had worked with Barney Kessel, Zoot Sims and Woody Herman, among others, before joining Shelly. The newest member of the quintet, a last-minute sub for pianist Russ Freeman (who was away on a short tour with Benny Goodman), was Victor Feldman. Feldman, who also played vibes and drums, was born in London, England on 7 April 1934. Largely self-taught, he played with Ted Heath, Woody Herman and the Lighthouse All-Stars.

This was the group booked into the San Francisco's Blackhawk for a two-week stand in September 1959. With the exception of Feldman, they had been working together at clubs and in concerts for well over a year. There was a bit of apprehension about Feldman, who was in effect learning the book on the job, but he fitted in from the start. The job at the Blackhawk was seen as nothing special, just a two-week out-of-town gig, but the band's performance the first night changed everyone's mind. Shelly relates what happened next:

The band was burning up there and everything felt right. You know there are certain times that you play that you almost feel that you leave your own body, and you're watching, and that you can do anything you want – and that was happening. So I called Les [Koenig] and said, 'Les, is there any way you can get up here with the machine and tape us up here? The band is outstanding.' And he said, 'OK'; he was that kind of guy. He came on up and we recorded three straight nights; he had the machine running all the time and we put out practically everything we recorded those nights – and that was four albums.

1. SUMMERTIME
BY GEORGE GERSHWIN & DU' BOSE HEYWARD

2. OUR DELIGHT
BY TADD DAMERON

S7577 Side 1 ◯ STEREO
(LKS 133)

SHELLY MANNE & HIS MEN
AT THE BLACK HAWK, VOL. 1

Shelly Manne, *drums*; Joe Gordon, *trumpet*;
Richie Kamuca, *tenor sax*; Victor Feldman, *piano*;
Monty Budwig, *bass*

Shelly Manne and His Men at the Blackhawk, Volumes 1–4 have long been cornerstones in the Contemporary catalogue and have held a special appeal for other musicians. Cannonball Adderley was so impressed by Vic Feldman's playing on the sides he hired Feldman for his own group, and incidentally added one of the numbers, 'Blue Daniel', to his group's book. There are fifteen performances in all on the four albums. Naturally the quality varies from number to number, but the overall level is consistently high. Perhaps the weakest performance comes on 'Poinciana' – the tune's changes are too monotonously similar to provide much interest. But balanced against that are some truly outstanding performances. Tadd Dameron's 'Our Delight' calls forth smoking solos by Gordon, Kamuca and Feldman, while Frank Rosolino's poignant waltz 'Blue Daniel' sustains its bittersweet mood throughout. There are three extended blues performances: 'Blackhawk Blues', an extemporaneous walking blues; Charlie Mariano's 'Vamp's Blues'; and a work-out on Bill Holman's 'A Gem from Tiffany', the band's theme. (There is an additional short take of 'A Gem from Tiffany' used as a set closer.) Two Benny Golson songs,

'Whisper Not' and 'Step Lightly', fit Shelly's men to a T. Cole Porter's 'I am in Love', one of his less frequently played numbers, turns out to be the sleeper of the set, with outstanding performances by all hands.

The Blackhawk was also the site, some seven months later, of an important meeting of East and West. Thelonious Monk, a true giant in a business where that term is often inappropriately applied, was visiting San Francisco for only his second time. The group he brought in for the three-week stand was composed of tenor saxophonist Charlie Rouse, bassist John Ore and the ubiquitous Billy Higgins, who had just joined Monk's quartet. This group, with two added horns, was recorded by Riverside records the night of 29 April 1960; the reason the recording appears in this narrative is that the additional musicians were Joe Gordon and Harold Land.

At this late date, the reasons behind this meeting have been lost. Harold Land can't remember whose idea it was originally: 'Joe Gordon and I got the call to do a live date with Monk ... but I can't recall how that came about, unless it was just Monk's idea and he asked for us.' Whatever the reason, Land remembers the time as a happy occasion. 'I think everybody has such a love for Monk's music – and him, for that matter; I know I always had and I'm sure Joe felt the same way.' In any case, the meeting was a memorable one.

The Los Angeles musicians flew up a few days early to rehearse, but there is no sign of the impromptu nature of the session on the recording; the band sounds as if Gordon and Land had been regular members of Monk's ensemble. Five originals of Monk's – including one brand-new composition – were taped for the album. 'San Francisco Holiday' (mistakenly labelled 'Worry Later' on the album sleeve) gets its recording debut here. The other Monk compositions had been in the book for some time. 'Let's Call This' and 'Four in One' both receive driving performances, while Monk's most famous tune, 'Round about Midnight' elicits moving solos by Rouse, Gordon, Land and Monk. There is also a rousing version of 'I'm Getting Sentimental over You' and a brief taste of Monk's closing theme 'Epistrophy'. Harold Land and Joe Gordon both delve deeply into Monk's music; neither simply 'runs the changes'. The result is a very satisfying album.

The year 1960 also marked the return of one of LA's major jazz voices to the recording scene. Actually, Teddy Edwards had been around all the time; he just hadn't been invited to record for several years. Part of his problems stemmed from extra-musical difficulties. 'I was going through a bad physical scene – the gall-bladder scene, plus tooth trouble,' he would later tell Les Koenig. 'I had oral surgery three times, and wasn't able to play for months on end. For a long while I didn't seem to get much action. I was taking whatever came up ...' Despite such distractions, he always strove to improve himself.

For instance, if I had a burlesque job, I'd just say to myself, 'I'll practise on this job.' I'd practise how to play the melody, my intonation, my approach to different tunes, changes, tempos. You have time to practise then, you know, because you're playing chorus after chorus behind those girls. So it all adds up. Playing with lousy rhythm sections in a strange way actually helps your time because you've practically got to carry the time yourself.[3]

It is also true that Teddy's straight-ahead, no-nonsense tenor style had been out of favour for several years. As he would later sardonically comment to another interviewer, 'The West Coast thing came along and I guess I didn't fit in.'[4] In any event, a combination of improved health and changing musical tastes helped him to return to playing jazz full-time in 1959. He and several like-minded musicians formed a quartet that year. The others were pianist Joe Castro, Leroy Vinnegar and – yes – Billy Higgins. The group was a co-operative affair, in the tradition of 'whoever gets the gig is the leader'. They appeared on the ABC-TV 'Stars of Jazz' show as the Leroy Vinnegar Quartet and recorded for Atlantic as the Joe Castro Quartet. When it came time to record for Contemporary in the summer of 1960 they were billed as the Teddy Edwards Quartet.

The group had, by that time, been together – off and on – for over a year. Billy Higgins had spent some of that time in New York with Ornette, of course; he had also recorded with Thelonious Monk at the Blackhawk and worked with John Coltrane's quartet at the Monterey Jazz Festival during the same period! Joe Castro, the group's pianist, was born 15 August 1927 in Miami, Arizona, but had been raised in the San Francisco bay area. He had gigged up and down the Coast and in Hawaii with his own trio in the early fifties, and spent some time in New York a few years later. He had also worked with singers June Christy and Anita O'Day. When all four members of the quartet were available at the same time, they worked club dates at the Intime in Los Angeles.

The album *Teddy's Ready* was recorded 17 August 1960. There are no surprises here; the music is mainstream modern. Teddy Edwards's style had not changed appreciably since the late 1940s, but his voice had matured and his command of the horn here is total. Joe Castro also shows himself to be a fully developed pianist, whose playing is at the same time technically brilliant and funky. Everybody's talents are perhaps best displayed on Charlie Parker's 'Scrapple from the Apple', which is taken at a flying tempo. On the A sections of the head it's just Teddy and Leroy; Joe Castro and Billy Higgins jump in on the bridge. The pattern continues for the first chorus of Teddy's and Joe Castro's solos, and Leroy Vinnegar also walks unaccompanied during the A sections of his first chorus. The other performances on the album are equally relaxed and swinging. There is a 'Blues in G' by Teddy Edwards and a blues with gospel roots, 'The Sermon', by Hampton Hawes. Two of the remaining tunes are Edwards originals, 'You Name It' and 'Higgins' Hideaway'. The latter is an AABA tune with the successive A sections in B flat, C and G. Billy Strayhorn's 'Take the "A" Train' and a ballad performance of 'What's New?' complete the programme.

Less than a year later Teddy Edwards once again entered the Contemporary studios, this time for a momentous reunion with another survivor of the bebop era, Howard McGhee. Howard's odyssey through the 1950s was if anything more painful than Teddy's. The man who had helped Charlie Parker keep afloat (and alive) during Bird's darkest days in California later succumbed to the same illness, but nobody seemed willing to lend Maggie a hand. His feelings about the period are best summed up in the title of an album he cut following his recovery: *Nobody Knows You when You're Down and Out*. Maggie was once again fit and able when Les Koenig invited him to record with Teddy Edwards. The sessions took place on 15 and 17 May 1961.

The rhythm section for this recording was an exceptionally strong one. Pianist Phineas Newborn Jr was born on 14 December 1931 in Whiteville, Tennessee, but spent most of his early life in Memphis. For years he laboured in the local R & B vineyards, although there were tours with Lionel Hampton. In

1955 he moved to New York, where he soon made a name for himself. A brilliant technician, he was sometimes accused of lacking emotion in his playing. In truth he was a performer the quality of whose work varied widely on different occasions. At the time of this recording he was at the top of his form, and had just worked an engagement with Teddy Edwards at LA's Zebra Lounge. Bassist Ray Brown and drummer Ed Thigpen, who were in town with the Oscar Peterson Trio, got the call to complete the rhythm section.

Howard McGhee contributed two originals to the album, one written especially for the occasion. 'Together Again' refers back to the pairing of Edwards and McGhee in the sextet that had recorded 'Up in Dodo's Room' in 1947. Much water had gone under the bridge since then, but both of the veterans had proved resilient and both were eager to advance with the flow of jazz.

1. TOGETHER AGAIN!
BY TEDDY EDWARDS
2. YOU STEPPED OUT OF A DREAM
BY NACIO HERB BROWN & GUS KAHN
3. UP THERE
BY RAY BROWN

S7588 Side 1 STEREO
(LKS 193)

TOGETHER AGAIN!
Teddy Edwards & Howard McGhee
TEDDY EDWARDS, tenor sax; HOWARD McGHEE, trumpet
PHINEAS NEWBORN Jr., piano; RAY BROWN, bass
ED THIGPEN, drums

The tune has a minor-key, hard-bop-flavoured theme, and the solos by Teddy and Maggie are very much in the same bag. 'You Stepped Out of a Dream' finds Maggie in Harmon mute; his solo burns with a fire that had lost none of its heat since his younger days. Howard's trumpet remains muted in Ray Brown's tune 'Up There'; the title no doubt refers to the tempo at which the piece is taken. 'Perhaps' is an old Charlie Parker Latin-flavoured blues line. At Howard's suggestion, each soloist on this occasion plays six choruses; two in the original key of C, two in F and two in B flat. Erroll Garner's 'Misty' is given a tender yet soulful performance by Teddy Edwards. The album closes with another original of McGhee's, 'Sandy'. The up-tempo number has some original and thought-provoking chord changes.

Together Again remains a very satisfying album – it wears like a comfortable pair of sneakers. Howard McGhee and Teddy Edwards were at the cutting-edge of jazz when they first got together in the late forties. By 1961 they were considered in the mainstream rather than the avant-garde, but both had continued to progress and increase the mastery of their horns. Backed by an exceedingly able rhythm section, they prove that good jazz, like a fine wine, improves with age.

That same May saw another established musician enter the recording studios to chart the progress he had made over the course of the decade. Bud Shank had enjoyed wide popularity early in the fifties when – in company with just about any youngster who picked up an alto sax – he had been touted as 'the new Bird'. It was a case of too much too soon; Shank was certainly a competent player, but he was at the time neither an innovator nor even a highly original soloist. But as the decade and the fortunes of West Coast jazz waned, Shank had quietly been improving. His playing gained a rhythmic punch and emotional commitment that had been missing in his earlier work.

New Groove, recorded for Pacific Jazz in May 1961, shows Shank's work on both alto and baritone sax to good advantage. The sidemen on this date had – with the exception of drummer Mel Lewis – been working club dates with Shank at the Drift Inn in Malibu. Trumpet man Carmell Jones was born in Kansas City, Missouri in 1936 and began his career playing in local groups around that city. He moved to LA in 1960 and began freelancing; the job with Bud Shank was his first steady gig with a name group. Guitarist Dennis Budimir, a native Angeleno, was born on 20 June 1938. He had first gained attention while playing alongside Eric Dolphy in the Chico Hamilton Quintet. Bassist Gary Peacock was born in Burley, Idaho, on 12 May 1935. He began his musical studies on piano and switched to bass following a tour in the army. Mel Lewis had recently returned to LA following a tour with the Gerry Mulligan Concert Jazz Band.

Three of the album's six tunes were written by Shank: 'New

Groove', a blues with a fashionably funky line; 'The Awakening', a touching ballad; and 'White Lightnin'', another blues which is taken at a flying tempo. There are also performances of Tyree Glenn's 'Sultry Serenade', Monk's 'Well You Needn't' and an original of Gary Peacock's, 'Liddledabllduya' (a tonsorial reference). Bud plays baritone on 'The Awakening' and 'Sultry Serenade', and his work on the big horn demonstrates the increased emotional directness of his playing. On the other numbers he plays alto with a new-found aggressiveness; his burning solo on 'White Lightnin'' is especially impressive. Carmell Jones shows his indebtedness to Clifford Brown throughout; he is at his lyrical best on 'The Awakening'. Dennis Budimir is tentative at times, but once launched into a solo he displays some outstanding chops. Gary Peacock's bass lines are very imaginative and hint of things to come; he would later move to New York and become an important figure in avant-garde jazz circles. As always, Mel Lewis manages to be propulsive yet subtle at the same time.

Another forward-looking album cut a few months later featured Joe Gordon, who had left Shelly Manne and struck out on his own. At the time of the recording Gordon was gigging around town mainly in the company of young alto saxophonist Jimmy Woods. Woods, born in St Louis, 29 October 1934, had played in a high-school band alongside Quincy Jones and spent several years paying R & B dues in the bands of Roy Milton, Big Maybelle and Jimmy Witherspoon. He moved to Los Angeles in 1958 and began playing club dates at night while attending LA City College by day. Both Gordon and Woods were interested in exploring the newer directions in jazz.

Gordon's album, *Lookin' Good*, was recorded by Contemporary in July 1961, with a rhythm section composed of pianist Dick Whittington, bassist Jimmy Bond, and drummer Milt Turner. Whittington was a native Angeleno, born 24 July 1936. Largely self-taught, he was playing Sunday-afternoon concerts at the Lighthouse while still a student at Santa Monica City College, and had worked with Sonny Criss and Dexter Gordon. Milt Turner was born in Nashville, 14 March 1935, and attended Tennessee State University. From 1957 to 1960 he was on the road with Ray Charles; he later gigged around LA with Phineas Newborn, Teddy Edwards and Paul Horn. Bassist Jimmy Bond was still working with Paul Horn at the time this record was cut.

All eight of the album's compositions were written by Joe

Gordon – who had taken up composing only a year before – and all demonstrate a thoughtful, original talent. 'Terra Firma Irma' is in the tradition of tunes like Duke Pearson's 'Jeannine'; it is based partly on a modal scale and partly on regular chord changes. There are two waltzes: the funky 'Non-Viennese Waltz Blues' (actually in 6/4) and the minor-key 'Mariana'. 'Co-op Blues' is the only 'standard' number; it's simply a medium-tempo E flat blues. 'You're the Only Girl in the Next World for Me' packs a rhythmic punch, while 'Heleen' is a lyrical ballad with intriguing chord progressions. 'Diminishing' is based on the same sequence of ascending chords a minor third apart as was the Paul Horn composition 'Mr Bond'.

Jimmy Woods, despite his years in R & B groups, is actually the more 'advanced' soloist. His alto work is rooted in Bird, of course, but he uses unexpected intervals and his tone at time takes on the voicelike cry that Ornette Coleman and Eric Dolphy were using to such great effect. Joe Gordon's work here is more firmly in the post-bop tradition, but he too is his own man. Although he was a friend of Clifford Brown's, his trumpet shows less indebtedness to Brownie than that of many of his contemporaries. And when he uses a Harmon mute on 'A Song for Richard', he manages *not* to sound like a Miles Davis clone. Together Gordon and Woods make an outstanding team. This album should have vaulted both into prominence, but although it was favourably received, it did not mark a major breakthrough for either musician. Tragically, Joe Gordon had only a few years to live when he made this album. Late in 1963 he was severely burned in a fire; he died in a Santa Monica hospital on 4 November 1963.

There remains one final album from this period to examine. In the summer of 1961 a new group began rehearsing. The group's co-leaders – Red Mitchell and Harold Land – were both musicians of proven stature, and their new quintet would be one of the strongest and most fascinating units to come out of LA in the decade. Although it would last only about a year due to the deteriorating club scene, the group did leave one outstanding record of their existence: the Atlantic album *Hear Ye!*

The Red Mitchell–Harold Land Quintet was a compatible unit formed of like-minded musicians. Trumpeter Carmell Jones was still improving following his tenure with Bud Shank. The group's pianist, Frank Strazzeri, had only been in California a little over a year. Born in Rochester, New York, 24 March 1930,

Strazzeri had studied at the nearby Eastman School of Music before deciding to opt for the jazz life. He had played with Charlie Ventura, Terry Gibbs and Woody Herman before moving to the Coast. Drummer Leon Petties had been a close friend of Harold Land's in San Diego, and had worked with Buddy Collette and Shorty Rogers after moving to Los Angeles.

The Atlantic album was recorded in December 1961, when the group had been together for about half a year. All of the numbers recorded were from the band's working book, and all of the tunes were written by members of the group. Harold Land contributed a blues, 'Triplin' Awhile', and the sombre-toned 'Catacomb'. Red Mitchell also contributed two numbers, 'Rosie's Spirit' and 'Hear Ye!' The title tune is in three and exhibits some gospel roots. Carmell Jones wrote 'Somara', a hard-bop-flavoured number, and Frank Strazzeri contributed an exciting up-tempo piece, 'Pari Passu'.

Red Mitchell's bass is treated as a major voice in the quintet, not simply because the bassist is co-leader but because his phenomenal chops make such a role feasible. On 'Triplin' Awhile', for instance, Land and Mitchell state the theme in octaves with a rapid string of eighth-note triplets, while on 'Hear Ye!', Red's arco bass sings the lead with the tenor sax. Harold Land's tenor sax is muscular and authoritative; he flies through the up-tempo numbers with ease, but never parades his technique for technique's sake. Carmell Jones offers fleet and lyrical trumpet lines that show his lineage from Clifford Brown. Frank Strazzeri lends solid support to the soloists and imaginative, flowing lines on his own solos, while Leon Petties sparks the group with driving yet unobtrusive drumwork.

This was a first-rate post-bop unit, the equal of any on either coast during its limited existence. Unfortunately, the lack of opportunities for club dates spelled its demise about a year after it was formed, 'which was a shame', Harold Land comments, 'because we had a good group and it was different in its approach'. The musicians, of course, were aware of the potential difficulties going in. 'There has been so little of this kind of music organized here,' Red Mitchell told Leonard Feather at the time of the recording. 'Curtis had a fine group, but it didn't last too long. We realized, too, that forming a group like this in Los Angeles and trying to keep it together was not the easiest thing in the world.'[5] That the band survived as long as it did was a tribute to the tenacity of all concerned.

At this admittedly arbitrary point the narrative comes to a close. The Los Angeles jazz scene of the 1960s and beyond is certainly as interesting and variegated as that of the 1950s, but it lies outside the scope of this book. In any case, jazz writers since 1960 or so have tended (quite rightly) to focus on the similarities rather than the differences between jazz produced in LA and that produced in New York or elsewhere (although they have continued to give Los Angeles and its jazz musicians short shrift in jazz texts and histories).

A little over ten years separate the Capitol recordings of Shorty Rogers and His Giants from the Atlantic recordings of the Red Mitchell–Harold Land Quintet. During that decade Los Angeles attracted, for the first time, the attention of a large segment of both the national and international jazz audience. Unfortunately much of this attention, at least in the earlier part of the decade, was focused on music that had only a peripheral relationship to jazz. At the time, few jazz writers bothered to distinguish between the music of lasting worth and that of little value; later, in a reaction to the excessive publicity given the style known as West Coast jazz, they tended to dismiss any music produced in LA altogether.

It is easy to denigrate much of the jazz produced in LA during the 1950s. Certainly such albums as *Chet Baker Sings* or the innocuous series of recordings by the Dave Pell Octet have little to offer the serious jazz listener. (Dave Pell himself once termed his music 'mortgage-paying jazz'.) On the other hand – as I hope I have shown – there are a great many recordings from that period that deserve better than to be dismissed simply because they were once tagged with the epithet 'West Coast jazz'. Perhaps the time has come to judge each recording on its own merits, and each artist on his or her individual accomplishments.

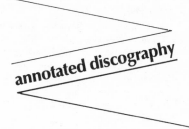

annotated discography

Jazz records are, alas, ephemeral products. They go in and out of print with breathtaking speed, in an apparently random and haphazard manner. The only inviolable rule seems to be that the more you desire a given record, the more likely it is that record will soon go out of print. There is one consolation: if you wait long enough, the record you want will probably be reissued by somebody, somewhere, some time – usually just after you've bought a scratched copy of the original release at an outrageous price on the second-hand market.

There seems little point, therefore, in attempting an up-to-the-minute discography, since it would almost certainly be out of date by the time a given reader comes across it. Nor have I attempted an exhaustive listing of all issues of the albums I mention; this discography is aimed at those readers who wish to listen to the performances discussed in the book, and not at the specialist collectors. In most cases I have given only the title and catalogue number of the original twelve-inch album, or (especially in the case of those performances recorded in the pre-LP era) the most comprehensive recent repackaging. Many of the albums listed, long out of print in the original American editions, are available in European or Japanese reissues. And since most of the reissues use the original titles – and many even reproduce the original album covers – a reader shouldn't have much trouble determining which album to order.

A special word on the Contemporary and Pacific Jazz catalogue and issue numbers is in order here, since the majority of albums I discuss were originally issued by those labels. As this is written, most of the Contemporary albums are once again available, either through the current Contemporary catalogue or through reissues on the OJC (Original Jazz Classics) label. The exceptions are, for the most part, albums which were originally issued on ten-inch LPs and never reissued in the twelve-inch format. The Contemporary 2500 series were ten-inch LPs; the 3500 series were and are twelve-inch monaural albums; the 7500/7600 series are twelve-inch stereo albums. The prefixes used by Contemporary – C, M (monaural), and S (stereo) – are essentially irrelevant and I have ignored them. Since the OJC

217

reissues use the original Contemporary album covers, I have listed the original Contemporary numbers, followed by the OJC reissue number (if applicable) in brackets.

The Pacific Jazz catalogue (long out of print) is a bit more complicated. The prefix PJLP- denotes a ten-inch LP; the PJ-1200 series were twelve-inch LPs. There was also a PJM-400 series and a JWC-500 [Jazz West Coast] series of twelve-inch albums; the latter were anthologies. In 1957 Richard Bock changed the name of his label from Pacific Jazz to World Pacific, and albums originally issued with the PJ- or PJM- prefix were then issued with a WP- or WPM- prefix, but in all cases albums sharing the same issue number [i.e. PJ-1232 or WP-1232] were identical. (For that reason, I have not added the prefix in the 1200 series.) In the 1960s, many of these albums were reissued in the PJ-1/99 series, although there were original albums in that series as well. A few Pacific Jazz albums were issued in stereo in the PJ/WP-1000 series. Pausa records has recently reissued a few of the Pacific Jazz albums; where these are listed I have given the Pausa issue number first, followed by the original Pacific Jazz number in brackets.

Records marked* are ten-inch LPs.

1 - *Diz and Bird in Lotus Land*
DIZZY GILLESPIE:
  The Development of an American Artist, Smithsonian R-004 (P2 13455)
JAZZ AT THE PHILHARMONIC
  Bird and Pres: The '46 Concerts, Verve VE-2-2518
CHARLIE PARKER:
  The Genius of Charlie Parker. Savoy 12014
  Charlie Parker on Dial, Vols. 1-3, Spotlite 101-103
  The Very Best of Bird, Warner Brothers 2 WB 3198

Four of the Dizzy Gillespie Sextet Dials (sans Parker) are found on the Smithsonian album. The Slim Gaillard Bel Tone session was last available on the Savoy album. The three albums in the Spotlite series (also available on the Japanese Stateside label) offer all of the extant Dial recordings cut by Parker in California, including numerous alternate takes. Volume one includes the 'Night in Tunisia' and 'Lover Man' sessions, as well as the rare Gillespie-Parker test recording of 'Diggin' with Diz'. Volume two issues the complete 'Cool Blues' session, Volume three the 'Relaxin' at Camarillo' session. (Three additional albums, Vols. 4-6, complete the set and make available the Dials recorded by Parker in New York.) A less exhaustive but more easily obtainable collection of Parker's Dials is offered on the Warner Brothers two-disc set.

2 - *The Central Avenue Scene*
DEXTER GORDON:
  The Chase, Spotlite SPJ 130 (Dial Masters series)
WARDELL GRAY:
  Central Avenue, Prestige 24062

HOWARD McGHEE:
Trumpet at Tempo, Spotlite SPJ 131 (Dial Masters series)
CHARLES MINGUS:
Mingus in California, Smithsonian [to be issued]
Red Norvo Trio, Savoy SJL 2212
FRANK MORGAN:
Frank Morgan, GNP Cresendo GNPS 9041
ANTHOLOGY:
Black California, Savoy SJL 2215

The two Spotlite albums offer the master takes of all the Dials recorded in California by Dexter Gordon and by Howard McGhee, including the Howard McGhee-Teddy Edwards 'Up in Dodo's Room' session and the two tunes cut by McGhee following Parker's aborted 'Lover Man' session. The two-LP Prestige *Central Avenue* set includes the jam at the Hula Hut with Wardell Gray, Dexter Gordon and Sonny Criss; the Art Farmer *Farmer's Market* session; and the Teddy Charles session, as well as recordings cut under Wardell Gray's own name. And while none of the performances on the Savoy two-LP *Black California* set is specifically talked about in this chapter, the album does offer selections by Sonny Criss and others that capture the ambience of the California jazz scene of this period.

3 – *Shorty Rogers and His Giants*
MILES DAVIS:
The Complete Birth of the Cool, Capitol M-11026
SHORTY ROGERS:
Modern Sounds, *Capitol H294
*Fourteen Historic Arrangements and Performances with Stan Kenton/
    June Christy/The Giants*, Pausa 9016
Shorty Rogers and Art Pepper/Popo, Xanadu 148
Shorty Rogers and His Giants, RCA LPM-1195
Cool and Crazy, *RCA LPM-3138
Big Shorty Rogers Express, RCA LPM-1350
Shorty Rogers Courts the Count, RCA LJM-1004
HOWARD RUMSEY'S LIGHTHOUSE ALL-STARS:
Sunday Jazz a la Lighthouse, Contemporary 3501 [OJC-151]
Lighthouse All-Stars, Vol. 3, Contemporary 3508
LENNIE TRISTANO:
Crosscurrents, Capitol M-11060

The Pausa album reissues the Capitol ten-inch *Modern Sounds* set and offers as well five Rogers arrangements recorded by Stan Kenton (including 'Jolly Rogers', 'Art Pepper' and 'Round Robin') and three cuts from a June Christy vocal session featuring Rogers arrangements. *Big Shorty Rogers Express* reissued the performances of the original ten-inch *Cool and Crazy* album with additional material recorded in 1956. All of the Shorty Rogers RCA albums are currently being reissued on the French RCA Masters series.

4 - The Gerry Mulligan Quartet
CHET BAKER:
  The Trumpet Artistry of Chet Baker, Pausa 9011 [reissue of PJ-1206]
GERRY MULLIGAN:
  Gerry Mulligan, Prestige 12016
  The Genius of Gerry Mulligan, Pausa 9010 [reissue of PJ-8]
  Gerry Mulligan Quartet, Pacific Jazz 1207
  Lee Konitz Plays with the Gerry Mulligan Quartet, Pacific Jazz PJM-406
    [also issued as WP-1273]
  *The Complete Pacific Jazz and Capitol Recordings of the Original Gerry
    Mulligan Quartet and Tentette with Chet Baker,* Mosaic MR5-102
  California Concerts, Pacific Jazz 1201

Prestige 12016 (a two-LP set) offers the Mulligan ten-piece band
recordings cut for that label in New York, as well as the quartet sides
recorded for the Fantasy label. The five-LP Mosaic set (a limited
edition available only by mail order) is truly exhaustive and reissues all
the material originally found on PJLP-1, PJLP-2, PJLP-5, PJLP-10,
PJ-1207 and PJM-406, as well as many previously unissued takes. (An
alternate take of 'Swinghouse' from PJLP-5 was somehow overlooked,
however.) All of the Mosaic albums are highly recommended. Unfortunately, the Mulligan Quartet and Sextet sides with Jon Eardley
(originally issued on PJ-1201 and various anthologies) are currently
unavailable. The Pausa Chet Baker set features a representative sampling of the Chet Baker Quartet, Sextet and Ensemble.

5 - The West Coast Sound
LAURINDO ALMEIDA:
  Quartet Featuring Bud Shank, *Pacific Jazz PJLP-7
  Brazilliance, Pausa 9009 [reissue of PJ-1412]
CHET BAKER:
  Chet Baker Ensemble, *Pacific Jazz PJLP-9
MAYNARD FERGUSON:
  Dimensions, Emarcy 36044
STAN GETZ:
  Interpretations, Norgran 1000
  At the Shrine, Norgran 2000
BOB GORDON:
  Meet Mr. Gordon, *Pacific Jazz PJLP-12
HERBIE HARPER:
  Herbie Harper Quintet, *Nocturne 1
SHELLY MANNE:
  Vol. 1: The West Coast Sound, Contemporary 3507 [OJC-152]
  Volume 2, *Contemporary 2511
  The Three and the Two, Contemporary 3584 [OJC-172]
LENNIE NIEHAUS:
  The Quintet, Vol. 1, *Contemporary 2513
  The Octet, Vol. 2, *Contemporary 2517
HOWARD RUMSEY'S LIGHTHOUSE ALL-STARS
  Volume 3, Contemporary 3508
  Vol. 4: Flute and Oboe, Contemporary 3520 [OJC-154]

BUD SHANK:
   Bud Shank Quintet, *Nocturne 2 [reissued with additional material on
   Pacific Jazz 1205]
ANTHOLOGIES:
   Jazz West Coast, Vol. 1, Pacific Jazz JWC-500
   Jazz: The 50's Volume I, Pacific Jazz PJ-LA892-H

   Most of the recordings listed here are long out of print; the exceptions
are the Pausa and OJC reissues. *Brazilliance* features many of the
Laurindo Almeida–Bud Shank performances from the original ten-
inch LP as well as material dating from a later collaboration in the
1960s. The anthology *Jazz: The 50's Volume I,* a Blue Note/Pacific Jazz
recording issued during the 1970s, may occasionally be found in the
remainders section of larger record shops. It and its companion *Volume
II* offer a representative cross-section of Pacific Jazz recordings, but
many of the selections have been heavily edited.

6 – California Hard (I)
CLIFFORD BROWN:
   The Complete Blue Note and Pacific Jazz Recordings of Clifford Brown,
   Mosaic MR5-104
   The Best of Max Roach and Clifford Brown in Concert, GNP Crescendo
   GNPS 18
   Jazz Immortal, Pacific Jazz PJ-3
   Brown and Roach, Inc., Emarcy 36008

   Clifford Brown and Max Roach, Emarcy 36036
   Best Coast Jazz, Emarcy 36039
   Clifford Brown All-Stars, Emarcy 36102
   Jam Session, Emarcy 36009
HERB GELLER:
   Herb Geller Plays, *Emarcy 26045
   The Gellers, Emarcy 36024
DEXTER GORDON:
   Daddy Plays the Horn, Bethlehem BCP-6008
   Dexter Blows Hot and Cool, Dootone DTL-207
HAMPTON HAWES:
   The Trio, Vol. 1, Contemporary 3505
   All Night Session, Vols. 1-3, Contemporary 7545-7547
STAN LEVEY:
   Stanley the Steamer, Bethlehem BCP-6030
DINAH WASHINGTON:
   Dinah Jams, Emarcy 36000

The Mosaic five-record set includes the Art Blakey *A Night at Birdland* recordings, as well as the Clifford Brown Ensemble sessions recorded by Pacific Jazz. All of the Clifford Brown–Max Roach Emarcy albums are currently available through reissues by Polygram records. (Four of the Hampton Hawes sides cut for Discovery are available on the Savoy *Black California* anthology, listed elsewhere.)

7 – *Riding the Crest*
CHICO HAMILTON:
   Chico Hamilton Quintet, Pacific Jazz 1209
   Quintet in Hi-Fi, Pacific Jazz 1216
JIM HALL:
   Jazz Guitar, Pacific Jazz 1227
LIGHTHOUSE ALL-STARS/JAZZ STATESMEN:
   Double or Nothin', Liberty LRP 3045
SHELLY MANNE:
   My Fair Lady, Contemporary 7527
JACK MONTROSE:
   Jack Montrose Sextet, Pacific Jazz 1208
   Arranged/Played/Composed by Jack Montrose, Atlantic 1223
BILL PERKINS/JOHN LEWIS:
   2^0 *East*, 3^0 *West*, Pausa 9019 [reissue of PJ-1217]
SHORTY ROGERS:
   The Swinging Mr. Rogers, Atlantic 1212 [reissued as Atlantic 90042-1]
   Martians Come Back, Atlantic 1232
   Big Shorty Rogers Express, RCA LPM-1350
SONNY ROLLINS:
   Way Out West, Contemporary 7527
CY TOUFF:
   Cy Touff, His Octet and Quintet, Pacific Jazz PJ-1211
   Havin' a Ball, World Pacific PJM-410 [slightly revised reissue of the above]
ANTHOLOGIES:
   Jazz West Coast, Vol. 2, Pacific Jazz JWC-501
   Jazz: The 50's Volume II, Pacific Jazz PJ-894-H

8 – *California Hard (II)*
PEPPER ADAMS:
  Pepper Adams Quintet, Mode 112
  Critics' Choice, Pacific Jazz PJM-407
CHET BAKER:
  Chet Baker and Crew, Pacific Jazz 1224
  Quartet: Russ Freeman and Chet Baker, Pacific Jazz 1232
THE CURTIS COUNCE GROUP:
  Vol. 1: Landslide (originally *The Curtis Counce Group*), Contemporary 7526
  Vol. 2: Counceltation (originally *You Get More Bounce with Curtis Counce*),
    Contemporary 7539 [OJC-159]
  Vol. 3: Carl's Blues, Contemporary 7574
  Exploring the Future, Dootone DTL-247
HERB GELLER:
  Fire in the West, Jubilee JGS 1004
HAROLD LAND:
  Grooveyard (originally *Harold in the Land of Jazz*), Contemporary 7550
    [OJC-162]
RED MITCHELL:
  Red Mitchell Quartet (originally *Presenting Red Mitchell*), Contemporary
    7538 [OJC-158]
ANTHOLOGY:
  The Hard Swing, Pacific Jazz JWC-508 [selections by the Elmo Hope
    Quintet; Pepper Adams Quintet; Jack Sheldon–Joe Maini Quintet; Chet
    Baker Quintet; and Art Blakey's Jazz Messengers]

9 – *Art Pepper*
CHET BAKER–ART PEPPER:
  Playboys, Pacific Jazz 1234
ART PEPPER:
  Discoveries, Savoy SJL 2217
  Early Art, Blue Note BN-LA591-H2
  The Complete Pacific Jazz Small Group Recordings of Art Pepper, Mosaic
    MR3-105
  Meets the Rhythm Section, Contemporary 7532
  Art Pepper Plus Eleven: Modern Jazz Classics, Contemporary 7568
  Gettin' Together, Contemporary 7573 [OJC-169]
  Smack Up, Contemporary 7602 [OJC-176]
  Intensity, Contemporary 7607
BILL PERKINS/RICHIE KAMUCA/ART PEPPER:
  Just Friends, Pacific Jazz PJM-401

The Savoy *Discoveries* two-LP set features the Art Pepper Quartet
and Quintet recordings originally issued by Discovery. (Four of the
Quartet performances are also available on the Savoy *Black California*
anthology.) The Blue Note set offers selections recorded for the Jazz
West and Intro labels. The Mosaic set includes both Chet Baker–Art
Pepper Sextet sessions, as well as the Art Pepper–Bill Perkins Quintet
and Art Pepper Nine selections.

10 - The Los Angeles Underground
PAUL BLEY AND ORNETTE COLEMAN:
  Live at the Hilcrest Club, 1958, Inner City 1007
ORNETTE COLEMAN:
  Something Else, Contemporary 7551 [OJC-163]
  Tomorrow is the Question, Contemporary 7569
  The Shape of Jazz to Come, Atlantic 1317
CHICO HAMILTON:
  Gongs East, Discovery DS-831 [reissue of Warner Brothers W-1271]
ANTHOLOGY:
  Black California, Savoy SJL 2215 [includes eight performances by the Roy
  Porter big band]

11 - Into the Sixties
TEDDY EDWARDS:
  Teddy's Ready, Contemporary 7583
  Teddy Edwards and Howard McGhee: Together Again, Contemporary 7588
JOE GORDON:
  Lookin' Good, Contemporary 7579 [OJC-174]
PAUL HORN:
  Something Blue, Hifijazz 615
HAROLD LAND:
  The Fox, Contemporary 7619 [reissue of Hifijazz 612]
SHELLY MANNE:
  At the Blackhawk, Vols. 1-4, Contemporary 7577-7580
RED MITCHELL/HAROLD LAND:
  Hear Ye!, Atlantic 1376
THELONIOUS MONK:
  Quartet Plus Two at the Blackhawk, Riverside RLP 1171 [reissued with
  additional material on Milestone 47033, *In Person*]
BUD SHANK:
  New Groove, Pacific Jazz PJ-21

DIAL
R E C O R D S

6-5-47
Contemporary
American Music

1018-A

MISCHIEVOUS LADY
DEXTER GORDON QUINTET

DEXTER GORDON......Tenor Sax
MELBA LISTON......Trombone
CHARLIE FOX......Piano
RED CALLENDER......Bass
CHUCK THOMPSON......Drums
Supervision—Ross Russell

(D-1081-D)

DIAL
R E C O R D S

12-4-47
PART ONE

1028-A

THE DUEL

DEXTER GORDON......Tenor Sax
TEDDY EDWARDS......Tenor Sax
JIMMY ROWLES......Piano
RED CALLENDER......Bass
ROY PORTER......Drums

(D-1143)

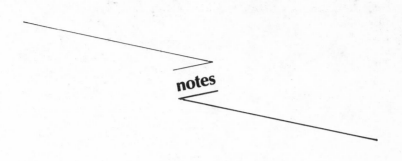

notes

Preface (pp. 1–3)
[1] Grover Sales, *Jazz: America's Classical Music* (Englewood Cliffs, New Jersey: Prentice-Hall, 1984), p. 168.

1. – *Diz and Bird in Lotus Land* (pp. 5–22)
[1] Quoted in Dizzy Gillespie, *To Be or Not ... to Bop: Memoirs* (Garden City: Doubleday, 1979; London: Quartet Books, 1983), p. 248.
[2] Ibid, p. 243.
[3] Hampton Hawes and Don Asher, *Raise Up Off Me: A Portrait of Hampton Hawes* (1974; rpt. New York: Da Capo, 1979), p. 13.
[4] Quoted in Ross Russell, *Bird Lives! The High Life and Hard Times of Charlie (Yardbird) Parker* (New York: Charterhouse, 1973; London: Quartet Books, 1973), p. 324.
[5] 'Ross Russell', *Bird: The Legend of Charlie Parker*, ed. Robert Reisner (1962; rpt. New York: Da Capo, 1977; London: Quartet Books, 1974), p. 197.
[6] Ibid, p. 198.
[7] Ibid, p. 201.

2. – *The Central Avenue Scene* (pp. 23–50)
[1] Quoted by Leonard Feather, *Inside Jazz* (1949; rpt. New York and London: Da Capo, 1980), p. 14.
[2] Art and Laurie Pepper, *Straight Life: The Story of Art Pepper* (New York: Schirmer, 1979), p. 42.
[3] Quoted ibid, p. 46.
[4] Quoted by Lester Koenig, notes to Contemporary 7588.
[5] John Tynan, 'Teddy Edwards: Long, Long Journey', *Down Beat* 24 May 1962: 19.
[6] Ibid.
[7] Quoted by Michael Ullman, *Jazz Lives: Portraits in Words and Pictures* (1980; rpt. New York: Perigee Books, 1982), pp. 93–4.
[8] Buddy Collette, personal interview, 30 September 1982. All further unreferenced quotations by Buddy Collette are from this interview.
[9] Ullman, op cit, pp. 94–5.
[10] Quoted by Ira Gitler, *Jazz Masters of the Forties* (1966; rpt. New York:

227

Collier, 1974; London: Collier-Macmillan, 1975), p. 204.

[11] Ibid, p. 206.

[12] Ibid, pp. 206–7.

[13] Ibid, p. 209.

[14] Ross Russell, *Down Beat* 3 December 1964: 17.

[15] Ibid.

[16] Ullman, op cit, p. 95.

[17] Quoted by Sally Placksin, *American Women in Jazz: 1900 to the Present, Their Words, Lives, and Music* (New York: Seaview Books, 1982; London: Pluto, 1985), p. 180.

[18] Ibid, p. 181.

[19] Interview with Paul Bullock and David Hoxie, *Jazz Heritage Foundation*, Vol. III No. 1, January 1982.

[20] Ibid.

[21] Ibid.

[22] Ibid.

[23] Quoted by Doug Ramsey in notes to Prestige 24062.

[24] Hampton Hawes and Don Asher, *Raise Up Off Me* (1974; rpt. New York: Da Capo, 1979), pp. 33–4.

3. – *Shorty Rogers and His Giants* (pp. 51–67)

[1] Quoted in Joe Goldberg, *Jazz Masters of the Fifties* (New York: Macmillan, 1965; London: Da Capo, 1980), p. 69.

[2] Quoted by Martin Schouten in notes to Capitol M-11060.

[3] Shorty Rogers, personal interview, 20 January 1983. All further unreferenced quotations by Shorty Rogers are from this interview.

[4] Quoted by Leonard Feather, 'Rumsey's Thirty Years with All that Jazz', *Los Angeles Times* Calendar Section, 27 May 1979, p. 3.

4. – *The Gerry Mulligan Quartet* (pp. 69–85)

[1] Quoted in Joe Goldberg, *Jazz Masters of the Fifties* (New York: Macmillan, 1965), p. 14.

[2] André Hodeir, *Jazz: Its Evolution and Essence* (1956; rpt. New York: Da Capo Press, 1975), p. 134.

[3] Quoted by Bob Rosenblum in notes to Artists House 9411.

[4] Ibid.

[5] Ibid.

[6] Notes to Pacific Jazz PJ-8.

[7] Ibid.

[8] Notes to Pacific Jazz PJLP-1.

[9] Notes to Columbia CL 1307.

[10] Notes to Pacific Jazz PJ-8.

[11] *Down Beat* 20 May 1953: 4.

[12] Quoted by Pete Welding in notes to Mosaic MR5-102.

[13] Ibid.

[14] Goldberg, op cit, p. 16.

[15] Quoted in Rosenblum, op cit.

[16] John Tynan, 'Straight Talk from Russ Freeman', *Down Beat* 14 March 1963: 20.

5. – *The West Coast Sound* (pp. 87–105)

[1] Letter to the author, 12 June 1983.

[2.] Notes to Contemporary 2511.
[3.] Ibid.
[4.] Notes to Contemporary 3584.
[5.] Ibid.
[6.] André Hodeir, *Jazz: Its Evolution and Essence* (1956: rpt. New York: Da Capo Press, 1975), p. 276.
[7.] John Tynan, 'The Real Story of Bossa Nova', *Down Beat* 8 November 1962: 21.
[8.] Ibid, 22.
[9.] Ibid.
[10.] Quoted by Richard Bock in notes to PJ-8.
[11.] *Down Beat* 9 September 1953: 15.
[12.] *Down Beat* 19 May 1954: 16.
[13.] Quoted by Bob Rosenblum in notes to Artists House 9411.

6. – *California Hard (I)* (pp. 107–124)
[1.] Harold Land, personal interview, 10 March 1983. All further unreferenced quotations by Harold Land are from this interview.
[2.] Hampton Hawes and Don Asher, *Raise Up Off Me* (1974; rpt. New York: Da Capo, 1979), pp. 12–13.
[3.] Ibid, pp. 77–8.
[4.] Ibid, p. 78.
[5.] Notes to Contemporary 3505.

7. – *Riding the Crest* (pp. 125–146)
[1.] Notes to Pacific Jazz PJ-1208.
[2.] 'Chico's Changed', *Down Beat* 28 March 1963: 19.
[3.] Shelly Manne, personal interview, 25 September 1982. All further unreferenced quotations by Shelly Manne are from this interview.

8. – *California Hard (II)* (pp. 147–163)
[1.] Quoted by John Tynan in notes to Pacific Jazz PJM-407.
[2.] Notes to Contemporary 7574.
[3.] Quoted by Nat Hentoff in notes to Contemporary 7550.
[4.] Notes to Contemporary 7589.
[5.] 'First Generation Still Generating', Calendar Section, *Los Angeles Times*, 25 April 1982: 61.

9. – *Art Pepper* (pp. 165–182)
[1.] Art and Laurie Pepper, *Straight Life: The Story of Art Pepper* (New York: Schirmer, 1979), p. 218.
[2.] Ibid, pp. 48–9.
[3.] Notes to Blue Note BN-LA591-H2.
[4.] Pepper, op cit, p. 194.
[5.] Ibid, p. 196.
[6.] Ibid, pp. 218–19.
[7.] Notes to Contemporary 7568.
[8.] Notes to Contemporary 7602.

10. – *The Los Angeles Underground* (pp. 183–199)
[1.] Quoted by Vladimir Simosko and Barry Tepperman, *Eric Dolphy: A Musical Biography and Discography* (1974; rpt. New York: Da Capo, 1979), p. 39.

[2.] Interview with David Keller, *Jazz Heritage Foundation*, Vol. IV, No. 5, September/October 1983.
[3.] Simosko and Tepperman, op cit, pp. 32–4.
[4.] Keller, op cit.
[5.] Quoted in A.B. Spellman, *Black Music: Four Lives* (1966; rpt. New York: Schocken Books, 1970), pp. 107–8.
[6.] Ibid, p. 110.
[7.] Ibid, p. 111.
[8.] Notes to Contemporary 7551.
[9.] Spellman, op cit, pp. 123–4.

11. – *Into the Sixties* (pp. 201–216)
[1.] Notes to Contemporary 7619.
[2.] Ibid.
[3.] Notes to Contemporary 7583.
[4.] *Down Beat*, 24 May 1962: 18.
[5.] Notes to Atlantic 1376.

231

Riverside records, 156, 208
Roach, Max (d), Lighthouse All-Stars, 90, 93; with Clifford Brown, 107-14; and Stan Levey, 122; with Sonny Rollins, 144; and Bill Loughbrough, 151; with Kenny Dorham, 162; with Eric Dolphy, 187; and Ornette Coleman, 192
Roberts, Howard (g), 49, 134
Robinson, Jimmy (tp), 123
Robinson, Leroy 'Sweetpea' (as), 185-6
Robinson, Lester (tb), 187
Rogers, Michele, 56, 128
Rogers, Shorty (tp, arr), 55-6, 95; Finale, 12; with Will Bradley, 56; with Woody Herman, 56-7; with Butch Stone, 56; with Stan Kenton, 57-8; *Modern Sounds*, 58-9, 126; Lighthouse All-Stars, 61-3; *And His Giants*, 63-4, 126, 167; *Cool and Crazy*, 64-5, 129, 167; *Courts the Count*, 65-7; and Gerry Mulligan, 69, 77-8; with Shelly Manne, 87, 89, 91, 93, 205; Giants, 63-4, 90, 126; with Bud Shank, 100; with Lennie Niehaus, 101; with Lorraine Geller, 115; with Curtis Counce, 116, 147; with Hampton Hawes, 118; *The Swinging Mr Rogers*, 126-8; *Way Up There*, 128-9; *Big Band Express*, 129, 168; *Wherever the Five Winds Blow*, 129; and Jack Montrose, 130; with André Previn, 142; with Art Pepper, 166, 175, 177
Roland, Gene (tp, tb, arr), 56-7
Rollins, Sonny (ts), 113, 123, 142, 142-4, 145, 153, 168, 177
Rosolino, Frank (tb), 122-3, 145-6, 207
Ross, Annie (vcl), 46-7
Rouse, Charlie (ts), 208
Rowles, Jimmy (p), 35, 42, 71-2, 99-100, 155, 171
Royal, Ernie (tp), 28-9, 38, 71
Royal, Marshall (as), 29, 38, 43
Royal Roost (club), 45, 51-3
Roy Porter big band, 184-7
Rubin, Harry, 135
Rugolo, Pete (p, arr), 52, 57, 131
Rumsey, Howard (b), 1, 60-2, 76, 87, 90, 115, 145
Russell, George (p, comp), 52, 55
Russell, Ross, 9-11, 15-20, 26, 32, 35-6

Russo, Bill (tb), 89
Ruther, Wyatt (b), 188

Sales, Grover, 1
Sanborn House (club), 149
San Pedro High School, 166
Santa Monica City College, 213
Sarmento, Paul (tu), 91
Savoy records, 7-8, 22, 28, 31, 184-6
Sesac records, 189
Shank, Bud (as, bars, fl), and Shorty Rogers, 58; with Shorty Rogers, 64-5, 129, 175; with Gerry Mulligan, 78; with Chet Baker, 83; with Shelly Manne, 89-90; Lighthouse All-Stars, 90, 92-3; with Laurindo Almeida, 97-8; with Maynard Ferguson, 100; with Art Pepper, 176, 178; *New Groove*, 212-13; with Carmell Jones, 214
The Shape of Jazz to Come (Ornette Coleman), 198
Sheldon, Jack (tp), 117, 147-50, 156-7, 159, 169-70, 177-8, 180-1
Shelly Manne and His Friends, 142
Shelly Manne and His Men, Vol.2, 90-2
Shelly Manne and His Men at the Blackhawk, Vols. 1-4, 207
Shorty Rogers and His Giants, 63-4, 167, 175
Shorty Rogers Courts the Count, 65
Showplace (club), 189
Shreve, Dick (p), 145
Silver, Horace (p), 114, 145, 156-7, 159, 163, 177, 194
Simosko, Vladimir, 185
Sims, Zoot (ts), Finale, 12; and tenor duos, 33; Pontrelli's, 56; with Shorty Rogers, 66; with Gerry Mulligan, 84; with Clifford Brown, 110; with Lorraine Geller, 115; with Lawrence Marable, 116; with Johnny Mandel, 132; with Monty Budwig, 206
Sinatra, Francis Albert (vcl), 44
Singleton, Zutty (d), 8
Slack, Freddie (p), 118
'Slim and Slam' (Slim Gaillard and Slam Stewart), 6, 8
Smack Up! (Art Pepper), 180-2
Smith, Carson (b), 73, 77, 80, 110, 135-7
Smith, Hale, 188